Nomadic Indigenous Peoples and the Law

This book investigates the unique challenges faced by nomadic Indigenous peoples in claiming self-determination and rights to their ancestral lands.

Nomadic or mobile Indigenous peoples have been largely ignored in the wider context of Indigenous land rights, but such groups are often even more marginalised than other Indigenous peoples. Focusing on the Indian Forest Rights Act, this book explores how access to justice remains uneven and elusive for mobile Indigenous communities who have been dispossessed of their lands. Exposing the lack of recognition of usufruct rights and of customary land laws, which have caused a more acute displacement from ancestral lands for mobile Indigenous peoples, the book reveals how their nomadic livelihoods have excluded them from government policies and laws. The book further examines the gendered and intersectional aspects of this exclusion. In conclusion, the book maintains that legislation such as the progressive Forest Rights Act is necessary, but not enough, to protect the rights of mobile Indigenous peoples. In such cases, the book argues, legislation has to be supported by nuanced governance, which is sensitive to the particular challenges presented by Indigenous peoples who are further marginalised through nomadic lifestyles.

This book will be of interest to scholars and researchers working in the areas of Indigenous studies, socio-legal studies, human and minority rights, and gender and international development.

Indrani Sigamany is a researcher and a senior international development consultant, working in the fields of social justice, gender justice, and Indigenous land rights.

Part of the Indigenous Peoples and the Law Series
Series Editors
Dr Mark A. Harris
University of British Columbia, Canada
Professor Denise Ferreira da Silva
University of British Columbia, Canada
Dr Claire Charters
University of Auckland, New Zealand
Dr Glen Coulthard
University of British Columbia, Canada

A GlassHouse book

For information about the series and details of previous and forthcoming titles, see www.routledge.com/law/series/INDPPL

Nomadic Indigenous Peoples and the Law

Self-Determination, Land Rights and Gender Justice in India

Indrani Sigamany

Routledge
Taylor & Francis Group
a GlassHouse Book

First published 2026
by Routledge
4 Park Square, Milton Park, Abingdon, Oxon OX14 4RN

and by Routledge
605 Third Avenue, New York, NY 10158

Routledge is an imprint of the Taylor & Francis Group, an informa business

A GlassHouse book

British Library Cataloguing-in-Publication Data
A catalogue record for this book is available from the British Library

ISBN: 978-1-032-96445-4 (hbk)
ISBN: 978-1-032-96448-5 (pbk)
ISBN: 978-1-003-58948-8 (ebk)

DOI: 10.4324/9781003589488

Typeset in Sabon
by Apex CoVantage, LLC

To Nikhil and Anisha

Contents

Illustrations

Preface

The impetus for this research began in 2006 when, as a consultant, I stood at the front of a large room while the participants at the meeting constructed a joint list of recommendations derived from their group work. They were all mobile Indigenous peoples. While rapidly classifying their brightly coloured Post-it stickers to form priorities, I was struck by the predominance of issues associated with land rights. These ranged from land security and land tenure to access to grazing resources. This was a side event[1] at the United Nations Permanent Forum on Indigenous Issues (UNPFII) in New York, and my role as a consultant entailed facilitating a meeting for twenty-two representatives of various mobile Indigenous groups from more than a dozen countries.[2] My remit was to build the capacity of these mobile Indigenous peoples to participate in the UNPFII, which at that point did not include nomadic peoples. This was my first exposure to the acute struggle of Indigenous peoples for their rights, and was the beginning of a personal journey of involvement which has shaped my professional interest in Indigenous land rights and has informed the topic of this book.

A sincere thank you to each person who helped me in small and big ways with this lengthy research undertaking, which has resulted in this book. I cannot name every person who has helped me along the way, but you know who you are, and please know that I am extremely grateful to each of you.

A huge thank you to Professor Dawn Chatty, Oxford Department of International Development, University of Oxford, who continues to act as my professional mentor. A special note of gratitude to Nikhil Wilmink, for constant emotional support, encouragement, and for keeping the pressure on from Zambia. Towards the end, when night and day merged into one block

1 The side event was organised by the Standing Committee of the Dana Declaration on Conservation and Mobile Peoples, and the World Alliance of Mobile Indigenous Peoples (WAMIP).

2 The countries this group represented included Burkina Faso, Ethiopia, India, Jordan, Kenya, Mali, Inner Mongolia, Mongolia, Morocco, Namibia, Palestine, Senegal, Sudan and the United Arab Emirates.

of time with brief snatches of sleep in between, Nikhil was present, tirelessly editing through all hours of the day and night, with valuable and insightful suggestions, all done 'by remote' from another continent. A personal note of appreciation to Anisha Wilmink, who accompanied me in the field and took beautiful photos and who was a great source of encouragement; and to Professor G. Sigamany, whose commitment to social justice and legacy of courage and professional excellence continues to inspire and offer constant strength in spite of her very recent departure from our lives, and without her nurture and support this research effort would not have begun. A huge thank you to Tenzing Tshering who worked for days alongside me on the unmanageable and intimidating task of compiling the index. Tenzing tirelessly navigated the software with brilliance, and I am so grateful for his patience, kindness, and generosity with his time.

In the field in India, I am grateful to the many people from the Adivasi and pastoral communities whom I visited in Rajasthan, Gujarat, and Maharashtra, who gave of their time and hospitality so freely. Thank you to the staff of all the NGOs and civil society organisations who worked with me closely on my data collection: Astha Sansthan, Seva Mandir, Society for Promotion of Wastelands Development (SPWD); Anthra, Marag, Lokhit Pashu-Palak Sansthan (LPPS), Kalpavriksh, and Campaign for Survival and Dignity.

Specifically I would like to thank Dr Ginny Shrivastava, who made the crucial long-distance phone calls from India inviting me to use Astha's facilities and professional connections with tribal peoples, and who made sure in so many thoughtful ways that I was taken care of; Mangi Lal Gujjar from Astha and Juned Khan from SPWD, whose analytical minds and ability to think outside the box opened my eyes to valuable and alternative perspectives; Mr Sudhansu from the Ministry of Tribal Affairs (MoTA) Udaipur; Ramesh Bhatnagar, Sarfraj, Mohseen Ahmed, and other Astha field staff whose commitment and extremely hard work under strenuous living and travelling conditions in tribal areas are admirable. Thank you.

Thank you to Jagdish Purohit from SPWD, and Suresh Sharma and Shailendra Tiwari from Seva Mandir who so kindly volunteered their professional opinions and time. Suresh Sharma was especially helpful and hospitable, allowing me to accompany the team on field visits. And from Astha, R.D. Vyas, Vinod, Ramesh Nandvana, Bhanwar Singh, and all Astha staff who were so consistently kind and helpful. From Kalpavriksh, thank you to Ashish Kothari, Meenal Tatpati, Sheba Desor, and Neema Pathak. Madhu Sarin, from Campaign for Survival and Dignity, was so generously accessible, whether by phone or email – open to discussion and patient with every question. I have depended on the strong dedication of Indian civil society organisations to the cause.

Introduction

'When the Camel Grows Horns'

I caught a ride to the village of Bhasla[1] in the NGO vehicle transporting headquarters' staff from Udaipur city to a rural meeting on land rights. Abandoning the jeep when the road ended, we continued our journey on foot through the thinly forested Aravalli hills of southern Rajasthan in India. A splash of colour on a distant knoll indicated the forest community that was waiting for us, the women wearing saris of bright hues visible from a distance. The Bhasla village community organisation, called the *Adivasi Sangathan*, was led by Mirabai, a committed leader and a strong woman. Under Mirabai's leadership, they had already mapped their village boundaries and petitioned for their Community Forest Rights (CFR) claims, under the Scheduled Tribes and Other Traditional Forest Dwellers (Recognition of Forest Rights) Act, 2006 (hereafter known as the Forest Rights Act). The process of their land claims was being discussed at this meeting. Significant at this community meeting were the women, who, contrary to local convention, were sitting up front, rather than either behind the men or separately as in the other meetings I had attended in Rajasthan. Another important difference was that these women were not wearing the *gungat* over their faces.[2] Hindu women in Rajasthan[3] use the *gungat*, which is part of the practice of purdah, pulling the sari over their heads and down over their eyes.[4] The tribal women of Bhasla village were not veiled, which

1 Names of places and of people have been anonymised.

2 The *gungat* is a veil used by Hindu women in Rajasthan and Gujarat to cover the head and eyes and sometimes the whole face, using the end of the sari. It is used in the same manner as the purdah is used by Muslim women. In India, the purdah is part of the practice of female seclusion from public observation or from the sight of men and strangers.

3 Purdah is not historically part of the Hindu culture, and in India, Hindu women in the states of Rajasthan and Gujarat are considered to be complicit in patriarchal traditions in which the onus is placed on women to avoid sexual harassment by covering up.

4 In southern Rajasthan, the tribal women had adapted to the local mainstream Hindu custom of wearing the *gungat*. This process of Sanskritisation is not a tribal tradition in any other part of India. Historical evidence suggests that 'tribal societies have been less discriminatory against women and girls than other societies'. However, this is not uniform in all states, and in Rajasthan the tribal communities have assumed the patriarchal structures of traditional mainstream Indian cultures.

DOI: 10.4324/9781003589488-1

Figure 0.1 Community meeting for forest rights with a woman leader

was remarkable and significant, especially in Rajasthan, in which the historic gender inequality requires women to cover their heads.

The meeting began with a discussion of Bhasla's struggle to claim land rights. The unveiled Bhasla village women in the meeting were eager to share a particular experience from the day before the meeting, and were very vocal in describing a crucial episode in their journey towards justice. It involved dealing with bank officials and the deputy *Sarpanch*[5] in Udaipur. The officials had taken a bank account passbook from fourteen women applying for Rs. 45,000 per person, which was part of the *Mukya Mantri* (chief minister) scheme for constructing *pukka* houses, or permanent dwellings. The women were illiterate. When they collected their money, it was handed to them in an envelope by the deputy *Sarpanch*. Mirabai, the leader of the Bhasla village organisation, had taken her literate 11-year-old son with her and asked him to count the money before they left the bank. Every envelope was missing Rs. 500, which the *gram panchayat's*[6] deputy Sarpanch, in collusion with the bank manager, had taken as a bribe without informing the women. Incensed,

5 Sarpanch is the deputy head of the Gram Panchayat or the village council.
6 Gram Panchayat is the village council or village governing body.

the women stormed the bank demanding their money. They declared that they would only leave without their money 'when the camel grows horns'. And back home, when the rest of the village heard about it, they sent resources and joined in. The deputy *Sarpanch*, who was from their own tribe and from the same *panchayat*, was overwhelmed and had to return the money. This was perceived by the women as a victory that they owned, and could be seen as an example of the positive gender consequences of legal empowerment for Indigenous land rights.

The power and political acumen generated by their determination, resulting in a successful conclusion, was not lost on the women of Bhasla. They explained at the meeting that they felt empowered and strong. Some of them felt they needed to eschew the *gungat*, which was now perceived by them as keeping them in the background, and had, they felt, kept them sheltered from community decision making. They stated that although they had previously never been out of their village, they were now ready to travel to Udaipur – the 'big city' – to fight for their land rights and try to gain justice. The men at the meeting confirmed that they were now aware of the new-found strength and agency of the women, which had changed their own attitudes towards the women in their community and produced a realisation of the formerly hidden potential of women. The claims for CFR that this community had made had been with the participation of these politically mobilised women who, with a newly acquired agency and voice, affirmed that they were ready to fight for their lands. Within the context of gender equality, data such as how the women of Bhasla responded to being exploited as described earlier is evidence that even just the enactment of legislation protecting land rights can be empowering. Legislation has been shown to offer confidence in access to justice, even if the actual trajectory to access to justice can be rather more rocky.

The scenario playing out in the Bhasla community is part of the qualitative data empirically derived from field work in India from the states of Rajasthan, Gujarat, and Maharashtra. The context in this debate is how justice is accessed by communities marginalised by enforced migration and dispossession of their lands, and specifically examines two aspects. Firstly, how legislation strengthens Indigenous peoples' ability to claim legal land rights; secondly, whether the law provides marginalised communities with an effective instrument to access justice for land rights.

The earlier questions relate closely to the relationship between rights, access to justice, social exclusion, and land dispossession.[7] The significance for this book is the interrelationship between access to justice, inequity, and poverty, within the context of marginalised Indigenous communities who are often forced to migrate and are displaced from their ancestral lands. My

7 Anderson, 'Access to Justice and Legal Process'.

analysis in the book exposes the contradictions inherent in a progressive piece of rights-based legislation not necessarily being implemented with respect to rights to land. The analysis also specifically highlights the dimensions of gender inequality.

The Unique Experience of Land Dispossession

Displacement from ancestral lands has been more acute for mobile Indigenous peoples because of a lack of recognition of usufruct rights and of customary land laws. Furthermore, their livelihoods, which necessitate a nomadic way of life, have excluded them from government policies and laws, especially those which facilitate mobility between national borders. This book investigates and publicises effective legal and advocacy strategies used by mobile Indigenous peoples to access justice and claim rights to their ancestral lands. Specifically examining the Forest Rights Act 2006 in three states in India, it explores how access to justice remains uneven and elusive for Indigenous peoples dispossessed of their lands. Using empirical data, the book details the different strategies used by different mobile Indigenous groups in three states in order to retain their lands. Control of land is of fundamental importance for retention of Indigenous peoples' way of life, self-determination, and protection of climate. Indigenous land rights are an issue of global importance, with marginalised Indigenous groups around the world being displaced from their lands in violation of their human rights.

The Global Fight for Ancestral Lands

Indigenous peoples on a global scale are struggling to retain possession of ancestral lands and usufruct[8] rights. Many of them who are mobile[9] pursue pastoralist occupations such as herding animals or hunting and gathering, a continuation of ancient nomadic lifestyles and culture. These nomadic livelihoods have deep pre-historic roots and have endured as livelihoods which are currently continued in vast parts of South Asia, the Middle East, Africa, Central Asia, Europe, South America, and the subarctic.[10] The data gathered for this study include pastoralist communities in India who herd cattle in Gujarat, goats from the Konkan coast to the Deccan plateau in Maharashtra, and camels in Rajasthan.

8 'Usufruct' is the legal right to use and enjoy the benefits and profits of something belonging to another. Vemuri, 'Joint Forest Management in India'.

9 The terms 'nomadic' and 'mobile Indigenous peoples', which are used interchangeably, will be defined in Chapter 2 of this volume.

10 Honeychurch and Makarewicz, 'The Archaeology of Pastoral Nomadism'.

Currently, worldwide there are around 370 million Indigenous peoples, comprising five thousand groups living in about seventy countries.[11] The topic of Indigenous peoples' land rights is fraught with legal contradictions.[12] National and international land laws assume private individualistic ownership of land, or land owned by the sovereign state.[13] This is contrary to the collective use of land by Indigenous communities,[14] especially mobile populations,[15] who do not necessarily own the land they use, abiding instead by the customary practice of using common lands, known as 'usufruct' in legal terminology.[16] Mobile Indigenous peoples, who are identified by their nomadism, face double legal discrimination within the group of Indigenous peoples. For instance, human rights instruments such as the UN Declaration on the Rights of Indigenous Peoples of 2007[17] (hereafter known as 'the Declaration') do not specifically mention mobile or nomadic communities, who are also often invisible to their own governments, making it more difficult to advocate for land rights. The paucity of evidence of rights needed by mobile Indigenous peoples in international law has repeatedly been referred to by scholars such as Jeremie Gilbert: 'international human rights law does not refer to the specific situation of mobile peoples, and no treaties include any specific rights for mobile peoples. Instead, the focus is on universal human rights applicable to all'.[18]

The lack of specific rights for mobile Indigenous peoples contributes to an inability to control lands they have historically used, and repeatedly collides with the refusal of governments to relinquish power and to recognise legal rights. At the intersection of both mobile and settled Indigenous communities is the specific gender differential that forced migration affects women differently. When women are forced to migrate away from their traditional lives

11 Impe, *A Convention to Fight Discrimination*, 12.
12 Sigamany, 'Destroying a Way of Life', 159.
13 Gilbert, 'Land Rights and Nomadic Peoples', 78.
14 Gilbert and Doyle, 'A New Dawn Over the Land', 3.
15 Mobile Indigenous Peoples, whose pastoralist occupations of herding animals or hunting and gathering are a continuation of ancient lifestyles and culture. (At the moment, worldwide there are around 370 million Indigenous peoples, comprising 5000 groups living in about 70 countries, (Impe, *A Convention to Fight Discrimination*, 12) many of them struggling to retain possession of ancestral lands and usufruct rights. Mobile Indigenous peoples face a double legal discrimination within the group of Indigenous peoples. For instance, human rights instruments such as the UN Declaration for Indigenous Peoples of 2007 do not specifically mention mobile or nomadic communities, who are also often invisible to their own governments, making it more difficult to advocate for land rights.
16 *Oxford Dictionaries*, s.v. 'usufruct', accessed 12 August 2014, https://oxforddictionaries.com.
17 United Nations General Assembly, Declaration on the Rights of Indigenous Peoples (UNDRIP), Res. 61/295 A (13 December 2007).
18 Gilbert, 'Land Rights and Nomadic Peoples', 78.

in the forest environments, they face hardships that Indigenous men do not, such as sexual exploitation in mainstream society.

The exploitation of Indigenous peoples' lands has a long history dating back to the colonial period. The colonial laws in India, which originally initiated the forced migration of forest communities from their resource-rich lands, treated Adivasis as encroachers and criminalised them. Often it is the men who migrate in search of casual labour. Since their livelihoods and reproductive activities are both forest-based, women tend not to migrate at the same rate as men, and have been criminalised at a higher rate than men. Laws have been used to regulate social living within communities from the beginning of history, and range from local customary laws to national, regional, and international laws. They unintentionally reflect the biases of the political thinking of their time. Property laws have discriminated against women, for instance, and legal theories on land titles, such as *terra nullius*,[19] which I explain later, have reflected racial attitudes towards Indigenous communities.

The Inequality of Land Laws

The concept of *terra nullius* or 'empty lands' was used by European immigrants and colonials to expropriate Indigenous lands. The Europeans treated Indigenous peoples occupying their ancestral lands as if they had no rights to the lands and as if the lands belonged to no one.[20] *Terra nullius* is a principle that Indigenous peoples are still fighting against in an effort to reclaim lost ancestral lands, and to avoid forced migration. Laws can contradict each other within nations and between nations, where state laws can differ from national laws, and national laws can contradict international laws.[21] This makes the Indigenous struggle to negotiate the legal systems even more complex, and therefore makes the laws less effective.

One of the themes surfacing from this critical analysis of justice surrounds two aspects: first, the principles and semantics of the law while it is being formulated, and second, compliance by government organs once it has been enacted. The principles of justice underpinning a new piece of legislation are of particular significance when dealing with the rights of populations facing exclusion and marginalisation, such as women's rights or Indigenous rights. Normative human rights instruments, whether international or national, have contributed positively to alleviating the marginalisation of peripheral groups.[22] It can be argued, however, that they embody structural biases and inequalities towards these groups, which may negatively influence

19 *Terra nullius* means vacant lands.
20 Anaya, *Indigenous Peoples in International Law*, 15.
21 American Bar Association, *Access to Justice Assessment Tool*, 6.
22 Simmons, *Mobilizing for Human Rights*.

their compliance. The historical rationale for new laws, such as many land acquisition laws, created a hegemony of foreign laws and generated disparities between communities. I will develop this analysis to demonstrate how historical laws in India have adversely affected the land rights of Indigenous communities in the tribal belt.

Third World Approaches to International Law (TWAIL)

Third World Approaches to International Law, known as TWAIL, are strongly reflected as methodologies in the discussions in this book. My analysis is grounded in how international law has historically been founded on the premise of imperialism, designed to legitimise settler colonialism through the concept of *terra nullius*, or empty lands, thereby supporting the expropriation of Indigenous lands, both internationally and nationally. The postcolonial manifestation of land expropriation is substantiated in this book by case studies. These demonstrate how currently in India the law is being subverted, ignored, or even repealed by the government in an effort to use forest lands for extractive industry. The current government, which is committed to a neoliberal, free market capitalist economic strategy, continues to displace Indigenous communities, resulting in an impoverishing loss of livelihoods, habitat, and spiritual culture. These government policies mirror the discriminatory roots of international law, and TWAIL is the "expression of this confrontation in the discipline, theory, and practice of international law."[23]

Born in the mid 1950s, TWAIL developed as a postcolonial political movement of intellectuals from the Third World who were pushing back against the inherent imperialistic characteristics of international law. These imperialistic aspects are seen as delegitimising the regime of international law, making it a tool for furthering Western imperialism.[24] TWAIL scholarship challenges the legitimacy of international law, offering "an alternative, universal vision of international law and justice."[25] TWAIL scholars continue to produce "a substantive critique of the politics and scholarship of mainstream international law to the extent that it has helped reproduce structures that marginalize and dominate Third World peoples, especially aspects such as conquering, and dispossessing Third World communities."[26]

Historically, the development of an international body of law was founded on the legal philosophy and imperialistic interests of colonial powers during their search for new territories in which the concept of 'justice'

23 Mutua and Anghie, 'What Is TWAIL?'.
24 Mutua and Anghie, 'What Is TWAIL?'.
25 Anghie, 'Rethinking International Law'.
26 Anghie, 'Rethinking International Law'.

was determined by their agendas of conquest.[27] The way in which the law has been created, and by whom it has been both drafted and enacted, has not only provided us with a framework that gives people rights but has also denied people their rights. This dichotomy has led to the uncomfortable existence of judicial imperialism, in which the laws do not change the lives of people in the ways they were intended. In building the historical context for the Forest Rights Act 2006, I trace the imposition of Western law on countries such as India as a result of colonisation, and demonstrate how this created a fragmented and multi-layered legal incongruence, further excluding marginalised Indigenous communities from accessing justice.

Land encroachment of the Indigenous peoples by colonial powers occurred with the "slaughter of the children, women and men who stood in the way."[28] This was happening simultaneously in many parts of the world, causing "human suffering in turmoil on a massive scale."[29] The historical context includes a Eurocentric bias:

> the patterns of empire and conquest that engulfed indigenous peoples . . . and a state centred system, strongly grounded in the Western world view it developed to facilitate colonial patterns promoted by European states and their offspring, to the detriment of indigenous peoples.[30]

Despite considerable progress, contemporary laws have not been able to fully reject the mantle of colonial legacies, whether in aspects of the black letter of the law, or in how they are implemented.[31] This legal hegemony does not obscure the fact that human rights mechanisms in themselves are positive, as

27 International, regional and national legislation embodies the principle of self-determination in, for example, the 2007 UN Declaration of Rights for Indigenous Peoples, the 1948 United Nations Charter, and several regional declarations. Anaya, *Indigenous Peoples in International Law "Acknowledging that the Charter of the United Nations, the International Covenant on Economic, Social and Cultural Rights and the International Covenant on Civil and Political Rights, as well as the Vienna Declaration and Programme of Action, affirm the fundamental importance of the right to self-determination of all peoples, by virtue of which they freely determine their political status and freely pursue their economic, social and cultural development,"* Resolution adopted by the General Assembly 61/295. United Nations Declaration on the Rights of Indigenous Peoples (adopted on 13 December 2007, UNGA Res. 61/295 A (UNDRIP Add 1) 2.

28 Anaya, *Indigenous Peoples in International Law*.

29 Xanthaki, 'Indigenous Rights in International Law Over the Last 10 Years and Future Developments'.

30 Anaya, *Indigenous Peoples in International Law*. Bartolome de la Casas (1474–1566), Francisco de Vitoria (1486–1547), Hugo Grotius ("the most prominent of the 'fathers' of the Law,") Fransico Suarez (1548–1617), Domingo de Soto (1494–1560), Balthasar Ayala (1548–1584), and Alerico Gentilis (1552–1608), are the important European theorists who contributed to the origins of international law, and its Eurocentric bias.

31 Anaya, *Indigenous Peoples in International Law* vi.

they offer an acknowledgement of power imbalances and the need to protect minority rights.[32] I argue that present-day laws have evolved from a skewed rationale reflecting historical power imbalances, developed during a world order when colonial powers were advancing across foreign continents framing laws such as *terra nullius* to benefit their territorial expansion. These laws, used as "instruments of colonialism"[33] were intrinsically biased against Indigenous peoples and their rights to their ancient lands, and "sought to do away with or suppress indigenous identities."[34]

TWAIL, besides challenging international law, also developed the theory of the New International Economic Order which they call NIEO, pointing out that the new world order after all the wars,[35] which was developed by the UN system, was also shaped by "expansive and powerful trade and investment regimes."[36] B.S. Chimni writes that international institutions are definitely not "neutral actors in hot pursuit of the common good."[37] Concentrating specifically on international institutions, Chimni feels they have evolved "at the initiative of the first world."[38] These regimes maintained the economic inequalities created by large-scale predatory, market-dominated, neoliberal colonisation, which have been reinforced by expanding corporate power. By 'common good', Chimni is referring to the "legitimacy or justness of rules and policies" and their impact on the working class(es); the landless and poor peasants; women and other marginal sections.[39] He advocates reform by changing the rules and policies by which international institutions abide, and also by holding them responsible in international law for "the wrongful consequences that ensue from their acts of omission and commission."[40] This needs to be done by developing the law of international responsibility of international institutions.

The importance of TWAIL ideology for this book is that it offers the perspective that historical development of international laws, inherently imperialistic and Eurocentric, were designed to expropriate Indigenous lands, thus impoverishing Indigenous communities and reinforcing domination and marginalisation of the Third World.[41] Threaded through the debates in this

32 Xanthaki, 'Indigenous Rights in International Law Over the Last 10 Years and Future Developments'

33 Anaya, *Indigenous Peoples in International Law*, 3.

34 Anaya, *Indigenous Peoples in International Law*, vi.

35 Anghie, 'Rethinking International Law: A TWAIL Retrospective', 13 "the Peace of Westphalia in 1648, the Congress of Vienna in 1815, the League of Nations in 1919 and the UN in 1945 [and] the fall of the Berlin Wall in 1989."

36 Anghie, 'Rethinking International Law: A TWAIL Retrospective', 13.

37 Anghie, 'Rethinking International Law: A TWAIL Retrospective', 13.

38 Chimni, 'International Institutions Today'.

39 Chimni, 'International Institutions Today'.

40 Chimni, 'International Institutions Today'.

41 Anghie, 'Rethinking International Law: A TWAIL Retrospective', 111.

book are analyses which subscribe to the colonial origins of international law, and how it has been constructed with a systemic bias against lands and peoples in the global south.[42] Barriers to realising forest rights and to accessing justice are explored by deconstructing the evolution of postcolonial legal traditions, a legal chronology of land expropriation during colonial occupation, gender inequality, extractive neoliberal policies, and subversive forest governance structures and officialdom. The threads of this bias, even if not part of the principles of new rights-based legislation, continue to be reflected in the compliance to the law by implementing bodies, resulting in reinforced inequities. Laws such as *terra nullius* ensured the right to expropriate lands in the Americas, Africa, Australia, and Asia. The context includes the role of the state, and subversive forest governance structures, plus neoliberal economics in the context of dichotomies of international human rights legislation.

The 'Third World' terminology remains intrinsic to TWAIL, on the basis of it exposing the "hierarchical ordering of the international community"[43] both internationally and at the state level. This understanding of the term encompasses historic, linear, Eurocentric, and cultural roots inherent in the colonial and imperialistic experience, which includes independence from colonial rule.[44]

Creating a dichotomy between the postcolonial state breaking free of crushing imperialism, yet unable to lose the violence of imperial rule,[45] governments in nations such as independent India reinforce colonial instruments of rule. The displacement of Indigenous communities from ancestral lands continues. How contemporary laws are implemented or not implemented in countries such as India maintains inequalities and uneven access to justice for communities being displaced from ancestral lands. This, as discussed in the book, corresponds to the approach used by TWAIL scholarship, as does the "systemic inadequacies in the international order" that prevent justice from occurring.[46]

The historical rationale for new laws, such as many land acquisition laws, created a hegemony of foreign laws and generated disparities between communities. I develop this analysis using critical TWAIL tools to demonstrate how historical laws in India have adversely affected the land rights of Indigenous communities in the tribal belt. The "expropriation of law"[47] occurred with imperial domination, from which decolonised societies have had to purge themselves. The classic Western legal traditions still exist, though they continue to alienate local legal traditions in many countries in Asia, Africa,

42 Chimni, 'International Institutions Today: An Imperial Global State in the Making', 30.
43 Rajagopal, 'Locating the Third World in Cultural Geography', 20 3.
44 Rajagopal, 'Locating the Third World in Cultural Geography', 1.
45 Anghie, 'Rethinking International Law: A TWAIL Retrospective', 24.
46 Anghie, 'Rethinking International Law: A TWAIL Retrospective', 10 and 12.
47 Cohn, 'Some Notes on Law and Change in North India', 79 67.

and Latin America which have had a history of colonisation. Referring to India, Galanter writes: "Foreign in origin and in inspiration, notoriously incongruent with the attitudes and concerns of much of the population, [the Western legal tradition] displaced a major intellectual and institutionally complex one within a highly developed civilization."[48]

Conceptualising Universal Human Rights

Legal awareness of human rights has been slowly evolving since the transgressions of the Second World War forced an international commitment[49] called the Universal Declaration of Human Rights (UDHR 1948).[50] This was the beginning of a moral and legal response to the recognition of human rights followed by numerous normative developments, both national and international. The new treaties include specific legislation for different groups, such as women, children, and Indigenous peoples,[51] and have been heralded as tools to counter historical social, political, and economic injustice. "At their foundation, human rights are a set of moral principles about how people should treat each other, particularly how people should be treated by the state authorities."[52]

The normative framework for Indigenous rights, aspects of which can be used to advocate legally for land rights of mobile peoples, includes both international and national instruments. "These establish principles and minimum rules for administration of justice and offer fairly detailed guidance to states on human rights and justice."[53] Control of land is a continuous source of contention among Indigenous (tribal) peoples, governments, conservationists, and extractive industries. The competition for control, coupled with a historical lack of rights for Indigenous peoples which has resulted in displacement and impoverishment of the Indian tribal populations, also obliged the Indian government to enact the Forest Rights Act of 2006. This is in keeping with the articulation of new international legal standards on human rights for Indigenous peoples. Enacting a progressive law, however, has not necessarily ensured the implementation in a just and equitable manner in India. In violation of human rights, state and central governments in India are ignoring participatory and democratic requirements of the Act, such as informed consent and the right to self-determination. This begs the question of whether

48 Galanter, 'The Displacement of Traditional Law in Modern India', 65.
49 Galligan and Sandler, 'Implementing Human Rights', 23.
50 United Nations General Assembly, 'Universal Declaration of Human Rights' (adopted 10 December 1948, UNGA Res. 217 A (III) (UDHR art 5)).
51 United Nations Children's Fund, 'Convention on the Rights of the Child'; CEDAW.
52 Galligan and Sandler, 'Implementing Human Rights', 23.
53 United Nations Development Programme, *Access to Justice: Practice Note*, 5.

the new Act does actually serve as a powerful tool for them to protect and manage their own forests and advocate for their rights.[54]

The Forest Rights Act: Scheduled Tribes and Other traditional Forest Dwellers (Recognition of Forest Rights) Act 2006 recognises customary forest land rights, and usufruct and habitat rights of tribal and Indigenous peoples in India. The Act also aims to encourage community participation, and community management and protection and conservation of forests and wildlife. It is framed in progressive, rights-based language, and was the result of long and vigorous advocacy by forest dwellers and activists. However, the effectiveness of legal standards protecting the needs of Indigenous and tribal populations in India is questionable. The obligation for successful implementation of these standards is not being met satisfactorily by the Indian government and the Forest Department, leaving open the question of whether the Forest Department could be creating barriers to justice for Indigenous and tribal peoples. Two articles of the Act are pertinent here: firstly, that land can only be inherited and not transferred by any other means; secondly, that any government decision involving forest lands has to be endorsed by the *Gram Sabhas* (local village assemblies) concerned, which is a wonderfully participatory and democratic aspect of the Act. These particular aspects, however, are repeatedly violated by the government, which continues to transfer vast tracts of land to extractive industries without Gram Sabha permission.

Deeply embedded in the debate tied to forced migration of forest peoples from their lands are issues of poverty and inequality. Socio-economic hierarchies divide local communities, and benefits are often distributed unequally depending on local power structures, reinforcing inequality. Why are forest lands, which are the richest biodiversity areas, usually also areas of some of the most extreme poverty? On the basis of this rationale, the main question this book asks is: how accessible is justice for Indigenous peoples in their struggle for land rights since the enactment of new legislation? The law and land dispossession of Indigenous peoples have historically shared an interface, which has had a knock-on effect on the role of governance and administration in the enactment and execution of land rights laws in India such as the Forest Rights Act. Looking deeper into whether legislation respecting land rights has affected women's rights within tribal communities, I have examined the gender consequences of legal literacy. Extractive industries and the movement for conservation of biodiversity have contributed to the displacement of Indigenous peoples from their ancestral lands, while simultaneously dismissing their traditional conservation practices.

54 Council for Social Development, *State of Implementation of the Forest Rights Act*.

Embedded Patriarchy

Without a gender lens, critical analysis remains imperfect. Intersectionality[55] and the double marginalisation of women who are Indigenous is vital to understanding how land rights affect different sections in communities. Women continue to face more extreme discrimination when forced to migrate away from ancestral lands, because their livelihoods are based on the forest economy and they are the community keepers of ecological knowledge and conservation.

An analysis of legal frameworks through a gender lens reveals that historical laws enacted with a Eurocentric colonial bias also embodied a patriarchal element congruous with the times, which affected and continues to affect women's access to justice. If access to justice differs between different communities and groups, it also differs inside communities. For example, it can be argued that an Indigenous tribe has less access to justice than a community that is not Indigenous. However, if disaggregated, data on the tribal group itself might show that within that tribe, women may have less access to justice than men. In general, women tend to be less literate, less exposed to public institutions, and have been known to face more discrimination from public officials when seeking justice.[56] Formal and customary laws often reflect cultural structures such as patriarchy, within which women have fewer land rights and less financial power in households and communities. Both women and men might accept gender power differentials in a household, and in a wider context within legal institutions, without challenging this inequality. Laws and the ability to use these laws correspond to the inequality inherent in patriarchal cultures, in which expectations of women using legal institutions to claim their rights are low. Land and property rights differ between women and men, and patriarchal traditions dictate land inheritance laws. This has had negative consequences for women's economic independence, and remains disempowering for many groups of women. In tribal societies, some of which are matrilineal – for example in India, with the North East tribal groups such as the Khasis – land inheritance laws are not tradition-

55 Taylor, *Intersectionality 101*; defines intersectionality as "the concept that all oppression is linked. More explicitly, the Oxford Dictionary defines intersectionality as "the interconnected nature of social categorisations such as race, class, and gender, regarded as creating overlapping and interdependent systems of discrimination or disadvantage". The significance of using an intersectionality lens is to avoid reinforcing these systemic inequalities such as misogyny and race, and to be aware of injustices. As Taylor points out, "any feminism that purely represents the experiences of white, middle class, able-bodied, heterosexual etc. women will fail to achieve equality for all." Taylor, *Intersectionality 101*.

56 Gender justice is the recognition that women's equality needs to take into consideration that women experience multiple inequalities which overlap, as explained in the section of the text on intersectionality on page 20.

ally patriarchal, which contributes to shifting the gender balance of power. In general, however, globally, ownership of land in Indigenous groups also follows patriarchal lines of inheritance, which has to be borne in mind during any discussion of access to justice for minority groups. This indicates that within marginalised societies, marginalisation itself is not homogenous. As my case studies show, there can be further divisive marginalisation along gender lines, mobility, caste, or other hierarchies.

Indigenous Peoples and the Nature of Forced Migration and Displacement

Dependent on land for their survival, Indigenous peoples are ancient inhabitants of the land before it was either colonised or governed by a sovereign state.[57] Their social structures are often distinctive from mainstream populations,[58] and one of the characteristics of Indigenous populations is their symbiotic relationship with, and the deep respect they share for, their lands: "a profound cultural social and spiritual relationship with their lands and territories is characteristic of indigenous peoples and fundamental to their survival".[59] The UN Declaration on the Rights of Indigenous Peoples of 2007 acknowledges the "historic injustices as a result of, inter alia, their colonization and dispossession of their lands, territories and resources, thus preventing them from exercising, in particular, their right to development in accordance with their own needs and interests".[60] Mobile Indigenous peoples, a sub-group within the broader category of Indigenous peoples,[61] are dependent on usufruct of land for their survival, and earn their livelihoods from activities that rely on a mobile way of life, such as pastoralists who herd animals, slash-and-burn cultivators, or hunters and gatherers. There are also mobile seafaring (and other waterborne) peoples who sail and fish.[62] Since the mobile way of life is so physically demanding, a growing number are either resorting to regimes that are semi-nomadic only, or engaging in other settled occupations.

There is no legal definition of Indigenous people to which all countries subscribe, nor is the term defined in the UN Declaration. This was a deliberate decision, reflected in Article 33: "Indigenous peoples have a right to determine their own identity or membership in accordance with their customs

57 Gilbert and Doyle, 'A New Dawn Over the Land', 9.
58 Government of India, Ministry of Tribal Affairs website, accessed 2 February 2013, http://tribal.nic.in/.
59 Gilbert and Doyle, 'A New Dawn Over the Land', 3.
60 Gilbert and Doyle, 'A New Dawn Over the Land', 2.
61 Dana Standing Committee, *Dana Declaration.*
62 Dana Standing Committee, *Dana Declaration.*

and traditions".[63] This decision recognises and reflects the view that the complex and nuanced nature of the politics pertaining to Indigenous groups is too broad for a single definition.[64] One UN study attempts a definition:

> Indigenous communities, peoples and nations of those which, having a historical continuity with pre-invasion and pre-colonial societies that developed on their territories, consider themselves distinct from other sectors of the society now prevailing in those territories, or parts of them. They form at present non-dominant sectors of society and are determined to preserve, develop and transmit to future generations their ancestral territories, and their ethnic identity, as the basis of their continued existence of peoples, in accordance with their own cultural patterns, social institutions and legal systems.[65]

In many parts of the world, pressure from growing populations, their need for food, and, consequently, more intense demand for agricultural land often encroach on forest lands. Increasing extractive industries operating in the name of economic development, and governments that collude with them at the expense of conserved lands, pose a real threat. More than 40 per cent of land illegally acquired for development and mining belongs to tribal communities in India,[66] and in the five years following the enactment of the Forest Rights Act 2006, more than 500,000 hectares of forest land were destroyed to make way for mines, dams, and industrial projects.[67] This process of destruction of habitats is happening worldwide, having started in the 1400s, and is not confined to India or to the developing world.[68]

'Access to Justice'

The debate on access to justice explores the evolution of land laws and how, driven by the expropriation of land, land laws evolved in ways that produce

63 Gilbert, 'Indigenous Rights in the Making', 207.

64 Most countries employ the term Indigenous, but other countries use Aboriginal (Australia or Malaysia), First Nation (Canada) or Native Americans (USA). The Indian government uses the word Adivasi (or tribal) for the ancient communities who reside in the hills and forests.

65 Martínez Cobo, *Study of the Problem of Discrimination*, UN Doc E/CN.4/Sub.2/1986/7/Add 4, para. 369.

66 Sarin, 'Land Lessons from Australia'.

67 Campaign for Survival and Dignity, 'What Is the Forest Rights Act about?', *Forest Rights Act Website*, accessed 30 October 2013, https://forestrightsact.com/what-is-this-act-about/.

68 In the USA, for example, during the first four years under President Obama, his government leased around six million acres to the oil and gas industry. This was more than twice as much land as was set aside for protection, as compared to Bill Clinton's administration, which protected 26.9 million acres. To combat this global trend, which has connotations for the disappearance of flora, fauna and competition for shrinking space between human beings and wildlife, a global conservation movement has emerged.

and maintain inequality. This inequality, reinforced by historical bias, continues to be supported in the formulation of land laws, impacting contemporary access to justice, especially for certain groups of people who are on the periphery of societies. The chapter also examines the role of the state and the economics of survival, and challenges the assumed protective role of the state in the fair distribution of justice to marginalised communities.

Access to justice is influenced by various socio-economic, administrative, and political factors. Access to justice as defined by the United Nations Development Program (UNDP) is "much more than improving an individual's access to courts, or guaranteeing legal representation. It must be defined in terms of ensuring that legal and judicial outcomes are just and equitable".[69] Justice is a moral concept and a legal one, and is related to fairness and what is due. Legally, it relates to institutions which are obligated to dispense justice for the smooth running of society, and concerns corrective justice and distributive justice. The latter deals with the penal corrective systems; the former deals with the allocation of resources, and the negotiation of rights and obligations, both of which are socially oriented. The notion of 'fair' distribution in this study relates to relationships, wealth, privileges, and opportunities among mainstream and minority communities. The moral aspect of justice underpins the law, but is not synonymous with it. The law can be framed in an unjust manner, benefitting some groups at the expense of others, making the ability to access justice dependent on how equal a society is.[70] Social justice is the context for this review of access to justice. Access to justice signifies that citizens are able to use legal institutions to obtain solutions to their common justice problems. A politically neutral perspective would regard access to justice as a process that is part of the justice system, which in principle provides all citizens with equal means to use the legal system in order to claim their rights. The contrasting position takes a more politicised stand, recognising that true access to justice is dependent on equality.

Access to justice can be seen as the ability to use legal instruments in order to ensure that legal rights are recognised and awarded, and "the means by which rights are made effective".[71] The existence of a law that grants rights to land, for example, can lead to the assumption that justice will now be fulfilled. The concept of law and justice is therefore inextricably linked to rights, working on the assumption that human rights,[72] or other rights such as land rights, are conceded by legislation. If rights to land are enacted by

69 UNDP, *Access to Justice: Practice Note*, 5.

70 *Oxford Dictionaries*, s.v. 'usufruct', accessed 12 August 2014, https://oxforddictionaries.com.

71 Cappelletti and Garth, 'Access to Justice', 185.

72 Rights provide a minimal level of protection for the individual or group against others and the state. The beneficiary of rights could be individuals or groups, such as children, women and minorities. American Bar Association, *Access to Justice Assessment Tool*, 5.

law, in order to claim these rights an individual or community needs access to justice. Rights themselves, enshrined within the law, are distinguished as substantive rights and procedural rights. Legislation, especially rights-based legislation, incorporates substantive rights. For example, land rights incorporate the right to hold the land, to live on it, and to conserve and manage it; these are substantive rights. Procedural rights outline the rules and regulations that allow an individual or a group to be supported by the judiciary. The framing of these rules as legislation, the courts, the lawyers, the government bodies, and civil society organisations who assist people in claiming their rights are all part of the procedural process. These institutions within the legal system have to be effective and functional in order to provide solutions that are fair for citizens seeking justice and in order for access to justice to be realised.[73] Problems arise when these expectations are thwarted by dysfunction and justice becomes inaccessible.

The Consequences of Legal Imperialism

The Scheduled Tribes and Other Traditional Forest Dwellers (Recognition of Forest Rights) Act, 2006 ('the Forest Rights Act') has tremendously affected the lives of Indigenous forest communities in India. This book critically examines and evaluates how the Forest Rights Act has changed the dynamics of land expropriation of Indigenous tribal peoples and their access to justice. The book's inter-disciplinary approach incorporates a historical overview which sets the context for current government policy with its evident postcolonial links. The historical analysis connects with a socio-legal analysis to reveal how colonial ideology shaped the current expropriative land laws, creating a dichotomy with India's postcolonial activist judiciary which innovates and advocates for human rights. The economic impact of the extractive industry created a neoliberal environment, which has similarities of the colonial prioritisation of profit over community rights, and has created a form of internal colonisation. The more severe consequences of these neoliberal policies affected women who have been resisting entrenched patriarchal patterns and land loss. The gender inequity has eroded women's power base connected to their ecological knowledge and conservation. Based upon extensive fieldwork in India and by grounding the FRA in India's history of colonialism and post-colonialism, the book argues that the FRA has not necessarily helped mobile Indigenous peoples in their struggle to reclaim their ancestral lands and to advocate for their rights. Instead, the FRA may have made them more vulnerable to displacement and state-supported development, which is consistent with

73 American Bar Association, *Access to Justice Assessment Tool*, 1.

forms of legal imperialism that maintain inequalities and perpetuates as it reproduces impoverishment.

Conclusion

Although people can consciously act to change their social and economic circumstances, critical research recognises that their ability to do so is "constrained by various forms of social, cultural and political domination".[74] This book investigates contemporary societal conflicts, inconsistencies, and contradictions, with a focus on eradicating causes of oppression and exclusion through agency and empowering goals.[75] This focus occurs within a framework of rights and responsibilities of communities and governments, which in turn is grounded in the context of inequality and justice. If justice is the principle underpinning law, then the impact of new laws, such as the Forest Rights Act 2006, needs analysing in reference to whether they have facilitated justice for tribal populations made vulnerable by being dispossessed of their lands.

Barriers to realising forest rights, and to accessing justice, are explored by deconstructing the evolution of postcolonial legal traditions, a legal chronology of land expropriation during colonial occupation, gender inequality, extractive neoliberal policies, and subversive forest governance structures and officialdom.

Inequality is conceptualised by examining the development of human rights legislation for Indigenous populations, in the context of the increasing land dispossession that they face. Within the context of justice, it has been argued that greater equality makes societies stronger, and that inequality is divisive and socially corrosive.[76] This argument makes the success of the Forest Rights Act more important, because it could theoretically reduce the growing impoverishment of Indigenous populations being dispossessed of their lands, and ease the social problems faced by the Adivasis. These communities facing land dispossession can, in theory, use the Forest Rights Act to reclaim customary land rights to their forest habitation.

There are four major aspects of accessing justice that have emerged from the scholarship on the subject outlined earlier. First, historically, the ways in which the law has been created, and by whom it has been both drafted and enacted, have not only provided us with a framework that gives people rights, but have also denied people their rights. This has led to the uncomfortable existence of judicial imperialism, in which the laws do not change

74 Myers, 'Qualitative Research in Information Systems', 7.

75 Myers, 'Qualitative Research in Information Systems', 7. See also Ngwenyama and Lee, 'Communication Richness in Electronic Mail' and Hirschheim and Klein, 'Realizing Emancipatory Principles'.

76 Wilkinson and Pickett, *The Spirit Level*.

the lives of people in the ways they were intended. Second, socio-economic inequalities within countries have impaired the legal literacy and capacities of individuals and communities to use legal institutions on a more equal basis, meaning that access to justice is shaped both by the socio-economic culture of a country and by other inequalities such as those related to class or gender. This in turn is tied to the third aspect of the evolution of human rights norms. These norms have institutionalised the concept and created a global awareness that every individual and community has rights that need to be legally protected, and which base the concept of justice on a social contract. The fourth and final point that has emerged from the scholarship are the differences in how legal rights are either recognised or enacted by judiciaries or governments. This boils down to a moral framework that decides whether human beings are entitled to certain rights at all. This morality, as outlined earlier by thinkers such as Rawls and Sen, influences the framing of international and national laws and, more importantly, how these laws are implemented at all levels, whether global, national, or local. If the moral beliefs of individuals who hold power in governments do not respect these rights, access to justice and 'just' laws that respect land rights become untenable. Egalitarian and inclusive governance is therefore a basic prerequisite for legal rights and access to justice.

In critically examining how the Forest Rights Act has changed the dynamic of land expropriation of Indigenous tribal peoples and their access to justice, I seek to establish a framework that contextualises legal control of community forest land rights through access to justice which emphasises an inter-disciplinary and nuanced approach. This book aims to provide evidence of the effects of the Forest Rights Act 2006 on the lives of Indigenous forest communities in India. The intention is to contribute towards the scholarship on access to justice for marginalised mobile Indigenous peoples through the introduction of social legislation.

Annex

1. Methodology

The analysis, evidence, and clarity for this research was shaped by the methodology, specifically the primary data from the field, and applies social-scientific and historical methods to study access to justice for marginalised groups. The empirical aspect of this research was chosen in order to examine the law from two critical standpoints, a critical-theory approach and an Indigenous-positionality approach. The critical-theory approach asks the questions about the unstated (and, generally, unexamined) assumptions in the interpretation of statutory law. The Indigenous-positionality approach, dependent on the ethnographic fieldwork, asks how law and its implementation is interpreted, deployed, contested, and perhaps alterably, by grassroots Indigenous activism. This is a deeply inter-disciplinary approach which draws on theory and method from a range of relevant disciplines, which serves to demonstrate both the richness of such an approach, as well as the unexpected general lessons that flow from it.

This empirical study draws on qualitative primary data, supported by secondary conceptual sources.[77] The Critical Research approach was chosen under the assumption that "social reality is historically constituted and that it is produced and reproduced by people,"[78] and that critical research teases out contemporary societal conflicts, inconsistencies, and contradictions, with a focus on eradicating causes of oppression and exclusion with empowering goals.[79]

77 "Qualitative research methods are designed to help researchers understand people and the social and cultural contexts within which they live." Myers, 'Qualitative Research in Information Systems.'

78 Myers, 'Qualitative Research in Information Systems.'

79 Myers, 'Qualitative Research in Information Systems.'; Management Information Systems Quarterly no page number; Also see Ngwenyama and Lee, 'Communication Richness in Electronic Mail' and Hirschheim and Klein, 'Realizing Emancipatory Principles in Information Systems Development.'

The primary sources comprised the collection of new data through field visits and interviews from a number of different sources, mainly communities and activists connected to forest rights and legislation in India during five months in a period of over two years. The major primary data was gathered with the help of NGO teams who have access to remote tribal communities; and from multiple case studies of tribal peoples in various forest community sites, identified in order to ensure different experiences of the use of Forest Rights legislation.

I used multiple qualitative methods to develop a conceptual understanding, comprising field observation; open-ended, unstructured and semi-structured in-depth interviews with groups of men and women from forest communities; group discussions with village councils (*Gram Sabha*); meetings interviewing key players and local leaders; and my researcher impressions and reactions. I also used visual participatory research approaches (PRA), and group activities to record the understandings and perspectives of the case study groups, such as PRA tools for mapping with mobile Indigenous peoples to derive data of the grazing corridors for their pastoral activities, how the Forest Rights Act was being used by them, and how it changed land use and dispossession. The data has been examined for variables such as gender, exclusive rules, and power dynamics between the community and local government.

I interviewed key civil society activists who are part of the Government of India review committee on FRA, and key NGO/civil society persons and academics who worked intensively on getting the Forest Rights Act passed by the Central Government.[80] It was vital that the methodology I had planned to use not only provided evidence to evaluate the success of the FRA but also helped me draw out the questions within the debates around access to justice, and around the political morality embodied both in the law and in its implementation.

Using a multiple case study method, I tested the conceptual framework empirically in three states in India through in-depth interviews with stakeholders and field observations. The four indicators that I used for choosing an appropriate community to study included whether the communities were forest dwellers or dependent on the forests for their livelihoods, namely hunting and gathering minor forest produce; whether they were dealing with issues of land dispossession; and whether they used the Forest Rights Act to make claims.

80 Astha Sansthan, *Astha: A Field Based Resource Organization. Annual Report 2007–2008*, 2007–2008, https://www.astha.ngo. Quote from Astha's Annual Report 2007–2008: "The Resource Unit, working with the Campaign for Survival and Dignity (CSD) conducted a Sit-In, in New Delhi, in November 2007, and during this period, many M.P.s, senior Political Party leaders and Ministers were contacted to make them aware of just how important it was to get the Rules framed so that the Scheduled Tribes and Other Traditional Forest Dwellers (Recognition of Forest Rights) Act could be implemented."

The three states selected during 2012 to 2014 were Gujarat, Rajasthan, and Maharashtra, which fulfilled the criteria earlier. This included the Maldhari community of pastoralists in Mera District, Gujarat; the Dhangar mobile Indigenous communities who undertake an annual 300 km migration from Dahanu in the coastal Konkan to the Deccan Plateau in Maharashtra; the Raika camel herders in the Rajsamand District of the Kumbhalgarh forests in western India's Rajasthan; Adivasi forest peoples, who were engaged in land right struggles in the Aravalli Hill range of Udaipur district in Rajasthan.

Bibliography

Anaya, J.S. *Indigenous Peoples in International Law*. Oxford University Press, 2004.

Anderson, M.R. 'Access to Justie and Legal Process: Making Legal Institutions Responsive to Poor People in LDCs'. *IDS Working Paper* 178 (2003), 178

Chimni, B.S. 'International Institutions Today: An Imperial Global State in the Making'. *EJIL* 30 (2004).

Council for Social Development (CSD). *State of Implementation of the Forest Rights Act – Summary Report*. CSD, 2012.

Dana Standing Committee. *Dana Declaration on Mobile Peoples and Conservation*. Conference, Wadi Dana Nature Reserve, Jordan, 3–7 April 2002. http://danadeclaration.org/main_declarationenglish.shtml.

Galanter, M. 'Making Law Work for the Oppressed'. *The Other Side* III (1983), 7

Gilbert, J. 'Indigenous Rights in the Making: The United Nations Declaration on the Rights of Indigenous Peoples'. *International Journal on Minority and Group Rights* 14(2/3) (2007), 207–30.

Gilbert, J. 'Land Rights and Nomadic Peoples: Using International Law at the Local Level'. *Nomadic Peoples* 16(2) (2012), 78–83.

Gilbert, J., and C. Doyle. 'A New Dawn Over the Land: Shedding Light on Collective Ownership and Consent'. In S. Allen and A. Xanthaki (eds), *Reflections on the UN Declaration on the Rights of Indigenous People*. Hart Publishing, 2011, 1–68.

Hirschheim, R., and H.K. Klein. 'Realizing Emancipatory Principles in Information Systems Development: The Case for ETHICS'. *Management Information Systems Quarterly* 18(1) (1994), 83–109.

Honeychurch, W., and C.A. Makarewicz. 'The Archaeology of Pastoral Nomadism'. *Annual Review of Anthropology* 45 (2016), 341.

Impe, A.-M. *A Convention to Fight Discrimination*. Union View, 2011.

Martínez Cobo, J. *Study of the Problem of Discrimination against Indigenous Populations*. Special Rapporteur of the Sub-Commission on Prevention of Discrimination and Protection of Minorities. United Nations, 1986.

Myers, M. 'Qualitative Research in Information Systems'. *Management Information Systems Quarterly* 21(2) (June 1997), 241–42.

Ngwenyama, O.K., and A.S. Lee. 'Communication Richness in Electronic Mail: Critical Social Theory and the Contextuality of Meaning'. *Management Information Systems Quarterly* 21(2) (June 1997), 145–67.

Pastoralism CCoELoEA. 'Pastoralists Turn Variability into Food'. *Misereor*, 2021. www.celep.info/wp-content/uploads/2021/06/Pastoralists-turn-variability-into-food-FULL-1.pdf, accessed 18 August 2021.

Pathak, N. *Community Conserved Areas in India: A Directory*. Kalpavriksh, 2009.

Sarin, M. 'Land Lessons from Australia'. *The Hindu*, 9 March 2013. www.thehindu.com/opinion/editorial/land-lessons-from-australia/article4488891.ece.

Sigamany, I. 'Destroying a Way of Life: Indigenous Peoples, the Forest Rights Act of India and Land Displacement of Indigenous Peoples'. In I. Satiroglu and N. Choi

(eds), *Development-Induced Displacement and Resettlement: New Perspectives on Persisting Problems*. Routledge, 2015, 159–69.
Simmons, B. *Mobilizing for Human Rights: International Law in Domestic Policy*. New York, Cambridge University Press, 2009.
Taylor, B. *Intersectionality 101: What Is It and Why Is It Important?* Womankind Worldwide, 2019.
United Nations Commission on Sustainable Development (UNCSD). *Indigenous Peoples Caucus Major Group Closing Statement*. United Nations, 2005.
United Nations Declaration on the Rights of Indigenous Peoples (UNDRIP), United Nations, 2007.
United Nations Department of Economic and Social Affairs (UN DESA). *Indigenous Peoples' Caucus #39 Statement by Victoria Tauli Corpuz*. United Nations, 2002.
United Nations Development Programme (UNDP). *Access to Justice: Practice Note*. United Nations, 2004. www.undp.org/content/dam/aplaws/publication/en/publications/democratic-governance/dg-publications-for-website/access-to-justice-practice-note/Justice_PN_En.pdf.
United Nations Disaster Risk Reduction Program (UNDRR). *Hyogo Framework for Action 2005–2015: Building the Resilience of Nations and Communities to Disasters*. ISDR, 2005.
United Nations Framework Convention on Climate Change (UNFCCC). *The Rio Declaration*. United Nations, 1992.
United Nations International Strategy for Disaster Reduction (UNISDR). *Indigenous Knowledge for Disaster Risk Reduction: Good Practices and Lessons Learned from Experiences in the Asia-Pacific Region*. United Nations, 2008.
Vemuri, A. 'Joint Forest Management in India: An Unavoidable and Conflicting Common Property Regime in Natural Resource Management'. *Journal of Development and Social Transformation* 5 (2008), 81.
Wilkinson, R., and K. Pickett. *The Spirit Level: Why Greater Equality Makes Societies Stronger*. Bloomsbury Press, 2011.

Notes

American Bar Association, R. O. L. I. (2012). *Access to Justice Assessment Tool. American Bar Association, Rule of Law Initiative*. Washington, DC, American Bar Association, 105.
Anaya, J.S. *Indigenous Peoples in International Law*. Oxford University Press, 2004.
Anghie, A. 'Rethinking International Law: A TWAIL Retrospective'. *The European Journal of International Law* 34 (2023), 7.
Chimni, B.S. 'International Institutions Today: An Imperial Global State in the Making'. *European Journal of International Law* 30 (2004), 1.
Cohn, B.S. 'Some Notes on Law and Change in North India'. *Economic Development and Cultural Change* 8 (1959), 79.
Galanter, M. 'The Displacement of Traditional Law in Modern India'. *Journal of Social Issues* 14 (1968), 65.
Honeychurch, W., and C.A. Makarewicz. 'The Archaeology of Pastoral Nomadism'. *Annual Review of Anthropology* 45 (2016), 341.
Impe, A.-M. *A Convention to Fight Discrimination*. Union View, 2011.
Mutua, M., and A. Anghie. 'What Is TWAIL?'. *American Society of International Law* 94 (2000), 31.
Myers, M. 'Qualitative Research in Information Systems'. *Management Information Systems Quarterly* 21 (1997).
Rajagopal, B. 'Locating the Third World in Cultural Geography'. *Third World Legal Studies* 15 (1999), 20.

Sansthan, A. *Astha: A Field Based Resource Organization*. Annual Report 2007–2008, 2007–2008, unpublished. https://www.astha.ngo

Taylor, B. *Intersectionality 101: What Is It and Why Is It Important*? Womankind Worldwide, 2019.

Vemuri, A. 'Joint Forest Management in India: An Unavoidable and Conflicting Common Property Regime in Natural Resource Management'. *Journal of Development and Social Transformation* 5 (2008), 81.

Xanthaki, A. 'Indigenous Rights in International Law Over the Last 10 Years and Future Developments'. *Melbourne Journal of International Law* 10 (2009), 27.

Chapter 1

Legal Mechanisms for Indigenous Peoples and the Forest Rights Act of India

Introduction

Historically, most Indigenous communities were nomadic, herding animals to pasture and employing agricultural techniques such as slash-and-burn agriculture, which allows land to regenerate while the communities move on. Many Indigenous communities have since settled and chosen either agriculture or other livelihoods. Culturally, however, Indigenous peoples still tend to live communally and use land collectively. National and international land laws primarily assume private individualistic ownership of land, or land owned by the sovereign state.[1] This contrasts with the collective use[2] of land by Indigenous communities, especially mobile populations,[3] who do not necessarily seek to own the land they use, abiding instead by the customary practice of using vast swathes of common lands for grazing corridors.

In the past, the concept of *terra nullius* or 'empty lands' was used to expropriate Indigenous lands by settlers who colonised and denied the rights of Indigenous communities inhabiting those lands.[4] *Terra nullius* is a principle that Indigenous peoples continue to fight against in an effort to reclaim lost ancestral lands, especially since their identity is often tied to a collective relationship to lands and resources. This foundational relationship with land is recognised as central to ensuring the physical well-being of present and future generations as well as providing the resources that enable their social, cultural, and spiritual lives.[5] The lack of access to their lands, territories, and

1 United Nations General Assembly, Declaration on the Rights of Indigenous Peoples (UNDRIP), Res. 61/295 A (13 December 2007).
2 Gilbert and Doyle, 'A New Dawn over the Land', 3.
3 The terms 'nomadic' and 'mobile Indigenous peoples', which are used interchangeably, and refer to communities whose historic livelihoods necessitate a nomadic way of life. Many mobile indigenous peoples are pastoralists. See Introduction Chapter Endnote 10, for a more detailed description.
4 Gilbert and Doyle, 'A New Dawn over the Land', 5.
5 Tugendhat and Dictaan-Bang-oa, *Realizing Indigenous Women's Rights*, 2.

DOI: 10.4324/9781003589488-2

natural resources could serve as a threat to Indigenous cultures so distinctly tied to ancestral lands.[6]

In India, land displacement of tribal peoples began under colonial rule when forests were recognised as a rich source of revenue and converted to sovereign territory beginning in the seventeenth century. Current land struggles focus on threats from both development and conservation. Large-scale industrial extraction and production, such as fishing, logging, hydroelectric dams, and monoculture plantations, have taken place in resource-rich forests, displacing Indigenous communities. Similarly, environmental conservation has relied on excluding communities and undermining ancestral land rights.[7]

The struggle of forest peoples in India against the historic loss of land since 1874 eventually led to the birth of the Scheduled Tribes and Other Traditional Forest Dwellers (Recognition of Forest Rights) Act 2006, also known as the Forest Rights Act. The discourse on Indigenous peoples' land rights is complex, especially when situated within the legal frameworks of national land laws. The discussion of the Forest Rights Act here is connected to international legal frameworks through an analysis of the extent to which expansion in international rights-based approaches for Indigenous communities complements the development of national legislation. The Forest Rights Act 2006 precedes the UN Declaration on the Rights of Indigenous Peoples 2007 (UNDRIP)[8] by one year. UNDRIP mirrors some of the land rights reflected in the Forest Rights Act of India, such as Free, Prior, and Informed Consent (FPIC), confirming the global recognition of Indigenous rights. Viewed within the context of Indigenous land rights and situated against the background of a broader international rights-based normative framework, I argue that national legislation and policies do not necessarily improve access to justice for communities and individuals on the national stage, unless strongly supported by administrative justice. I also question whether the international laws on Indigenous land protection can counter the national discrimination faced by Indigenous communities when being displaced from their ancestral lands. I have illustrated and substantiated the arguments for access to justice for Indigenous peoples and the effects of the Forest Rights Act on the lives of forest peoples in India with three case studies.

Terra Nullius

The *terra nullius* attitude and lingering expropriative mentality causing opposition to Indigenous rights to land is illustrated later in two relatively contemporary examples in India. In 2013, a struggle took place between the

6 United Nations, 'United Nations Permanent Forum on Indigenous Issues', 2004, accessed 29 January 2013, http://social.un.org/index/IndigenousPeoples/SecondDecade.aspx.

7 Jonas et al., *An Analysis of International Law*.

8 United Nations General Assembly, Declaration on the Rights of Indigenous Peoples (UNDRIP), Res. 61/295 A (13 December 2007).

Kondh tribes of Orissa and a global mining company called Vedanta, which was mining for bauxite in partnership with the Indian government. The central Government of India filed an affidavit in an attempt to acquire Kondh land, arguing that it would be in the public interest. This would effectively remove tribal rights.[9] It would also displace tribal peoples from the Niyamgiri hills, which were sacred to them, and destroy their livelihoods.[10] Another high-profile case in which thousands of tribal communities were displaced was the Sardar Sarovar Dam and Power Project on the Narmada River in Gujarat in India. The social and environmental costs of this project were very high because no adequate measures were taken by the government to protect the tribal communities, whose habitat and livelihoods would be wiped out when the plains were flooded by the dam waters. The project was highly controversial from the late 1980s onwards, and the World Bank withdrew its funding in the 1990s.[11]

These examples reveal the lack of responsibility and accountability that states, international institutions, and multinational corporations assume towards the rights of Indigenous peoples. Often this pro-profit development at the expense of the livelihoods and habitats of marginalised Indigenous communities has encompassed a lack of political morality and political will of the government in India, and has culminated in an inability to abide by national and international legal norms for the protection of Indigenous peoples. The normative framework outlined later explicates the national and international response to the long history of land dispossession that continues to be driven by a corporate commitment to free-market capitalist values often concealed under the justification for 'development'.[12]

The Forest Rights Act: Scheduled Tribes and Other Traditional Forest Dwellers (Recognition of Forest Rights) Act 2006

Substantive Rights and Access to Justice

The Scheduled Tribes and Other Traditional Forest Dwellers (Recognition of Forest Rights) Act 2006, of India, referred to as the Forest Rights Act throughout this book, grants enhanced rights to forest peoples over lands that they have occupied or used, often for generations.[13] The Forest Rights

9 Sigamany, 'Destroying a Way of Life', 163.
10 Sambhav,'CentreSettoDiluteTribalRights',www.downtoearth.org.in/news/centre-set-to-dilute-tribal-rights-over-forestland-40389 (no page numbers), no page numbers.
11 Sambhav, 'Centre Set to Dilute Tribal Rights'.
12 Raya, *Indigenous Women Stand against Violence*.
13 Government of India, The Scheduled Tribes and Other Traditional Forest Dwellers (Recognition of Forest Rights) Bill (adopted 15 December 2006, No. 158-C of 2005).

Act recognises that the 'historical injustice' of land dispossession of Indigenous peoples of India, called Adivasis,[14] needs to be addressed.[15] The Forest Rights Act, reflecting a global move towards the recognition of human rights, is founded on principles of social justice, and was formulated on the cusp of evolving international laws for Indigenous peoples,[16] creating a powerful tool for Indigenous peoples in their struggle to reclaim lost land and usufruct rights.

The main purposes of the Act were to revoke historical injustice endured by the Adivasis in relation to lost lands, to restore customary rights to them, to increase tribal participation in the management of forest lands, and to contribute to a more structured conservation approach.[17] One of the strongest aspects of the Forest Rights Act is that it recognises community forest rights. This is especially significant given that most tribal and pastoralist communities behave communally. The Forest Rights Act is part of India's legal system, and recognises usufruct and habitat rights of tribal and Indigenous peoples in India.[18] It was the result of long and vigorous advocacy by forest dwellers and activists. The Government of India states that the Forest Rights Act

> is a result of the protracted struggle by the marginal and tribal communities of our country to assert their rights over the forestland on which they were traditionally dependent. This Act is crucial to the rights of millions of tribal people and other forest dwellers in different parts of our country as it provides for the restitution of deprived forest rights across India, including both individual rights to cultivated land in forestland and community rights over common property resources. The notification of Rules for the implementation of the Forest Rights Act, 2006 on 1st Jan 2008, has finally paved the way to undo the 'historic injustice' done to the tribals and other forest dwellers.[19]

14 'Adivasi' is the Indian name for the original inhabitants of the Indian subcontinent. The Indian government uses several terms interchangeably: Adivasi, tribal, Scheduled Tribes, or SC for the ancient communities who reside in the hills and forests. Dash and Khotari, 'Forest Rights and Conservation in India', 151.

15 Government of India, The Scheduled Tribes and Other Traditional Forest Dwellers (Recognition of Forest Rights) Act, 2006.

16 United Nations General Assembly, Declaration on the Rights of Indigenous Peoples (UNDRIP), Res. 61/295 A (13 December 2007). 1.

17 Bose, Arts and van Dijk, 'Forest Governmentality', 664; Government of India, The Scheduled Tribes and Other Traditional Forest Dwellers (Recognition of Forest Rights) Bill (adopted 15 December 2006, No. 158-C of 2005).

18 Indian Tribal Heritage, 'The Scheduled Tribes and Other Traditional Forest Dwellers (Recognition of Forest Rights) Act, 2006'; Dash, 'Redefining Biodiversity Conservation in India', 33.

19 Government of India, The Scheduled Tribes and Other Traditional Forest Dwellers (Recognition of Forest Rights) Bill (adopted 15 December 2006, No. 158-C of 2005).

In India, the expropriation of forest lands began in 1874, when the colonial government converted all forest lands into sovereign property for the purposes of extractive industry. During this process, Indigenous tribal peoples and other traditional forest dwellers lost their customary ancestral rights of ownership and usufruct. These resource-rich lands were officially labelled 'schedule areas', and the Adivasi populations were called 'Scheduled Tribes'. This language and concept are still in use, and in the 1950s the compiled 'schedule' or list of forest and hill tribes was incorporated into independent India's constitution. Under colonial occupation, new laws were enacted to ensure the arrogation of forest lands. The new forest legislation included Scheduled Districts Act XVI 1874, the Government of India Act 1919, and the Government of India Act 1935.[20] The new laws not only facilitated colonial control of forest lands but displaced forest peoples, forcing migration and criminalising communities who attempted to maintain their forest-based livelihoods, under the Criminal Tribes Act and the Indian Forest Act 1927.[21]

Independent India after 1947, much to the detriment of forest peoples, did not revise the existing forest laws, such as the Indian Forest Act 1927, which were designed to expropriate forest lands. New laws after independence, such as the Wild Life (Protection) Act 1972 and Forest Conservation Act 1980, were strongly influenced by the colonial laws that facilitated the extraction of natural and mineral resources. The Indian government continued colonial policies that forced the migration of Adivasis and other traditional forest dwellers and prioritised wildlife protection over improvement in the quality of forest peoples' lives in areas such as housing and livelihoods. Under the British occupation, the Forest Department had full administrative control of the scheduled areas of the forests. The Indian postcolonial government retained similar control, with new policy mechanisms such as the National Forest Policy of 1988 and the Joint Forest Management programme. They continued to use the Forest Department, which maintained and reinforced the colonial type of discrimination and exclusion of Adivasis, perpetuating 'ecological imperialism and dispossession'.[22]

In establishing a new legal tradition, independent India had to move away from what Galanter calls 'expropriation of law',[23] referring to a colonial legal system of 'imperial domination and repression'.[24] The British legal system was superimposed onto India's discrete, multilingual, and multicultural kingdoms ruled by rajas and maharajas. With this modern new legal system came the foreign machinery of bureaucracy and protocol, which was introduced

20 Bhengra, Bijoy and Luithui, *Report on the Adivasis of India*, 10.
21 Sigamany, 'Destroying a Way of Life', 159.
22 Sigamany, 'Land Rights and Neoliberalism', 369; Springate-Baginski et al., *The Indian Forest Rights Act 2006*, 12.
23 Galanter, 'The Displacement of Traditional Law', 67.
24 Sigamany, 'Land Rights and Neoliberalism', 369.

into the newly unified colony under British rule. These new traditions shaped the postcolonial nation, but were alien to Hindu law, Sharia law, and tribal legal traditions. Galanter points out how they were alien to Indian legal traditions: "Foreign in origin and in inspiration, notoriously incongruent with the attitudes and concerns of much of the population, [the Western legal tradition] displaced a major intellectual and institutionally complex one within a highly developed civilization".[25]

Modern India had to begin the process of extricating itself and shrugging off the inherited classic legal forms of control, some parts of which, unfortunately, were to remain permanent fixtures of postcolonial law in India. For Adivasis, this has meant engaging with unfamiliar legal structures, which has created permanent alienation, especially because Indigenous legal practice relies on informal tribunals with mediation and a win-win tradition representing 'a multiplicity of systems with no fixed authoritative body of law, no set binding precedents, no single legitimate way of applying or changing the law'.[26] Local tribunals, which could have peaceably settled disputes under traditional formats, were not recognised by the government's courts, throwing Indigenous peoples into a contentious, Western tradition with its win-lose punitive litigation. Language barriers, geographical isolation, and illiteracy exacerbate legal disempowerment.[27] Indigenous legal traditions in India relied on communal ties, status, and mediation, concepts that were quashed under the Western 'equality before the law' and win-lose principles.

> The new courts not only created new opportunities for intimidation and harassment and new means for carrying on old disputes, but they also gave rise to a sense of individual rights, not dependent on opinion or usage, and capable of being actively enforced by government, even in opposition to community opinion.[28]

This permanent cultural dichotomy obstructs Adivasi access to the judicial system when they are being displaced or dispossessed of their lands, and raises the question of whether even revolutionary, progressive rights-based legislation will always be alien to Indigenous communities.

The Forest Rights Act of 2006 has been 'India's largest statutory development' in the field of Adivasi rights.[29] The Act has generated continuing polarised debates in India, with some heralding it as the long-awaited legal mechanism that the Adivasis and other forest dwellers need, not only to reclaim their ancestral lands and as a means to eventually pull themselves out of the economic

25 Galanter, 'The Displacement of Traditional Law', 65; Kidder, 'Western Law in India', 170.
26 Galanter, 'The Displacement of Traditional Law', 71.
27 Sigamany, 'Land Rights and Neoliberalism', 372.
28 Galanter, 'The Displacement of Traditional Law', 70.
29 Saravanan, 'Political Economy', 199.

deprivation that forced migration has induced but also to be able to halt forced migration. The arguments in favour of the Forest Rights Act are that tribal peoples' ancestral claims to their lands have been recognised.

> It is estimated that at present about 40 lakhs (4,000,000)[30] tribal and forest dwellers [have] no legal status to their land. Without any legal documents to the lands they occupy, cultivate, and graze their cattle on, they are extremely vulnerable. For any development purpose or industrial project, they may be evicted without compensation, as has happened several times before.[31]

Firstly, the previous pieces of legislation, the Forest Conservation Act of 1980 and the Indian Forest Act of 1927, were not conservation-friendly. Both used the legislation to expropriate land for government revenue and timber industries. 'In fact, it is estimated that since 1980, 40,000 hectares of land has been diverted annually for non-forestry purposes; in the period 2001–06 alone, 5.73 *lakh* hectares were diverted for non-forestry projects.'[32] Secondly, it is thought that secure tenurial rights correlate with sustainable management of land.[33]

Others see it as a politically motivated law that 'will neither benefit the tribal communities nor enhance conservation. Rather, it serves as a cloak to justify non-tribal intervention, with potentially disastrous consequences'.[34] In contrast, there exists unease among government officials from the Ministry of Environment and Forests and from the Forest Department who have had to relinquish control over forest lands. In this chapter I examine whether the Forest Rights Act has improved access to justice for tribal communities, or made them more vulnerable. The expectation for new social legislation such as the Forest Rights Act in India is that it should increase justice for those whom the legislation seeks to protect. This newly acquired social and economic justice should theoretically, according to the terms of the Forest Rights Act, enable Indigenous forest peoples to claim ancestral land rights, to continue their forest-based livelihoods, and to conserve the forests. In practice, however, a very different narrative of social justice has been emerging.[35]

30 One lakh is one hundred thousand. Forty lakhs would be four million.
31 Ramnath, 'Surviving the Forest Rights Act', 38.
32 Ramnath, 'Surviving the Forest Rights Act', 38.
33 Ramnath, 'Surviving the Forest Rights Act', 38.
34 Saravanan, 'Political Economy', 199.
35 For the purpose of this article, the term 'justice' is defined as '(1) fairness; (2) moral rightness; (3) a scheme or system of law' (http://dictionary.law.com/Default.aspx?typed=justice&type=1). The term 'social justice' will be defined as 'justice in terms of the distribution of wealth, opportunities, and privileges within a society' (www.oxforddictionaries.com/definition/english/social-justice), accessed 2014.

Salient Features of the Forest Rights Act

In India, in response to the expectation of a 'minimum core' of social economic rights stipulated by the UN Committee on Economic, Social and Cultural Rights (UNCESCR), the Forest Rights Act 2006 provides a legal framework for the protection of substantive rights for tenurial security of vulnerable forest peoples and Indigenous groups. The Act, framed in rights-based language, 'can in some way, be called contemporary India's largest land regime change – from the forest administration to the rightful owners of forestland'.[36] It has the potential to change forest governance and to empower forest communities. The Forest Rights Act was passed in 2006 and became effective on 1 January 2008. The law notes that it is intended to address the 'historical injustice' suffered by tribal peoples and other forest dwellers who have lived for generations in the forests yet whose 'rights on ancestral lands and their habitat were not adequately recognised in the consolidation of State forests during the colonial period as well as in independent India'. The law also explicitly states that its purposes include addressing the consequences of development by the state: The Act is meant to address the 'long standing insecurity of tenurial and access rights of forest dwelling Scheduled Tribes and other traditional forest dwellers including those who were forced to relocate their dwelling due to State development interventions'.[37]

The Indian government maintained for several decades the economic policies that the British had pursued, starting with the expropriation of forest lands for the British timber economy, and continuing after independence. One departure from colonial policy by the Indian government was an attempt to protect biodiversity and to counter the deforestation that had occurred during the colonial era. This set in motion extensive conservation efforts[38] supported by new legislation.[39] The nature of the new conservation legislation, however, further excluded forest peoples from their lands, while mainstream populations and industrial interests encroached steadily.[40] In 1988, as part of the National Forest Policy, the Supreme Court ordered a regularisation of forest encroachment.

36 Sambhav, 'Centre Set to Dilute Tribal Rights'.

37 The Scheduled Tribes and Other Traditional Forest Dwellers (Recognition of Forest Rights) Act 2006. Preamble.

38 Gadgil and Guha, *This Fissured Land*, 109.

39 New legislation for conservation was passed, such as the Forest Conservation Act of 1980. 'The Wild Life Protection Act of 1972 had already severely restricted the rights of Adivasis in the wildlife sanctuaries and removed their rights in national parks. The 1991 amendment to the Act took this a stage further. The 147 wildlife sanctuaries and 75 national parks (of which 18 are tiger reserves) covering 4.26 per cent of the land mass are planned to increase. These moves, with the financial backing of the World Bank and other international agencies, have forced Adivasis to further restrict or altogether abandon their survival activities in the forests.' Bhengra, Bijoy and Luithui, *Report on the Adivasis of India*, 10.

40 Bose, Arts and van Dijk, 'Forest Governmentality', 669; Ramnath, 'Surviving the Forest Rights Act', 37; Bhullar, 'The Indian Forest Rights Act 2006', 25.

The Ministry of Environment and Forests (MoEF), however, misinterpreted this order and used it as an excuse for forced forest evictions throughout the whole country, triggering mass protests before the 2004 elections. The new UPA (United Progressive Alliance) government promised to address the issue. In response to the advocacy efforts of Adivasi communities, other forest dwellers, pastoralist communities, and civil society tribal rights organisations, the Ministry of Tribal Affairs (MoTA) began drafting the Forest Rights legislation. The Forest Rights Act of 2006 is a legal mechanism that tribal and other forest people can use to access justice and reclaim ancestral land from which they have been displaced. The Act was welcomed by many in India, especially Adivasi tribal communities, other traditional forest people such as mobile Indigenous peoples, and activists who were part of the struggle for justice for Indigenous peoples in India dispossessed of their lands. A great number of people in India may benefit from the Forest Rights Act:

> Twenty-three percent of [India's] geographical area has been designated as forest, upon which an estimated two hundred million people depend for their livelihoods to varying degrees. The Forest Rights Act has particular significance for the forested, tribal inhabited, and mineral rich but most impoverished belt of central and eastern India. Here ancestral tribal lands, despite being protected by the Constitution, have largely been declared state forests without following the due legal process of enquiring into the pre-existing rights of the customary tenure holders. It is this population of the country's poorest people, numbering perhaps one hundred million, who have suffered institutionalised disenfranchisement during colonial rule and after independence, who stand to benefit the most from proper implementation of the Forest Rights Act.[41]

The government ministry responsible for implementing the Forest Rights Act is the Ministry of Tribal Affairs (MoTA), rather than the Ministry of Environment and Forests (MoEF). The MoEF may be required to surrender significant power, revenue, and land under the Forest Rights Act, causing a conflict of interest, and many advocates for forest dwellers questioned the likelihood that the MoEF would administer the law fairly. Thus, the assignment of responsibilities under the law to the MoTA was viewed as a victory for forest dwellers and their supporters.

Who Does the Act Cover?

Two groups of people are granted substantive rights under the Forest Rights Act: 'Forest Dwelling Scheduled Tribes' who are defined as 'members or

41 Sarin and Springate-Baginski, *India Forest Rights Act*, 6.

community of the Scheduled Tribes who primarily reside in and who depend on the forests and forest lands for bona fide livelihood needs and includes the Scheduled Tribe pastoralist communities'.[42] This definition caused a controversy, as it excluded the majority of potential tribal and non-tribal claimants who may not be dwelling on forest land but are dependent on it, such as the Dhanger pastoralists I describe in Chapter 2. The Ministry of Tribal Affairs (MoTA) had to issue a special clarification that those dependent on but not necessarily living on forest land were also eligible.[43] The semantics of the Forest Rights Act has caused problems for mobile Indigenous communities because initially the Act only described 'Scheduled Tribes' (Adivasis) and excluded pastoralists. Pastoralists and civil society organisations all over India took up this issue, and the wording of the Act was changed to include 'other traditional forest dwellers', which includes pastoralists.[44] 'Other traditional forest dwellers' are now defined as any member or community who has, from 1930 and before, "primarily resided in and who depends on the forest or forest lands for bona fide livelihood needs".[45] It is important to note that not only individual but also community rights are recognised.

The proof of residence that is required in order to prove occupation of land is restrictive, and it could be argued that it is discriminatory for some groups. Eligible Scheduled Tribes are required to prove occupation of their land prior to 13 December 2005. For other traditional forest dwellers, the requirement is for "any member or community who has for at least three generations [75 years] prior to the 13th day of December, 2005 primarily resided in and who depends on the forest or forest lands for *bona fide* livelihood needs".[46] Seventy-five years goes back to at least 13 December 1930, which makes this provision restrictive as it

> would render the claims of nomadic tribes and members of the more vulnerable non-ST forest dwelling tribes, who may have relied on other means of livelihood since the year 1930, ineligible. The discriminatory nature of this provision is borne out by the fact that no such requirement is imposed on the FDSTs [Forest Dwelling Scheduled Tribes].[47]

42 The Scheduled Tribes and Other Traditional Forest Dwellers (Recognition of Forest Rights) Act 2006, Chapter One, Section 2 (c); Government of India, The Scheduled Tribes and Other Traditional Forest Dwellers (Recognition of Forest Rights) Bill (adopted 15 December 2006, No. 158-C of 2005).

43 Springate-Baginski et al., *The Indian Forest Rights Act 2006*, 3.

44 The Scheduled Tribes and Other Traditional Forest Dwellers (Recognition of Forest Rights) Act 2006.

45 The Scheduled Tribes and Other Traditional Forest Dwellers (Recognition of Forest Rights) Act 2006, 2.

46 The Scheduled Tribes and Other Traditional Forest Dwellers (Recognition of Forest Rights) Act 2006, 2.

47 Bhullar, 'The Indian Forest Rights Act 2006', 25.

It is difficult for forest people to legitimately produce evidence of residence going back to the colonial recording days of the 1930s, especially when many of them have not been literate. The Act may exclude certain groups of people if they do not satisfy all the conditions for rights. If this happens, it could be used to evict forest dwellers and pose a barrier to seasonal pastoralists who do not occupy the land in the traditional sense, but who need usufruct rights.

> In fact, the Forest Rights Act created new restrictions on the use of forest resources, which were previously easily accessible to the community. The new restrictions, which cover grazing and collecting dry fuel woods, fodder, and other non-timber forest products, may affect the livelihood of the marginalised forest-dependent people and may in practice lead to new types of forest tenure conflicts,

confirming that despite legislation, tribal communities have a lack of power and poor access to justice.[48]

In order for pastoralists to use the land, the government requires papers dating back seventy-five years under the Forest Rights Act. This is particularly difficult for mobile Indigenous peoples who had not engaged in the traditional legal system of filing deeds and paying taxes.

> International and local legislation is too removed from groups such as mobile indigenous peoples. The aim of such legislation should be to help groups live together. At present [the Forest Rights Act] is divisive and only considers the needs of states and of individuals. They don't consider collective groups such as mobile indigenous peoples and they don't create horizontal links within communities.[49]

Many non-tribal people quickly bought up land in tribal settlement areas before the legislation had been approved, proving the law to be ineffective, and consequently engendering a 'massive displacement of tribals who were pushed into positions of labourers on their own lands'.[50] Rule 13 issues a detailed list of both documentary and oral evidence. However, the Gram Sabha has the decision-making power to determine proof of residence, which could introduce an arbitrary aspect into the decision and could in principle be discriminatory towards the claimant.[51]

48 Bose, 'Individual Tenure Rights, Citizenship, and Conflicts: Outcomes from Tribal India's Forest Governance', 8.
49 Saravanan, 'Political Economy', 205.
50 Saravanan, 'Political Economy', 203.
51 Bhullar, 'The Indian Forest Rights Act 2006', 26.

Free, Prior, and Informed Consent (FPIC)

FPIC is considered a very significant right in land rights legislation such as the ILO Convention 107 (1957) and UNDRIP,[52] and is mentioned in the Forest Rights Act, Chapter 3, Section 4 (e): "the free informed consent of the Gram Sabhas in the area concerned to the proposed resettlement and to the package provided has been obtained in writing". In India, this has resulted in the renewing of Gram Sabhas, or village councils, who, in theory, have to consent to their land being used by the government for development purposes. This capacity to consent is powerful and promotes voice and self-determination for this still-marginalised group of Indigenous peoples.

Customary Land Rights

The fact that the Forest Rights Act also respects community forest rights in addition to individual rights is a revolutionary advance in land rights, changing the concept of generic property laws. Both individual and community forest rights are recognised in Section 3 (1). Property laws that are conventionally based on individual ownership now incorporate the recognition of communal land rights. This is particularly significant for Adivasis, who, as demonstrated by the case studies in this book, use their land communally both for purposes of food harvesting and for gathering minor forest produce for livelihoods.

Substantive rights, outlined in Chapter 2, Section 3 (1) of the Act, include the right to live in the forest and to use the land for habitation and livelihood. Customary usufruct rights, and rights to collect minor forest produce for livelihood, are recognised. None of the rights to land granted under the Act can be either sold or otherwise transferred, which ensures that ancestral lands stay with Adivasi communities.

Economic Development and State Violence

A most significant aspect is recognition of past government development schemes causing the excessive and unfair displacement of forest peoples without compensation or rehabilitation, and the clawing back of forest land rights for displaced communities. The procedures, however, do not specify how the loss of land can be restored or compensated.[53] Economic development schemes

52 United Nations General Assembly, Declaration on the Rights of Indigenous Peoples (adopted 13 December 2007, UNGA Res. 61/295 A (UNDRIP Add 1)). 'Indigenous peoples shall not be forcibly removed from their lands or territories. No relocation shall take place without the free, prior and informed consent of the Indigenous peoples concerned and after agreement on just and fair compensation and, where possible, with the option of return' (Article 10).

53 United Nations General Assembly, Declaration on the Rights of Indigenous Peoples (adopted 13 December 2007, UNGA Res. 61/295 A (UNDRIP Add 1)), 13.

are essential for any country, and for any government to be able to implement. It is when economic development schemes are implemented in an unjust manner, dismissing the rights of marginalised communities, that neoliberal values usurp human rights. Communities do not have control over the 'experts' who make decisions on the basis of impact evaluations or assessments. Adivasis have no control if these are manipulated to serve the interests of the powerful.[54] Violence, including state violence, is regularly used as a mechanism to circumvent the legal process and to validate state decisions to expropriate land for extractive industries and economic development. Adivasis have been regularly evicted, or their houses burnt down.[55]

Governmental Bureaucracy

Title deeds can be claimed for up to four hectares of land, and the registration of land titles in joint names of both spouses. The right for conversion of Pattas, or leases or grants, is, in principle, very good, but it is not recognised by the Forest Department, who classifies this land as forest land. Their official land records are poorly compiled, moreover, creating a conflict of interest and poor judicial administration on the part of the Forest Department. The rights for conversion and settlement of all forest villages[56] into revenue villages means that they become eligible for development and welfare resources. Sarin and Springate-Baginski clarify that 'forest villages' were 'created by the forest departments themselves in the past to ensure availability of bonded labour for forestry operations'.[57] This reveals another conflict of interest for the Forest Department in the judicial administration of the Forest Rights Act.

The land rights that can be claimed under the Forest Rights Act include both individual land rights and Community Forest Rights (CFR), which are claims made by the community for shared forest lands. The procedure for claiming rights under the Forest Rights Act begins at the village level.

54 United Nations General Assembly, Declaration on the Rights of Indigenous Peoples (adopted 13 December 2007, UNGA Res. 61/295 A (UNDRIP Add 1)) 61.

55 United Nations General Assembly, Declaration on the Rights of Indigenous Peoples (adopted 13 December 2007, UNGA Res. 61/295 A (UNDRIP Add 1)), 61.

56 Forest villages are defined in the Forest Rights Act as 'the settlements which have been established inside the forests by the forest department of any State Government for forestry operations or which were converted into forest villages through the forest reservation process and includes forest settlement villages, fixed demand holdings, all types of taungya settlements, by whatever name called, for such villages and includes lands for cultivation and other uses, permitted by the Government'. Government of India, The Scheduled Tribes and Other Traditional Forest Dwellers (Recognition of Forest Rights) Bill (adopted 15 December 2006, No. 158-C of 2005), Definitions.

57 Sarin and Springate-Baginski, *India Forest Rights Act*, 10.

The Gram Sabha – a village assembly, which under the Forest Rights Act rules must comprise not less than one-third women – invites claims, verifies them, and prepares a map outlining the area of each claim it recommends for recognition. "This is a key although diluted provision of the Act designed to provide a democratic, accessible and transparent forum for claiming rights instead of the normal vesting of such authority in inaccessible and unaccountable officials."[58] The rules still have many omissions, including no clarification on either how to claim rights or restrictions on rights claimed. Procedures are lacking in how to claim complex rights such as usufruct rights. This is harmful to pastoral and transhumant communities and those called Primitive Tribal Groups (PTGs). Another obstacle to the decision process for claims is that the Gram Sabha, which technically consists of all the adult voters within a certain administrative boundary, can entail thousands of villagers from different settlements, which would comprise their 'village'. This becomes unmanageable and creates yet another impediment to the process.[59]

In Rajasthan, where my field work took place, the experience of the Forest Rights Act has been that the awards have been uneven. The process to file a claim itself is not simple, which restricts access to justice for individuals and communities with limited literacy, and who are dependent on civil society organisations to protect them. If the District Level Committee (DLC) rejects a claim, the claimant can appeal to the High Court. This would cost them money, which would also be a restriction to accessing justice. So far, up to 2014, when the data for this study were collected, no one had approached the High Court. The DLC rejection rate was low in Udaipur District, with seven rejections out of roughly thirteen thousand claims. According to the Forest Rights Act, the Sub District Level Committee (SDLC) is not empowered to reject claims, but only to examine them. In Udaipur District, the SDLC had illegally assumed the responsibility to reject claims.[60] Since the seven claims were rejected illegally, those seven people can appeal against the rejections. The Gram Sabha can reject a claim, which has to be sent to the SDLC, which then scrutinises the Gram Sabha rejections. The SDLC can in turn send the claim to the DLC for a final decision. If the claimant does not agree with the DLC, they can complain to the state level monitoring committee within sixteen days of rejection.

An Incompatibility Between the Rights of Tribal Communities

The unfortunate articulation of how the Forest Rights Act relates to other existing laws reflects an incompatibility between rights of tribal communities

58 Sarin and Springate-Baginski, *India Forest Rights Act*, 16.
59 Sarin and Springate-Baginski, *India Forest Rights Act*, 18.
60 Interview with Mangilalji from Astha, Rajasthan.

and conservation and wildlife laws. Forest peoples have always lived in areas that are now labelled as wildlife habitats. Conservation and biodiversity protection laws are often at variance with rights of forest peoples. The Forest Rights Act does not provide adequate clarification on these contradictions, nor therefore adequate protection for forest peoples. Section 13 of the Act states:

> Save as otherwise provided in this Act and the Provisions of the Panchayats (Extension to the Scheduled Areas) Act, 1996 (PESA), the provisions of this Act shall be in addition to and not in derogation of the provisions of any other law for the time being in force.

Under the Forest Rights Act, the Gram Sabha is defined as a village assembly. The PESA, however, defines Gram Sabhas as 'hamlets' or 'a group of hamlets' or 'forest villages', 'traditional villages', and so on. This inconsistency has created a lot of harm and confusion, and has given the government officials who oppose decentralised decision making a loophole through which they can disregard Gram Sabha decisions. That government officials searching for a loophole in order to circumvent compliance with the law is an indication of poor judicial administration.

As one can see from this review, a number of significant substantive rights are granted by the terms of the Forest Rights Act. If implemented as written, the Forest Rights Act has the potential to improve the lives of many who live in the forests and rely on its produce to live, but who have been treated unjustly in the past. To sum up, the inconsistencies within the Forest Rights Act are many, and the implementation of it is neither consistent with the spirit of the law, nor fair towards the communities. The law therefore can be perceived as inadequate for successful land reform.

Deeply Divided Activists and Environmentalists

A key purpose of the Act, besides recognition of land rights, is to acknowledge the traditional role of forest peoples in the conservation and management of forest resources.[61] Besides the recognition of the ecological contribution of Indigenous peoples to their environment, this 'is amongst the most powerful and significant rights for re-commoning the enclosures and restoring community controlled democratic forest governance within customary village boundaries'.[62] Since Indigenous women play a vital role in forest ecology, and are the traditional keepers of knowledge of biodiversity and natural forest resources, this recognition of traditional Indigenous conservation practices restores the empowerment of women in traditional conservation roles.

61 Bhullar, 'The Indian Forest Rights Act 2006', 24.
62 Springate-Baginski et al., *The Indian Forest Rights Act 2006*, 10.

While the Act itself, couched in rights-based language, acknowledges:

> Whereas the forest rights on ancestral lands and their habitat were not adequately recognized in the consolidation of the state forests during the colonial period as well as in independent India resulting in *historical injustice* [emphasis mine] to the forest dwelling Scheduled Tribes and other traditional forest dwellers who are integral to the very survival and sustainability of the forest ecosystems,[63]

Ramnath claims that the Act is "an excellent attempt at trying to appease two warring parties", referring to both conservationists and tribal rights activists.[64]

Parties critical of the Forest Rights Act feel that it will contribute to further loss of biodiversity and degradation of forests and wildlife. They feel that giving tribal peoples their land back will amount to no land in the government's keeping. They are against the Gram Sabhas having decentralised authority over the lands. There is a fear that non-tribal forest dwellers will deceive forest dwellers and dominate them, creating more social tensions, not only between tribal and non-tribal communities but also within tribal communities. The Act bans all hunting and does not allow traditional rights of hunting or trapping for forest peoples.[65] There are certain drawbacks in implementing the procedural aspects of the Forest Rights law.[66] The major consideration is that India is a very large diverse country, with federal and state divisions, and each state presents different cultural, geographical, and administrative complications for implementation. The states themselves implement the Forest Rights Act to widely varying degrees. The North Eastern frontier states, with their predominantly tribal populations, have had collective jurisdiction over their lands since colonial times.[67] Certain tribal communities in the North East collectively exercise jurisdiction over forest lands, which at times comprise between three and four hundred kilometres.[68] These states, in order to protect their historical customary tenurial agreements, made arrangements with the Ministry of Tribal Affairs to clarify and

63 Government of India, The Scheduled Tribes and Other Traditional Forest Dwellers (Recognition of Forest Rights) Bill (adopted 15 December 2006, No. 158-C of 2005).

64 Ramnath, 'Surviving the Forest Rights Act', 37.

65 Ramnath, 'Surviving the Forest Rights Act', 37; Saravanan, 'Political Economy'; Wani, *Nought without Cause.*

66 'The part of the law which deals with practice, process and procedure, as distinct from substantive law, which prescribes the content of the rights and duties dealt with in the law.' Dictionary of Law – Oxford Reference (accessed 2016). (www.oxfordreference.com/view/10.1093/oi/authority.20110803100347458).

67 The North East states of India are Arunachal Pradesh, Assam, Manipur, Meghalaya, Mizoram, Nagaland, Tripura and Sikkim.

68 Bhullar, 'The Indian Forest Rights Act 2006', 27.

confirm their customary ownership rights to most of the forest lands, making the relevance of the Forest Rights Act insignificant in their territories.[69]

Several mechanisms that have impaired administrative justice have been outlined by Wani.[70] New regulatory procedures use evidence which Wani calls 'reductionist'; they "break down complex environmental and ecosystem functions into a set of services."[71] Cost-benefit studies use arbitrary evidence that suits the government stakeholders, and do not necessarily take into consideration the cultural impacts of projects. Another mechanism used is 'mitigation and not prevention':

> Market instruments such as monetary compensation of resources lost, based on arbitrary valuation of their environmental services and compensatory offsets, are used to justify decisions that result in large scale and irreversible environmental impacts. Mitigation measures, however, such as the ones to curb pollution of forest losses have the potential to have their own impacts as they come in the form of restricting access to land and changing land use by restricting access to those whose livelihoods depend on them.[72]

Wani points out that these are never mentioned in reports or impact evaluations. He says: "in the entire process of impact assessment, developers and bureaucracy – those with the money and power – decide what are acceptable impacts and if mitigation is adequate".[73]

Forest Department officials historically charged an unofficial 'fee' to mobile Indigenous peoples to enter the forest for grazing. This practice had grown since Independence in the early 1950s, when the forests were part of the eminent domain of the government. Mobile Indigenous peoples considered this a 'tax' and not a 'bribe'. Pastoralists claimed that 'taxes' such as this, paid to local officials, were more efficient than legal mechanisms since settlements in court using the Forest Rights Act did not happen quickly, and, in their experience, lawyers 'cheated' them. National legislation therefore held very little interest for mobile Indigenous peoples, validating the assertion that administrative justice is not complied with.

Administrative injustice refers to

> when the government, or those working on its behalf, act in ways that appear wrong, unfair or unjust, [and does not ensure] that public bodies and

69 Springate-Baginski et al., *The Indian Forest Rights Act 2006*, 10.
70 Wani, *Nought without Cause*, 60.
71 Wani, *Nought without Cause*, 60.
72 Wani, *Nought without Cause*, 60.
73 Wani, *Nought without Cause*, 60.

> those who exercise public functions make the right decisions . . . [and that] mechanisms for providing redress when things go wrong

are not accessible to citizens, consumers, individuals or groups.[74] India's Forest Rights Act, one of the goals of which is to rectify the sort of administrative injustice outlined earlier, can be viewed within the larger context of international progression on human rights. Although the Forest Rights Act did not flow in any automatic sense from international legislation and agreements, and was an Indian response to a national issue, it did mirror international normative changes in Indigenous rights, the most significant of which are outlined in the next section.

Land Laws in India and the Right to Fair Compensation and Transparency in the Land Acquisition, Rehabilitation and Resettlement Act, 2013 (LARR)

The LARR Act refers to the Right to Fair Compensation and Transparency in Land Acquisition, Rehabilitation and Resettlement Act, 2013. It is also known as the LARR Act or New Land Act. Internationally, the LARR Act can be said to rank among the best country safeguard systems for land in the Global South because it incorporates principles of self-determination with local decision making, transparency, just and fair compensation, rehabilitation and resettlement, and an improved living status.

In theory, LARR Act's implementation of national safeguards are liable for local scrutiny and more rigorous accountability standards with social impact studies of land acquisition. Free and prior informed consent (FPIC) is mandatory. This is meant to provide litigation and local judicial processes resulting in a jurisprudence that favours communities vulnerable to development-induced displacement and resettlement.[75] The law requires the states to align state laws with the central law. The law was drafted by the Congress government when it was still in power in 2013, but since has been subject to several amendments starting in early 2015 by the current National Democratic Alliance (NDA) government led by the right wing Bharatiya Janata Party (BJP) party under Prime Minister Modi.[76]

The legal concept of land rights in India became institutionalised in 1950 after Indian independence when the right to property became a fundamental

74 United Kingdom Administrative Justice Institute, *What Is Administrative Justice?* 2.

75 Kabra and Das, 'Global or Local Safeguards?', 195. Sigamany, Indrani (2019) Book Review: Country Frameworks for Development Displacement and Resettlement: Reducing Rish, Building Resilience. Edited by Susanna Price and Jane Singer. LSE Review of Books, 2020 Website; Phadnis, 'Ongoing Land Conflicts Affecting Lives, Livelihoods of Over 6.5 mn People'.

76 Government non-compliance and subversion has been reflected in the LARR Ordinance, and state amendments to the LARR Act. Wahi, Bhatia, Gandhi, Jain, Shukla, and Chauhan, *Land Acquisition in India*, 39.

right, and later in 1978 when it was included as a constitutional right.[77] Later is a brief history of these land laws and how they are being amended by the 2019 elected ruling coalition, the National Democratic Alliance (NDA) led by Modi's Bharatiya Janata Party (BJP).

The LARR Act is based on sound principles of participation and equality. The Preamble uses concepts such as:

"in consultation with institutions of local self-government and Gram Sabhas"[78];
"a humane, participative, informed and transparent process for land acquisition";
"with the least disturbance to the owners of the land and other affected families and provide just and fair compensation to the affected families whose land has been acquired or proposed to be acquired or are affected by such acquisition";
"make adequate provisions for such affected persons for their rehabilitation and resettlement";
"ensuring that the cumulative outcome of compulsory acquisition should be that affected persons become partners in development leading to an improvement in their post-acquisition social and economic status".[79]

Land Laws in India and Amending the LARR Act

Prior to Indian independence, the significant law which facilitated the forcible acquisition of land leading to a loss of livelihoods and inevitable destitution was the original Land Acquisition Act of 1894. Creating a lasting, and an arguably permanent culture of a coercive process of land expropriation, it reinforced the postcolonial unequal dynamic between the government and vulnerable communities inhabiting resource-rich lands.[80] The earliest pieces of extractive legislation were the Land Acquisition (Mines) Act which was enacted in 1885 and the Indian Tramways Act 1886. This was part of the colonial government law regime in which land laws were enacted in order to expropriate land regarded by the government as a valuable resource for extractive industry.

Land acquisition in India has been governed by several pieces of legislation covering rehabilitation and resettlement. After Indian Independence, the first of these Acts dates back to the Resettlement of Displaced Persons (Land Acquisition) Act 1948.[81] The Land Acquisition Act of 1948 was directed at

77 Wahi, Bhatia, Gandhi, Jain, Shukla, and Chauhan, *Land Acquisition in India*, 4.
78 Gram Sabhas are local village councils comprising all adults in the village or hamlet.
79 Government of India, *The Right to Fair Compensation and Transparency in Land Acquisition, Rehabilitation and Resettlement Act, 2013* (Government of India 2013).
80 Wahi, *Land Acquisition in India: A Review of Supreme Court Cases from 1950 to 2016* 38; Jitendra, 'Government Introduces Land Amendment Bill Amid Protests, Walkout' *DownToEarth* (India 25 February 2015) News, 3, accessed October 2021 www.downtoearth.org.in/news/government-introduces-land-amendment-bill-amid-protests-walkout-48723.
81 The Resettlement of Displaced Persons (Land Acquisition) Act, 1948, https://legislative.gov.in/actsofparliamentfromtheyear/resettlement-displaced-persons-land-acquisition-act-1948 39.

the refugee crisis triggered by the partition into India, Pakistan, and East Pakistan. East Pakistan is now Bangladesh. When drafted, it was not necessarily directed at forest peoples who were displaced by extractive industry and state-led economic development. It was used as the major law till the LARR Act in 2013.

Some of the other land laws drafted after 1947 in independent India include the Damodar Valley Corporation Act of 1948, the Requisitioning and Acquisition of Immovable Property Act of 1952, the National Highways Act 1956, the Coal Bearing Areas Acquisition and Development act 1957, the Ancient Monuments and Archaeological Sites and Remains Act 1958, the Petroleum and Minerals Pipelines (Acquisition of Right of User in Land) Act of 1962, the Atomic Energy Act 1962, the Metro Railways (Construction of Works) Act of 1978, the Railways Act of 1989, and the Electricity Act of 2003.[82]

Provisions of the LARR Act

In their Review of Supreme Court cases from 1950 to 2016,[83] the Centre for Policy Research listed six significant changes created by the LARR Act which attempted to redress the historical imbalance of the earlier land laws in India, specifically the original Land Acquisition Act of 1894. The first change broadened the definition of 'persons interested' and 'affected family'. 'Persons interested' initially referred only to title holders but now includes tenancy and easement rights. The original category of title holders of families depending on land for their primary source of livelihood now includes the right to compensation for people who also lose their livelihoods. The second change includes detailing 'public purpose' to avoid illegitimate acquisition by the government in the name of 'public purposes.'

The third change involves several provisions in the LARR Act around Free, Prior, and Informed Consent (FPIC),[84] and requires 70 per cent consent of persons with interest in the land for direct government acquisitions and 80 per cent consent for public private partnership acquisition. The LARR Act also contains detailed social impact assessment provisions. These require greater public participation in acquisition proceedings before land is acquired, and provide for an independent expert group comprising gram panchayat[85] and social science experts to contribute to the report on the Social Impact Assessment. Unfortunately, this independent group only has the capacity to make recommendations. The social impact

82 Jitendra, 'Government Introduces Land Amendment Bill Amid Protests, Walkout'.

83 Centre for Policy Research, *Understanding Land Acquisition Disputes in India. CPR-Land Rights Initiative reviews Supreme Court cases on land acquisition from 1950 to 2016* (Centre for Policy Research 2017) 16.

84 FPIC – Free and prior informed consent.

85 Gram Panchayats are local village governing bodies who make decisions in the Gram Sabhas. Gram Sabhas are local village councils.

assessment committee comprises bureaucrats who are not bound by these recommendations. Acquisitions made under urgency clauses are exempt from these assessments.

The fourth change relates to the misuse of the urgency clause and limits it only to situations which involve national defence and security, or for emergencies arising from natural calamities requiring Parliamentary approval for any other emergencies. The fifth change involves a prescribed formula of enhanced compensation which is currently double the value of registered rural sale deeds, and four times the average value of registered urban sale deeds. The increase comprises 100% of the market value compared to 30% under the Land Acquisition Act, and adds the solatium amount to the market value. The provision under the LARR Act includes rehabilitation and resettlement awards and incorporates the provision of a constructed house to replace housing lost in the acquisition of land and, in some cases, replaces the land acquired with a grant of land.[86]

The BJP government proposed an ordinance Bill amending the LARR Act 2013 which began in December 2014, soon after Prime Minister Modi came to power. The LARR (Amendment) Bill 2015 purported to compensate farmers and to provide rehabilitation and resettlement benefits when their land was being expropriated for development. The Bill exempted five special categories of land use from requiring consent and from conducting Social Impact Assessments. The Bill has been extremely controversial because of how it diluted the rights and protective aspects of the LARR Act, and triggered very long and high-profile protests by farmers, supported by civil society organisations, and prominent activists. The opposition Congress Party staged a walkout from Parliament. Even allies of the NDA government, such as the Shiv Sena, Akali Dal, and Swabhimani Paksha, opposed the Bill, which was promulgated three times in the Rajya Sabha.[87] In August 2015, Prime Minister Modi finally announced the lapse of the ordinance ahead of the Bihar election.[88]

Critique of the LARR

The enlightened concepts contained in the legislation gave rise to expectations that land rights would be respected. I offer a critique that challenges the ideas that the LARR Act has led to land rights being respected, and that communities vulnerable to development-induced displacement and resettlement have been supported by the progressive measures drafted in this

86 Research, *Understanding Land Acquisition Disputes in India. CPR-Land Rights Initiative Reviews Supreme Court Cases on Land Acquisition from 1950 to 2016*, 16.
87 The Rajya Sabha is the upper house in India's Parliament and comprises the Council of 28 States.
88 Yadav, 'Even Under Attack, India's Democratic Institutions Are Pushing Back'.

legislation. The context for this debate is an ethical tension between, on the one hand, the protection of landowning communities and individuals and, on the other hand, the state's interest in industrial development. The legal privilege of eminent domain instituted by the state becomes oppressive when the state's neoliberal interests overrides human rights of communities and individuals, forcing displacement from ancestral lands and the loss of land-based livelihoods.

Two major limitations of the fair implementation of the law are how the states comply with aligning their laws with the central law, and how the central NDA government under Modi's BJP leadership is expropriating land. State governments, such as Karnataka, Maharashtra, and Tamil Nadu have rejected the protective provisions of the LARR Act regarding land rights of citizens. They have tried to enact other versions of the LARR Act which have served to "bypass or dilute [the] progressive provisions" of the LARR Act, and have resorted to the original Land Acquisition Act of 1894, which was specifically enacted to facilitate the forcible acquisition of land.[89] This action on the part of state governments in India specifically violates the LARR Act in which the law requires the states to align state laws with the central law.

In his three-year 2020 study, independent researcher Kumar Sambhav, founder of the data base Land Conflict Watch, revealed that the 703 current land conflicts in India has "affected lives and livelihoods of over 6.5 million people and over 2.1 million ha [hectares] of land is locked in conflicts."[90] They also found that a majority of these conflicts could have been avoided if the Forest Rights Act 2006 and the LARR Act had not been violated and if they had been properly implemented. Sambhav's study, which looks only at conflicts in which the public is one of the parties in the conflict, whether as individuals in a group or as a community, reveals that the state is pitted against the rights of the people in 95 per cent of the land conflict cases. Of the seven hundred and three land conflicts in India, 70 per cent of the conflicts have arisen from government activities which involved development and infrastructure projects or conservation policies which have displaced communities from the forests.[91]

The biggest threat of land expropriation by the government has been the creation of 'land banks' which has been an arbitrary, extra-legal process used by the government resulting in displacing citizens from their lands. A land bank serves to restrict access of local inhabitants to their ancestral lands in the forests or to lands they have traditionally harvested which are essential

89 Phadnis, 'Ongoing Land Conflicts Affecting Lives, Livelihoods of Over 6.5 mn People'.
90 Phadnis, 'Ongoing Land Conflicts Affecting Lives, Livelihoods of Over 6.5 mn People'.
91 Phadnis, 'Ongoing Land Conflicts Affecting Lives, Livelihoods of Over 6.5 mn People'.

to their livelihoods.[92] The eight states which have declared land bank statistics in state government websites include Andhra Pradesh, Chhattisgarh, Jharkhand, Madhya Pradesh, Odisha, Rajasthan, Tamil Nadu, and Uttar Pradesh. They have confiscated private and communal lands in land banks of up to 2.68 million hectares of land as a strategy to attract manufacturing and infrastructure investors.[93]

Once land has been banked by the government it has not been returned to the local people, which has created enormous land conflict and local opposition by the people whose livelihoods have been affected and who have been displaced. Some examples of land expropriation into land banks between 2017 and 2020 include the Odisha government which is building a wall around a 1,700-hectare piece of land on the periphery of a village. This includes forest land and has created a land dispute.[94] The Chhattisgarh government's plans to build a steel plant has resulted in them locking away a large piece of the people's land. In Jharkhand, the government has confiscated a large piece of forest land in a land bank for plans to build a firing range for the Indian army. The Jharkhand government has also sealed into a land bank, common land belonging to the Gram Sabha which they wanted to use to build the Koel-Karo dam. The plans for the dam project have been put on hold because of protests from the community.[95]

The Modi government's ordinance-driven amendments in early 2015 is an example used by Nielsen and Nilsen to illustrate how even progressive measures of a law such as the LARR Act can facilitate the process of economic restructuring in India, and exacerbate land dispossession of marginalised communities.[96] The neoliberal economic policies of successive Indian governments since 1991, which has deprived large swathes of the population of their lands and livelihoods, has also created an ubiquitous notion of unfairness and widening inequality. Pal points out that the compensation process for people being displaced could in effect be an attempt to "shift the focus from the event of land acquisition to the compensation process for those dispossessed and displaced."[97] If so, the strategy which pretends that a fairness exists could be perceived as cynical on the part of the government, which Pal

92 Tripathi, 'Conflicts Across India as States Create Land Banks for Private Investors, IndiaSpend'.
93 Tripathi, 'Conflicts Across India as States Create Land Banks for Private Investors, IndiaSpend'.
94 Tripathi, 'Conflicts Across India as States Create Land Banks for Private Investors, IndiaSpend'.
95 Tripathi, 'Conflicts Across India as States Create Land Banks for Private Investors, IndiaSpend'.
96 Nielsen and Nilsen, 'Law-Struggles, Law-Making and the Politics of Hegemony in Neoliberal India', 3.
97 Pal, 'Land Acquisition and "Fair Compensation" of the "Project Affected"', 2.

suggests has "legitimized the inevitability of acquisition of large tracts of land by the state for industrialization."[98]

The major dynamic created by the acquisition of land is a confusion of historically coercive land laws which has created social inequity and a power imbalance between the community and the state.[99] This is reinforced by executive non-compliance with the rule of law which is manifested in governance under the Modi regime. The key is whether the government is implementing the law rather than subverting the law in pursuit of neoliberal economic policies which override human rights.[100] The Centre for Policy Research confirms that the LARR Act creates channels for legally contesting political disputes with the state which empowers communities and helps pre-empt extra-legal conflict.[101] To conclude, the success of the LARR Act rests on government compliance with the rule of law, and administrative and bureaucratic reform targeting procedural efficiency and the elimination of inequities. Successful implementation of the law would allow the ability of the LARR Act legislation to mediate between the state and people being displaced, and support social and economic empowerment.[102]

An International Normative Framework for Indigenous Rights

International standards are applicable to all countries, including India. India ratified the first ILO Convention 107 (1957), and the Forest Rights Act 2006, recognised for its progressive rights, incorporates the spirit of such international treaties as the Committee on the Elimination of Racial Discrimination (CERD), the International Covenant on Economic, Social and Cultural Rights (ICESCR) and the ILO Convention 107 (1957). There is evidence, however, as outlined in this chapter, of a disjunction between this growing international awareness of Indigenous land rights within national legislation and access to justice being realised. International laws address aspects such as self-determination, self-governance, recognition of customary laws, and rights to territories and lands. These rights are not necessarily reflected in national judicial administration or the ways in which laws are implemented at national levels. While there is large-scale land expropriation in line with extractive industries, development, and conservation movements, there are also some successful national struggles.

98 Pal, 'Land Acquisition and "Fair Compensation" of the "Project Affected"', 38.
99 Wahi, *Land Acquisition in India: A Review of Supreme Court Cases from 1950 to 2016*, 38.
100 Wahi, *Land Acquisition in India: A Review of Supreme Court Cases from 1950 to 2016*, 39.
101 Wahi, *Land Acquisition in India: A Review of Supreme Court Cases from 1950 to 2016*, 39.
102 Research, *Understanding Land Acquisition Disputes in India. CPR-Land Rights Initiative Reviews Supreme Court Cases on Land Acquisition from 1950 to 2016*, 16.

Social justice norms, which guide national and international normative frameworks, are increasingly influenced by human rights norms. Human rights, "the dominant normative conception in the contemporary globalized world", have similarly shaped international history.[103] The French Revolution, the discontinuation of the slave trade in the USA and Europe, independence from colonial imperialism, and the US civil rights movement exemplify paradigm shifts in human rights norms. It was only in 1948, in response to the atrocities of the Second World War, however, that the Universal Declaration of Human Rights laid out the moral foundations of justice and freedom and was accepted internationally as a mainstream legal norm. International instruments, in line with these international legal norms and human rights frameworks, allow states to establish rights and obligations between themselves.[104] Table 2.1 lists the most important legislative enactments that comprise a normative framework for Indigenous rights.

A Normative Framework for Indigenous Rights

- Universal Declaration of Human Rights, 1948 (No. 217)
- International Convention on the Elimination of All Forms of Racial Discrimination, 1965 (No. 9464)
- ILO Convention on Indigenous and Tribal Peoples, 1989 (No. 169)

103 Gauri and Gloppen, 'Human Rights-Based Approaches to Development', 485.

104 'Declarations: The term "declaration" is used for various international instruments. However, declarations are not always legally binding. The term is often deliberately chosen to indicate that the parties do not intend to create binding obligations but merely want to declare certain aspirations. An example is the 1992 Rio Declaration. Declarations can however also be treaties in the generic sense intended to be binding at international law. It is therefore necessary to establish in each individual case whether the parties intended to create binding obligations. Ascertaining the intention of the parties can often be a difficult task. Some instruments entitled "declarations" were not originally intended to have binding force, but their provisions may have reflected customary international law or may have gained binding character as customary law at a later stage. Such was the case with the 1948 Universal Declaration of Human Rights. Declarations that are intended to have binding effects could be classified as follows: (a) A declaration can be a treaty in the proper sense. A significant example is the Joint Declaration between the United Kingdom and China on the Question of Hong Kong of 1984. (b) An interpretative declaration is an instrument that is annexed to a treaty with the goal of interpreting or explaining the provisions of the latter. (c) A declaration can also be an informal agreement with respect to a matter of minor importance. (d) A series of unilateral declarations can constitute binding agreements. A typical example are declarations under the Optional Clause of the Statute of the International Court of Justice that create legal bonds between the declarants, although not directly addressed to each other. Another example is the unilateral Declaration on the Suez Canal and the arrangements for its operation issued by Egypt in 1957 which was considered to be an engagement of an international character.' See https://treaties.un.org.

- The Convention on the Rights of the Child, 1989 (No. 1577)
- The Convention on Biological Diversity, 1992 (No. 30619)
- The Vienna Declaration, 1993
- UN Declaration on the Rights of Indigenous Peoples, 2007 (No. 61/295)

International bodies engaged in setting human rights standards attempt to direct and facilitate the implementation at national levels. The Universal Declaration of Human Rights (UDHR 1948)[105] recognises equality, dignity, and respect for all individuals, and these rights are 'inalienable' and absolute. It was conceived in the hope that the atrocities of the Second World War would never be repeated,[106] and has informed international and national legislation through the moral foundations of justice and freedom.[107] The Convention on the Elimination of All Forms of Racial Discrimination 1965[108] applies to every individual and group, which includes mobile Indigenous peoples, and every state is required to submit a report every two years to the UN Office of the High Commissioner for Human Rights (OHCHR) on the status of discrimination in their country.

The United Nations Committee on Economic, Social and Cultural Rights (UNCESCR) describes a 'minimum core' obligation by which a state has to ensure an indispensable set of social economic rights such as the right to housing. The state has to comply with the essential level for each right, which is "determined generally by having regard to the needs of the most vulnerable group that is entitled to the protection of the right in question . . . [and] must be understood in international law".[109]

The International Labour Organisation (ILO) Convention on Indigenous and Tribal Peoples of 1989, No. 169 on the right to continue traditional occupations, and the 2007 UN Declaration of the Rights of Indigenous Peoples, are major legal contributions to the land rights of Indigenous peoples.[110] The ILO Convention on Indigenous and Tribal Peoples[111] contains a substantial component on land rights, which was not only groundbreaking at the time it was formulated, but is also legally binding, and which creates a crucial legal

105 United Nations General Assembly, 'Universal Declaration of Human Rights' (adopted 10 December 1948, UNGA Res. 217 A (III) (UDHR art 5)), www.un.org/en/universal-declaration-human-rights/index.html.

106 Galligan and Sandler, 'Implementing Human Rights', 26.

107 United Nations, 'The International Bill of Human Rights', 6.

108 United Nations General Assembly, 'International Convention on the Elimination of All Forms of Racial Discrimination' (adopted 21 December 1965, CERD Res 2106 XX (9464 art 21)).

109 Government of the Republic of South Africa v. Grootboom, 2001 (1) SA 46 (CC) at para. 31, in Gauri and Brinks, *Courting Social Justice*, 86.

110 Gilbert and Doyle, 'A New Dawn over the Land', 7.

111 ILO, *ILO Convention on Indigenous and Tribal Peoples 1989 (No. 169)*, 4.

tool for displaced Indigenous communities.[112] It is a revision of the ILO Convention 107 of 1957 and was the first important international legal treaty protecting Indigenous and tribal populations.[113] The ILO Convention addresses the need for respect of

> distinctive ways of life, and their traditions and customs. It is also based on the belief that indigenous and tribal peoples have the right to continue to exist with their own identities and the right to determine their own way and pace of development.[114]

The ILO Convention also uses the term 'self-management',[115] which is incorporated into newer legal standards such as the 2007 UN Declaration on the Rights of Indigenous Peoples (UNDRIP). UNDRIP is a convention, not a treaty. It is legally non-binding, which means it is neither ratified by states, nor can states be held legally accountable.

Once a government ratifies a treaty recognising the rights of Indigenous and tribal peoples, it has a responsibility to protect those rights and to implement the legal principles fully.[116] The vulnerability of Indigenous peoples means it is necessary to protect their distinctive way of life from extinction. The ILO Convention No. 169 calls for a 'special measure' of protection of cultures, environment, identity, and properties,[117] although nomadic peoples use land and property collectively, which complicates their property rights. It also calls for their right to 'participation' and to be 'consulted' on any policies that may affect them, whether to do with land, the constitution or welfare services. Only twenty-two states have ratified the ILO Convention No. 169, and India is not one of them.

The Convention on Biological Diversity (CBD) of 1992 is a significant legal instrument for the conservation of ecosystems by Indigenous peoples and local communities. Advocating a 'rights and incentives' approach to conservation, it "seeks to recognize certain rights over genetic resources and associated traditional knowledge while ensuring the fair and equitable sharing of benefits arising from the commercial and research utilization of such resources and knowledge".[118] The basic principle behind the CBD is that

112 ILO, *ILO Convention on Indigenous and Tribal Peoples 1989 (No. 169)*, 4.
113 ILO, *ILO Convention on Indigenous and Tribal Peoples 1989 (No. 169)*, 4.
114 ILO, *ILO Convention on Indigenous and Tribal Peoples 1989 (No. 169)*, 5.
115 ILO, *ILO Convention on Indigenous and Tribal Peoples 1989 (No. 169)*, 10.
116 ILO, *ILO Convention on Indigenous and Tribal Peoples 1989 (No. 169)*, 11.
117 ILO, *ILO Convention on Indigenous and Tribal Peoples 1989 (No. 169)*, 14.
118 Articles 8(j) and 10(c) recognise the 'rights of communities to their knowledge, innovations, practices, and customary sustainable use of stewardship affirming the rights of communities to local ecosystems and ways of life that nurture these ecosystems'. Abrell et al., *Bio-Cultural Community Protocols*, 13.

biodiversity is best conserved and managed by communities who depend on these resources. Article 8(j) states:

> Subject to its national legislation [state parties shall] respect, preserve and maintain knowledge, innovations and practices of indigenous and local communities embodying traditional lifestyles relevant for the conservation and sustainable use of biological diversity and promote their wider application with the approval and involvement of the holders of such knowledge, innovations and practices and encourage the equitable sharing of the benefits arising from the utilization of such knowledge, innovations and practices.[119]

The rights contained in the ILO Conventions have been expanded in the 2007 UN Declaration on the Rights of Indigenous Peoples (UNDRIP).[120] The 2007 Declaration is a landmark for Indigenous peoples, especially for pastoralists, since it refers to collective land rights, usufruct rights, and also customary land laws.[121] The articles that pertain to Indigenous peoples and their lands are as follows:

- (**Article 8, 1, and 2 b**) Indigenous peoples and individuals have the right not to be subjected to forced assimilation or destruction of their culture; and States shall provide effective mechanisms for prevention of, and redress for: (b) Any action which has the aim or effect of dispossessing them of their lands, territories or resources.
- (**Article 25**) Indigenous peoples shall not be forcibly removed from their lands or territories.
- (**Article 10**) No relocation shall take place without the free, prior and informed consent of the Indigenous peoples concerned and after agreement on just and fair compensation and, where possible, with the option of return. Indigenous peoples have the right to maintain and strengthen their distinctive spiritual relationship with their traditionally owned or otherwise occupied and used lands, territories, waters and coastal seas and other resources and to uphold their responsibilities to future generations in this regard.
- (**Article 26**) Indigenous peoples have the right to the lands, territories and resources that they have traditionally owned, occupied or otherwise used or acquired. Indigenous peoples have the right to own, use, develop and control the lands, territories and resources that they possess by reason of traditional ownership or other traditional occupation or use, as well as those

119 Jonas et al., *An Analysis of International Law*, 8.

120 United Nations General Assembly, Declaration on the Rights of Indigenous Peoples (adopted 13 December 2007, UNGA Res. 61/295 A (UNDRIP Add 1)).

121 Gilbert and Doyle, 'A New Dawn over the Land', 13.

which they have otherwise acquired. States shall give legal recognition and protection to these lands, territories and resources. Such recognition shall be conducted with due respect to the customs, traditions and land tenure systems of the Indigenous peoples concerned.

- (**Article 29**) Indigenous peoples have the right to the conservation and protection of the environment and the productive capacity of their lands or territories and resources. States shall establish and implement assistance programmes for Indigenous peoples for such conservation and protection, without discrimination.
- (**Article 32**) Indigenous peoples have the right to determine and develop priorities and strategies for the development or use of their lands or territories and other resources. States shall consult and cooperate in good faith with the Indigenous peoples concerned through their own representative institutions in order to obtain their free and informed consent prior to the approval of any project affecting their lands or territories and other resources.[122]

Among the significant principles within this legislation are self-determination and Free, Prior, and Informed Consent (FPIC), requiring governments to inform and obtain the consent of Indigenous peoples before taking any action involving their lands. It gives the latter veto rights. It does not, however, mention nomadic or mobile peoples in the text.

Human rights instruments such as UNDRIP do not specifically mention mobile or nomadic communities, who are also often invisible to their own governments, making it more difficult to advocate for land rights.[123] The Dana Declaration of 2002 is the first declaration unique to mobile Indigenous peoples, and therefore is crucial to the recognition of mobile Indigenous rights. The Dana Declaration brings together a 'comprehensive approach' to conservation and mobile peoples.[124] Framed during the first World Decade on the Rights of Indigenous Peoples (1994–2004) declared by the UN,[125] it calls for the inclusion of Indigenous peoples' knowledge in the development of policies of conservation in adaptive and collaborative management, drawing on the breadth of Indigenous conservation knowledge in a democratic and transparent manner.[126] Though not legally binding, since it is a declaration of civil society, it establishes the context for mobile Indigenous peoples' rights, and it also raises awareness of a group that has been unjustly marginalised throughout history.

122 Universal Declaration of Human Rights 1948, G.A. Res. 217A (III), U.N. Doc. A/810 at 71; Jonas et al., *An Analysis of International Law*, 8.
123 United Nations General Assembly, Declaration on the Rights of Indigenous Peoples (adopted 13 December 2007, UNGA Res. 61/295 A (UNDRIP Add 1)).
124 Dana Standing Committee, *Dana Declaration on Mobile Peoples and Conservation.*
125 Dana Standing Committee, *Dana Declaration on Mobile Peoples and Conservation.*
126 Dana Standing Committee, *Dana Declaration on Mobile Peoples and Conservation.*

The Coordinator of Indigenous Organisations of the Amazon Basin (COICA) called for the recognition of forest peoples' rights in 1988. In 1992, rights to 'ancestral domains' were supported in the Global Biodiversity Strategy.[127] The same year, the International Alliance of Indigenous and Tribal Peoples of the Tropical Forests pronounced the Forest Peoples Charter, which recognised the right to conserve their own lands and to control government and corporate development interventions.[128] The charter recognises forest peoples' right to conservation of their forest lands, and to regulate development activities by government and corporate stakeholders. The Earth Summit of 1992 recognised the importance of Indigenous participation for future conservation.[129] The World Conservation Union (IUCN) in 1996 adopted seven different resolutions on Indigenous Peoples.[130] In 1996, the Worldwide Fund for Nature International adopted a Statement of Principles on Indigenous Peoples and Conservation (WWF 1996),[131] and an important agenda item at the United Nations Summit on Sustainable Development in 2002 was conservation and people's impact on the natural environment, which remains part of the customary land use of Indigenous peoples.[132]

The laws listed earlier demonstrate that there is more international recognition of Indigenous rights to conserve the integrity of their lands, and that the international normative trajectory is moving in the right direction. It is not clear, however, whether the increased international legal instruments positively parallel the national rights of Indigenous peoples. That is, can they access international laws to help their national land rights?

Conclusion

By and large, there is inconsistency and contradiction between the growing international legal instruments on Indigenous rights and land laws and the national experience of land expropriation experienced by tribal and Indigenous communities. The significant issue to be addressed is how the law can support national Indigenous efforts and struggles to protect and continue to conserve their lands for their own use. International laws are extremely useful, and can hold nation states accountable to some degree. However, international laws are enacted in order for nation states to abide by good practice norms and allow them room to reform their own norms in line with international ones. How this can happen and what strategies individual states can

127 Alcorn, 'Indigenous Peoples and Conservation', 424.
128 Alcorn, 'Indigenous Peoples and Conservation', 424.
129 Chatty, 'Mobile Peoples and Conservation', 2.
130 Chatty, 'Mobile Peoples and Conservation'.
131 WWF, 'WWF's Statement of Principles on Indigenous Peoples and Conservation'.
132 WWF, 'WWF's Statement of Principles on Indigenous Peoples and Conservation'.

take to respect these rights and access to justice are questions that need to be recognised and addressed.

Forest communities are predominantly Indigenous. It is no secret that ancient Indigenous practices of conserving forest lands, nomadic strategies of allowing fragile desert lands to regenerate by mobility, and practices such as slash-and-burn agriculture correlate to the preservation of forests. These customary practices have preserved forests inhabited by Indigenous people and sustained 'sophisticated customary systems of caring for territories and resources'.[133] Yet, at national levels, legal recognition of and access to justice through international treaties and declarations is absent,[134] and Indigenous peoples still face discriminatory actions by their own governments, leading to displacement from their lands. The rights of Indigenous communities that are committed to international laws are often not within reach under national laws. Stakeholders and activists are advocating for more legal movement and access from 'international to local levels, particularly towards making international treaties and declarations increasingly relevant for and useful to Indigenous peoples and local communities who want to defend their rights and responsibilities' in relation to the integrity of their own local lands.[135]

The grassroots reality of the implementation of the Forest Rights Act is the product of competing political interests and conflicting values, as is often the case when injustice occurs. The impact of the Forest Rights Act for Indigenous access to justice is impeded by two central factors. Firstly, the legal framework of the Forest Rights Act is alien to Adivasis' legal traditions, thereby impeding the use of the Act as a tool to access justice. "Indigenous peoples suffer the continued marginalization from legislative and judicial systems and decision-making processes at all levels, as well as the impacts of discriminatory and fragmented legal and institutional frameworks".[136] These aspects directly undermine access to justice for Indigenous communities. Secondly, underlying political and economic ideologies of the elected government, which can similarly hinder justice, drive the legal response to any demands for justice.

In principle, newly enacted progressive legislation promises justice. I question whether this promise of justice is being realised through the Forest Rights Act, and whether administrative justice determines access to justice for marginalised groups in India. Economic necessity is often an argument used by the government to appropriate forest lands, and thereby disregard the Forest Rights Act. This argument, however, is problematic in two important ways. Firstly, the key is whether appropriating land for legitimate

133 Jonas et al., *An Analysis of International Law*, 4.
134 Jonas et al., *An Analysis of International Law*, 7.
135 Jonas et al., *An Analysis of International Law*, 4.
136 Jonas et al., *An Analysis of International Law*, 4.

development is done in a just and fair manner. If not, injustice often disproportionately affects the most marginalised in society, thereby exacerbating inequality and poverty in society. Secondly, any consideration, whether economic or pertaining to the political interests of the judiciary, should not stop the law from being upheld. These two arguments conflict with the neoliberal view that any laws impeding economic development should be reviewed due to economic development being seen as an absolute good. Sircar points out that in India, the assumption that more laws mean there will be more rights, and that rights automatically deliver justice, is "an equation that has informed and been informed by fundamental rights jurisprudence and law reform, the enactment of legislation to guarantee socio-economic rights, and many of the strategies of social movement activism in contemporary India".[137] This neoliberal privatisation ideology underpins the unceasing displacement of Indigenous forest dwellers from their land in India, despite the Forest Rights Act. The case studies in the next three chapters illustrate some of the many examples of this continuous land dispossession. The displacement of people from their lands by the government thus raises another more complex question in relation to administrative justice: what characteristics of the legal and political system enable those charged with carrying out the law to circumvent existing legal frameworks?

In practice, the implementation of this rights-based law echoes Sen's critique of the inherent weakness of the human rights–based approach. In many cases, the central and state governments in India ignore the requirements of the Act. This violates both the Forest Rights Act itself and the principles of human rights on which the Act is founded. In India, committing to free-market capitalist economic policies that violate laws that the government itself enacted can be perceived as unbalanced and confused. It leads to a dichotomy that demonstrates the 'hollowness' of human rights with suspect political commitment, alluded to by Sen's critique of human rights.

Bibliography

Abrell, E., et al. *Bio-Cultural Community Protocols. A Community Approach to Ensuring the Integrity of Environmental Law and Policy*. United Nations Environment Programme (UNEP) and Natural Justice, 2009.

Alcorn, J. 'Indigenous Peoples and Conservation'. *Conservation Biology* 7(2) (1993), 424–26.

Bhengra, R., C.R. Bijoy, and S. Luithui. *Report on the Adivasis of India*. Minority Rights Group, 1999.

Bhullar, L. 'The Indian Forest Rights Act 2006: A Critical Appraisal'. *Law, Environment and Development Journal (LEAD)* 4(1) (2008), 23–84.

Bose, P., B. Arts, and H. van Dijk. '"Forest Governmentality": A Genealogy of Subject-Making of Forest-Dependent "Scheduled Tribes" in India'. *Land Use Policy* 1 (2012), 664–73.

137 Sircar, 'Spectacles of Emancipation: Reading Rights Differently in India's Legal Discourse', 527.

Chatty, D. 'Mobile Peoples and Conservation'. *Anthropology Today* 18(4) (2002), 1–2.
Dana Standing Committee. *Dana Declaration on Mobile Peoples and Conservation.* Conference, Wadi Dana Nature Reserve, Jordan, 3–7 April 2002. www.cenesta.org/wp-content/uploads/2015/10/Dana-declaration-2002-en.pdf
Dash, T. 'Redefining Biodiversity Conservation in India'. *Policy Matters* 17 (2010), 33–40.
Dash, T. and A. Khotari. 'Forest Rights and Conservation in India'. In H. Jonas, H. Jonas, and S.M. Subramanian (eds), *Right to Responsibility: Resisting and Engaging Development, Conservation, and the Law in Asia.* Natural Justice and UNU-IAS Institute of Advanced Studies, 2013, 151.
Dash, T., and A. Kothari. 'Grabbing: Dangers of the Green India Mission'. In K. Kohli and M. Menon (eds), *Banking on Forests: Assets for a Climate Cure?* Kalpavriksh and Henrich Boll Stiftung, 2012, 151–74.
Gadgil, M., and R. Guha. *This Fissured Land: An Ecological History of India.* Oxford University Press, 1992.
Galanter, M. 'The Displacement of Traditional Law in Modern India'. *Journal of Social Issues* 14(4) (1968), 65–91.
Galligan, D., and D. Sandler. 'Implementing Human Rights'. In S. Halliday and P. Schmidt (eds), *Human Rights Brought Home: Socio-Legal Perspectives on Human Rights in the National Context*, vol. 3. Hart Publishing, 2004, 51–54.
Gauri, V., and D.M. Brinks. *Courting Social Justice.* Cambridge University Press, 2008.
Gauri, V., and S. Gloppen. 'Human Rights-Based Approaches to Development: Concepts, Evidence and Policy'. *Polity* 44(4) (2012), 485–503.
Gilbert, J. 'Land Rights and Nomadic Peoples: Using International Law at the Local Level'. *Nomadic Peoples* 16(2) (2012), 78–83.
Gilbert, J., and C. Doyle. 'A New Dawn Over the Land: Shedding Light on Collective Ownership and Consent'. In S. Allen and A. Xanthaki (eds), *Reflections on the UN Declaration on the Rights of Indigenous People.* Hart Publishing, 2011, 1–68.
Government of India Controller of Publications. *The Scheduled Tribes and Other Traditional Forest Dwellers (Recognition of Forest Rights) Bill, 2006.* Government of India, 2012.
Indian Tribal Heritage. *The Scheduled Tribes and Other Traditional Forest Dwellers (Recognition of Forest Rights) Act, 2006, Reports & Articles.* Indian Tribal Heritage, 2013. https://indiantribalheritage.org/?p=10148
International Labour Organisation. *ILO Convention on Indigenous and Tribal Peoples 1989 (No. 169): A Manual.* Project to Promote ILO Policy on Indigenous and Tribal Peoples, 2003.
Iwanka Raya, M. *Indigenous Women Stand against Violence. A Companion Report to the United Nations Secretary-General's Study on Violence against Women.* International Indigenous Women's Forum, 2006.
Jonas, H., et al. *An Analysis of International Law, National Legislation, Judgements, and Institutions as They Interrelate with Territories and Areas Conserved by Indigenous Peoples and Local Communities.* Natural Justice and Kalpavriksh, 2012.
Karanth, K.K., and R. Defries. 'Conservation and Management in Human-Dominated Landscapes: Case Studies from India'. *Biological Conservation* 43(12) (2010), 2865–964.
Kidder, R.L. 'Western Law in India: External Law and Local Response'. In A.M. Johnson (ed), *Social Systems and Legal Process.* Jossey-Bass, 1978, 155–80.
Ramnath, M. 'Surviving the Forest Rights Act: Between Scylla and Charybdis'. *Economic and Political Weekly* 37 (2008), 37–42.
Sambhav, K.S. 'Centre Set to Dilute Tribal Rights over Forestland'. *Down to Earth Magazine*, 2012. www.downtoearth.org.in/news/centre-set-to-dilute-tribal-rights-over-forestland-40389.

Saravanan, V. 'Political Economy of the Recognition of Forest Rights Act 2006: Conflict between the Environment and Tribal Development'. *South Asia Research* 29 (2009), 199–221.
Sarin, M., and O. Springate-Baginski. *India Forest Rights Act: The Anatomy of a Necessary But Not Sufficient Institutional Reform*. Research Programme Consortium for Improving Institutions for Pro-Poor Growth, 2010.
Sigamany, I. 'Destroying a Way of Life: Indigenous Peoples, the Forest Rights Act of India and Land Displacement of Indigenous Peoples'. In I. Satiroglu and N. Choi (eds), *Development-Induced Displacement and Resettlement: New Perspectives on Persisting Problems*. Routledge, 2015, 159–69.
Sigamany, I. 'Land Rights and Neoliberalism: An Irreconcilable Conflict for Indigenous Peoples in India?'. *International Journal of Law in Context* 13(3) (2017), 369–87.
Sircar, O. 'Spectacles of Emancipation: Reading Rights Differently in India's Legal Discourse'. *Osgoode Hall Law Journal* 49(3) (2012), 527–73.
Springate-Baginski, O., et al. *The Indian Forest Rights Act 2006: Commoning Enclosures*. Overseas Development Group, University of East Anglia, 2008. http://dlc.dlib.indiana.edu/dlc/bitstream/handle/10535/1269/Springate-Baginski_233001.pdf?sequence=1.
Tugendhat, H., and E. Dictaan-Bang-oa. *Realizing Indigenous Women's Rights: A Handbook on the CEDAW*. Tebtebba Foundation, Forest Peoples Programme, Asia Indigenous Women's Network (AIWN), 2013.
United Kingdom Administrative Justice Institute. *What Is Administrative Justice?* AA Discussion Paper. Nuffield Foundation Series, 2016.
United Nations. *The International Bill of Human Rights*. United Nations, 1996.
United Nations Children's Fund (UNICEF). *Convention on the Rights of the Child*. UNICEF, 1990. www.unicef.org/crc/.
United Nations General Assembly. *United Nations Declaration on the Rights of Indigenous Peoples (UNDRIP)*. United Nations, 2007.
United Nations General Assembly (UNGA). *Universal Declaration of Human Rights*. UNGA, 1948. www.un.org/en/universal-declaration-human-rights/.
United Nations Office of the High Commissioner for Human Rights (OHCHR). *International Convention on the Elimination of All Forms of Racial Discrimination 1965*. OHCHR, 1965. www.ohchr.org/en/professionalinterest/pages/cerd.aspx
Wani, M. *Nought without Cause*. Global Forest Coalition, Kalpavriksh, Vasundhara, 2008.
WWF. *WWF's Statement of Principles on Indigenous Peoples and Conservation*, 1996. wwf.panda.org/our_work/people/people_and_conservation/wwf_social_policies/indigenous_peoples/

Notes

Das, B., and A. Kabra. 'Global or Local Safeguards? Social Impact Assessment Insights from an Urban Indian Land Acquisition'. In J. Singer and S. Price (eds), *Country Frameworks for Development Displacement and Resettlement: Reducing Risk, Building Resilience*. Country Frameworks for Development Displacement and Resettlement: Reducing Risk, Building Resilience, 1st edn, Routledge, 2019.
India Go. *The Right to Fair Compensation and Transparency in Land Acquisition, Rehabilitation and Resettlement Act, 2013*. Government of India, 2013.
Jitendra. 'Government Introduces Land Amendment Bill Amid Protests, Walkout'. *DownToEarth*, India, 25 February 2015. News. www.downtoearth.org.in/news/government-introduces-land-amendment-bill-amid-protests-walkout-48723, accessed October 2021.

Nilsen, A.G., and K.B. Nielsen. 'Law-Struggles, Law-Making and the Politics of Hegemony in Neoliberal India: Towards a Critical Perspective on the 2013 Land Acquisition Act'. In A. Chakraborty and A. D'Costa (eds), *The Land Question in India: State, Dispossession, and Capitalist Transition*. The Land Question in India: State, Dispossession, and Capitalist Transition. Oxford University Press, 2017.

Pal, M. 'Land Acquisition and "Fair Compensation" of the "Project Affected": Scrutiny of the Law and Its Interpretation'. In A. Chakraborty and A. D'Costa (eds), *The Land Question in India: State, Dispossession, and Capitalist Transition*. The Land Question in India: State, Dispossession, and Capitalist Transition. Oxford Scholarship Online, 2017.

Phadnis, A. 'Ongoing Land Conflicts Affecting Lives, Livelihoods of Over 6.5 mn People'. *Business Standard*, New Delhi, March 17, 2020. www.business-standard.com/article/economy-policy/ongoing-land-conflicts-affecting-lives-livelihoods-of-over-6–5-mn-people-120031700149_1.html, accessed 4 February 2022.

Research CfP. *Understanding Land Acquisition Disputes in India. CPR-Land Rights Initiative Reviews Supreme Court Cases on Land Acquisition from 1950 to 2016*. Centre for Policy Research, 2017.

Tripathi, B. 'Conflicts Across India as States Create Land Banks for Private Investors, IndiaSpend'. *IndiaSpend*, India, 2017. www.indiaspend.com/cover-story/conflicts-across-india-as-states-create-land-banks-for-private-investors-12188.

United Nations. 'United Nations Permanent Forum on Indigenous Issues', 2004. http://social.un.org/index/IndigenousPeoples/SecondDecade.aspx, accessed 29 January 2013.

Wahi, N., A. Bhatia, D. Gandhi, S. Jain, P. Shukla, and U. Chauhan. *Land Acquisition in India: A Review of Supreme Court Cases from 1950 to 2016*, Centre for Policy Research, New Delhi, 2017. https://cprindia.org/briefsreports/land-acquisition-in-india-a-review-of-supreme-court-cases-1950-2016/

Yadav, M. 'Even Under Attack, India's Democratic Institutions Are Pushing Back'. *The Wire*. https://thewire.in/government/modi-government-pushback-democratic-institutions, accessed July 2021.

Chapter 2

A Critical Examination of Forest Rights Legislation, Indigenous Access to Justice, and Land Expropriation

Introduction

Mobile Indigenous peoples, usually pastoralists, move with their herds through specific regional grazing corridors. In the past, Indian camel herders' migratory corridors stretched from Afghanistan through present-day Pakistan[1] into India.[2] After Indian independence from British colonial rule, in 1947, when Pakistan was severed from India, the usufruct access of camel herders shrank to the relatively narrow borders within India. Usufruct, a key concept with regard to mobile Indigenous peoples, refers to the right to use and enjoy communal lands for the grazing of herds. This land right is especially important for hunting and gathering forest peoples, and for nomadic pastoralist communities who do not necessarily own land but move seasonally over a wide terrain. The seasonal migratory aspect is different from settled forest communities who base their livelihoods on gathering minor forest produce and small-scale agriculture. Nomadism is not conducive to accessing the law, or owning land, or even claiming land rights. Access to justice, therefore, is experienced differently by mobile Indigenous peoples in India, compared to Adivasi tribes living in or using the forests.

Since independence in 1947, pastoralists in India have had their migration routes severely restricted. The legal systems in India have changed over time. The current Forest Rights Act of 2006, according to NGO staff in Pune, was initiated by the tribal Adivasis who did not have a deep understanding of pastoralist politics.[3] Historically, the British proclaimed forest land to be known as 'revenue land', as a way of extracting money from people who used the

1 According to the interviews I had with the Maldhari community in Gujarat, some pastoralists, even today, have secret trading arrangements with Pakistan across the border.

2 Interviews with the, Maldhari community member, and Hanwant Singh Rathod, Raika Camel Herders of Sadri, Rajasthan, 2012. In 1938, the British in India fought their first war in Afghanistan in an attempt to consolidate their Indian borders against the threat of Russian imperialism in Central Asia.

3 Interview with Nitya Ghotke, Head of the NGO Anthra, working with the Dhangar mobile Indigenous community in the Deccan Plateau, Pune, 2012.

DOI: 10.4324/9781003589488-3

forest. Revenue land was therefore economically beneficial, as opposed to 'waste land', which was unproductive.[4] The Indian government continued this practice after independence. The pastoralists, however, who have alternate, usufruct needs, and who use land differently, did not recognise the new government-set boundaries. The concept of 'land alienation' had been generally unfamiliar to mobile Indigenous peoples in India, as they had not owned land of which they could be dispossessed. During pasturing, they were and still are persecuted by Forest Department officials and settled populations. Pastoralists, being on the move and therefore less likely to be part of a coordinated 'movement', have found it more difficult to organise for their own rights. More recently, activists in India have been working with pastoralists, raising awareness of the Forest Rights Act since its enactment in 2006.

The case studies are specific to pastoralist land needs, and form the basis for an analytical discussion of land violations faced by the community within the context of the Forest Rights Act. The case studies include the Maldhari[5] community of pastoralists in Mera District, Gujarat, with their magnificent herds of Kankrej and Gir cattle, represented in their political struggle against the erosion of the *gauchar* lands, which are grasslands used customarily as common grazing lands. The Dhangar pastoralists of Ahmednagar, Parner Block, Maharashtra are part of the second case study and have been displaced from their grazing territories by the Indian military's firing range, and by a sugar factory set up by a politician under dubious circumstances.

These diverse pastoralist communities used significantly different strategies to lay claim to their land rights. The Maldharis were not using litigation to access justice; rather, they were using political activism as a strategy; the Dhangar were being introduced to the Forest Rights Act but were not as yet using litigation to claim their land rights. In the next chapter, I describe the Raika and Bhasla communities from Rajasthan who were using the justice system to fight land displacement. These case studies highlight the particular aspect of the justice protection of marginalised communities by Indian government ministries, and provide an analysis of the interface of access to justice with administrative justice.

Knowledge of Mobile Indigenous Peoples

The Forest Rights Act respects and acknowledges Indigenous knowledge, which is reflected in the legal expectation within the law to restore customary rights to forest communities, to increase tribal participation in the management of forest lands, and to contribute to a more structured conservation

4 Waste land is a term used by the government to denote barren and unused land.

5 'Maldhari' is a generic name for the pastoralist clan who inhabit several states in India. The Maldharis and Rahabari clans, as well as the Bharvad, Ahir, Charan/Gadhvi and Jat communities, are all traditionally pastoralists.

approach.[6] All these aspects of the legislation is dependent on mobile Indigenous peoples (MIPs) holding ancient knowledge of managing highly varied natural environments for their livelihoods and food production.[7] This knowledge is often reflected in customary Indigenous laws, also referred to as traditional law. MIPs are adept at adapting to their changing environments, which includes but is not limited to aspects such as sustainable food production, conservation, disaster management, and sustainable water resource management.[8] Their unique knowledge and practice of pastoralism and of ethnobotanical knowledge is a stewardship which includes conserving and enhancing the genetic diversity of domesticated animals and plants.[9]

The flexible and adaptive management approaches[10] contained in Indigenous knowledge of mobile or nomadic ways of life has become more relevant and valuable under the current extreme climate challenges and global warming conditions which most scientists believe have been caused by destructive human activity of industrialisation and corporate development. An important aspect of Indigenous knowledge is the Indigenous experience of developing strategies of sustainability, particularly in the use of natural environments, and in responding to environmental change.

Mainstream food production systems, for example, depend on rainfall and predictability. Climate change exacerbates predictability. Forty per cent of the world's land has unpredictable rainfall.[11] The attempt by mainstream agriculture to control the variability of the natural environment creates struggles for sustainable agriculture and for food production. Indigenous communities such as pastoralists, on the other hand, have developed strategies over thousands of years which use variability to their advantage, working with the fluid changeability of climate.[12] Herder conservationists have deep knowledge of how to stabilise the grazing lands patterns, matching their mobility to the variable landscape, and how to track and combine forage plants which contain high concentrations of nutrients for herds.

A big issue and threat to the mobile Indigenous community specifically is that their knowledge, which is closely connected to their patterns of movement from one area of low natural resources to another, is largely

6 Bose, Arts and van Dijk, 'Forest Governmentality', 664; Government of India, The Scheduled Tribes and Other Traditional Forest Dwellers (Recognition of Forest Rights) Bill (adopted 15 December 2006, No. 158-C of 2005).

7 Celep.PastoralismistheFuture.Animatedvideo.2021www.celep.info/DocumentsbyCELEPand Members/pastoralismandclimatechange/.

8 World Summit on Sustainable Development, *Indigenous Peoples' Caucus #39 Statement by Victoria Tauli Corpuz* (United Nations Department of Economic and Social Affairs 2002).

9 Standing Committee, *Dana Declaration on Mobile Peoples and Conservation*.

10 Dana Standing Committee, *Dana Declaration on Mobile Peoples and Conservation*.

11 Celep. Pastoralism is the Future. Animated video, 2021, www.celep.info/DocumentsbyCELEP andMembers/pastoralismandclimatechange/.

12 Celep. Pastoralism is the Future. Animated video, 2021, www.celep.info/DocumentsbyCELEP andMembers/pastoralismandclimatechange/.

unrecognised by the mainstream, or Western, international community. National governments generally dismiss or deny that Indigenous knowledge systems exist, especially governments subscribing to neoliberal economic systems. Governments continue to subscribe to postcolonial 'fortress' conservation efforts which remove Indigenous communities from ancestral lands in order to create pristine landscapes devoid of people. There remains a relative paucity of research into the ability of mobile Indigenous peoples to respond to environmental variability and sustainably produce organic agricultural goods (e.g. livestock, dairy products, wheat, barley, wool) which they have been marketing domestically and transnationally. A few international organisations, such as in the United Nations, are highlighting the importance and contribution of Indigenous knowledge in declarations such as the Dana Declaration 2002,[13] the United Nations Declaration of Rights of Indigenous Peoples 2007 (UNDRIP),[14] the Hyogo Framework for Action 2005–2015, the Kyoto Protocol, and RIO+20, 2012.[15] All these declarations refer to the knowledge of Indigenous peoples, especially mobile Indigenous peoples. The United Nations International Strategy (UN/ISDR) for Disaster Reduction has published a collection documenting various Indigenous practices in disaster management in the Asia Pacific region.[16]

The Dana Declaration, which outlines a "comprehensive approach" for mobile peoples specifically in regard to conservation, documents the "traditional resource use practices and culture-based respect for nature" of mobile Indigenous peoples.[17] The Dana Declaration reinforces that "many mobile peoples are still making a significant contribution to the maintenance of the earth's ecosystems, species and genetic diversity – even though this often goes unrecognized," and acknowledges the "immeasurable and irreplaceable range of knowledge and skills."[18] Pastoralists at the Dana + 10 meeting in Jordan in 2012 took their demands to the 2012 Rio Conference on Sustainable Development. In the document entitled "The future we want", Principle 49 states:

> We stress the importance of the participation of indigenous peoples in the achievement of sustainable development. We also recognize the importance of the United Nations Declaration on the Rights of Indigenous

13 Committee, *Dana Declaration on Mobile Peoples and Conservation.*

14 United Nations, *United Nations Declaration on the Rights of Indigenous Peoples.*

15 Examples are: UNISDR, Dana Declaration, Hyogo Framework for Action 2005–2015, Kyoto Protocol, UNDRIP, and RIO.

16 I S D R International Strategy for Disaster Reduction, *Hyogo Framework for Action 2005–2015: Building the Resilience of Nations and Communities to Disasters*, 2005); UNISDR, *Indigenous Knowledge for Disaster Risk Reduction: Good Practices and Lessons Learned from Experiences in the Asia-Pacifi c Region*, 2008).

17 Committee, *Dana Declaration on Mobile Peoples and Conservation.*

18 Committee, *Dana Declaration on Mobile Peoples and Conservation.*

Peoples in the context of global, regional, national and subnational implementation of sustainable development strategies.[19]

And Principle 22 of Rio Declaration on Environment and Development of 2005 states,

> Indigenous peoples and their communities and other local communities have a vital role in environmental management and development because of their knowledge and traditional practices. States should recognize and duly support their identity, culture and interests and enable their effective participation in the achievement of sustainable development.
>
> The full and effective participation of Indigenous Peoples is vital for all discussions relevant to their communities and interests. For Indigenous Peoples water is central to our cultures, and to our relationship to our lands and territories. In fact, we are guided by our respect for Mother Earth when we practice our traditional knowledge and sciences.[20]

Pastoralists and mobile Indigenous peoples have been reminding the world that pastoral systems all over the world specialise in transforming the variability of natural environments into a resource without destroying its ecological fragility. The world needs to start listening to MIPS and valuing their knowledge and their cultural diversity.[21] If the knowledge and flexible management practices of mobile peoples and herder conservationists were to be officially recognised and integrated into national and international policy, conservation would be enriched, and mobile Indigenous production systems would continue unimpeded to contribute concretely to sustainability for the future. A key purpose of the Forest Rights Act, besides acknowledging the traditional role of forest peoples in the conservation and management of forest resources, is the recognition of land rights.[22]

Respecting Ancestral Land Rights

James Anaya, former Special Rapporteur on the rights of Indigenous peoples, emphasises the historical power imbalances in the law. These were rationalised

19 13th United Nations Commission on Sustainable Development, *Indigenous Peoples Caucus Major Group Closing Statement* (nited Nations Commission on Sustainable Development 2005).

20 United Nations, *The Rio Declaration* (United Nations 1992), https://sustainabledevelopment.un.org/rio20.

21 CELEP Coalition of European Lobbies on Eastern African Pastoralism, 'Pastoralists Turn Variability into Food' (*Misereor*, 2021), accessed 18 August 2021, www.celep.info/wp-content/uploads/2021/06/Pastoralists-turn-variability-into-food-FULL-1.pdf.

22 Bhullar, 'The Indian Forest Rights Act 2006', 24.

from the sixteenth century by philosophers such as Hobbes, Pufendorf, Wolff, and Vattel, who used a reference point of morality that did not respect equal rights of races to their ancestral lands. Human rights have become an acceptable norm with moral foundations that were (mis)used to justify imperialistic policies. Rawls cites Aristotle's conception of justice as avoiding taking advantage of other people, whether that means taking what belongs to them or depriving them of what is owed to them. The term for this is 'pleonexia',[23] and Rawls derives the principles of justice from this, calling it a 'fair' manner in which to cooperate socially, and conceiving the regulation of this justice as being advanced by institutions set up by society. "Laws and commands are accepted as laws and commands only if it is generally believed that they can be obeyed and executed. If this is in question, the actions of authorities presumably have some other purpose than to organise conduct."[24] This interpretation is echoed by Amartya Sen's grounds for critical assessment of justice in the context of human rights, which rests on "judgements about justice", which he bases on "freedom, capabilities, resources, happiness, well-being" and other "diverse considerations" that figure under the general headings of equality and liberty, the evident connection between pursuing justice and seeking democracy seen as "government by discussion, and the nature, viability and reach of claims of human rights".[25] This discourse illustrates the emergence of human rights norms that offer legal recourse for Indigenous communities to reclaim lost land rights. I posit that the historical evolution of the law has an embedded bias due to the imperialistic policies of land expropriation by colonisers. This has long residual consequences, which can influence contemporary state attitudes and policies and hinder the course of justice, as illustrated by my case studies later of India.

Historical Overview

In the precolonial Himalayan regions, communities often had different collective roles. Pastoralist communities were generally highly valued members because of their contributions of milk, dairy products, and wool, and for fertilising the farmlands using their animals. This high regard was fragile and not homogenous across the different regions of the country. The British introduced a land-based concept of political economy, based on a newly introduced taxation system which criminalised people who did not pay.[26] This established a legal "structural violence" to which nomadic tribes are subjected, which is reinforced by "development hegemony".[27] Pastoralists were marginalised during this period, leading to communities such as the Yadavs, the Patels,

23 Rawls, *A Theory of Justice*, 9.
24 Rawls, *A Theory of Justice*, 9.
25 Sen, *The Idea of Justice*, ix.
26 Heredia, 'Denotified and Nomadic Tribes', 6.
27 Heredia, 'Denotified and Nomadic Tribes', 6.

and Jats becoming sedentary. In Gujarat, for example, all cattle herding was traditionally dominated by the Patel community. When these communities settled and gained prominence, they slowly alienated the mobile populations, who had no land and no permanence. The 'home village', which was linked with a temple and their deities, acted as base camp from which the nomadic communities migrated and returned. The semantics of 'Indigenous' is different in India, as the pastoralists came in waves over the centuries and were not necessarily ethnically Indigenous to India.[28] The dearth of population statistics for mobile Indigenous peoples in India, which I have been unable to include in this study, might be evidence of just how marginalised they are.

Although pastoralist groups such as those described in this chapter are socially marginalised, not all are economically poor. Major omissions in Forest Rights Act rules hinder access to justice for pastoralists. This is outlined by Sarin and Springate-Baginski, who indicate that the rules are particularly unclear about rights and restrictions of usufruct claims to land.

They argue that there are no provisions "for claiming more complex rights such as community tenures over their habitats by PTGs,[29] or claims by nomadic and pastoral communities for whom the single village based Gram Sabha procedure is inadequate".[30] This omission has major consequences for the mobile Indigenous communities because transhumant communities moving seasonally across district and state boundaries are facing immense difficulties in claiming their rights. The subsequent case studies provide context to this argument by describing the challenges that are particular to the nomadic lifestyles of mobile Indigenous communities when accessing land rights in certain parts of India.

Case Study: 'All Land Is God's Land'

The Maldhari Pastoralist Community of Mera District, Gujarat

Pastoralist Maldhari communities exist in Gujarat, Rajasthan, Pakistan, and Afghanistan. 'Mal' means livestock, and 'dhari' means owner. It was explained to me that the name Maldhari is still in use in Iran, while in Mongolia it is Malchain. 'Mal', therefore, is a common word stretching across these Indian subcontinental regions and beyond. The Gujarat Maldharis whom I visited possess

28 The United Nations Declaration on the Rights of Indigenous Peoples (UNDRIP) Article 8 states: '1. Indigenous peoples and individuals have the right not to be subjected to forced assimilation or destruction of their culture. 2. States shall provide effective mechanisms for prevention of, and redress for: (a) Any action which has the aim or effect of depriving them of their integrity as distinct peoples, or of their cultural values or ethnic identities; (b) Any action which has the aim or effect of dispossessing them of their lands, territories or resources; (c) Any form of forced population transfer'. United Nations Declaration on the Rights of Indigenous Peoples (adopted 13 December 2007, UNGA Res. 61/295 A (UNDRIP Add 1)).

29 Primitive Tribal Groups, an official term used by the Government of India to describe certain Indigenous groups who live in relative isolation.

30 Sarin and Springate-Baginski, 'India Forest Rights Act', 28.

a deep conceptual understanding of land as shared and, like many pastoralists, are intensely communal. Maldharis[31] have a saying that 'all land is God's land',[32] and have collective customs such as 'bij', which is free distribution of milk among community members, as well as a sharing of boundaries, territories, and other resources. Maldhari communities are nomadic and semi-nomadic pastoralists[33] who herd cows, and in some areas keep goats, buffaloes, sheep, and camels. They are spread around several states in Northern India[34] and migrate seasonally. Published literature seems to differ on how long the Maldharis have lived in India, dating it from seven hundred to two thousand years.[35] Prior to 1940, before Indian independence, their migratory corridors included Afghanistan, Sind in present-day Pakistan, and the Indian states of Gujarat and Rajasthan. After independence, however, they could no longer cross the borders into Pakistan, severely limiting their pastoral migratory routes.

The Maldharis whom I studied in Mera District were watching as their lifestyle was eroding with the corporatisation of milk production in India, initiated in the state of Gujarat. Changing land requirements for farmers, who had had a mutually interdependent relationship with pastoralists, added to the exclusion of the latter, and the altered political landscape of contemporary India has not been kind to those who choose a nomadic way of life. Responding to these developments that have threatened their livelihoods and existence as pastoralists, the Maldharis of Mera District have organised themselves with the support of an organically initiated NGO, founded by a member of the Maldhari community, and has begun activist political strategies to reclaim their land rights.

Maldhari Community Profile

"Maldharis were traditionally tall, energetic and healthy",[36] with a diet rich in milk and dairy, including ghee,[37] supplemented with millet, garlic, chillies, and ancient grains such as 'banti' and 'kodra'. Conventionally, the Maldharis only kept certain numbers of animals in relation to their own capacity to support them, and did not expand beyond this capacity. If someone lost their livestock accidentally, the other pastoralists were required by community custom to support them. Their livelihood was based on preparing ghee

31 While 'Maldhari' is a generic name for the pastoralist clan who inhabit several states in India, India is home to many distinct pastoralist communities including the Maldharis and Rahabari clans, as well as the Bharvad, Ahir, Charan/Gadhvi and Jat communities.
32 Maldhari proverb.
33 Stanley, 'Wetland Ecosystems', 62.
34 Maldharis are found in the states of Maharashtra, Uttar Pradesh, Madhya Pradesh, Andhra Pradesh and Orissa.
35 Gadgil, 'Conserving Biodiversity'; Gadgil and Guha, *This Fissured Land.*
36 Quote by a, Maldhari community member when being interviewed as part of the data collection for my research.
37 Ghee is clarified butter, traditionally made at home.

from milk, and if they had surplus milk it was sold in the open market. Big markets were held within 50 km, and every 30 km small markets were held, facilitating quick sales of the surplus. Every three or four days, the women pastoralists sold the ghee and milk in the open market and bought other household goods. In addition to ghee, they sold some of their cattle to be used as transport as an additional source of income. Camels were only owned by communities who lived in sandy soil areas, such as in Kutch. The community that I visited in Mera District owned sheep, goats, and cows. Other sources of income included the collection and sale of wool, and the sale of cows, which were used for agricultural purposes as well as for dairy. The two main breeds of cows in Gujarat were the Gir and Kankrej.[38]

The cultural tradition known as 'bij' required free distribution of milk to neighbours at least two days per month. This milk was conventionally not allowed to be sold for money. Another communal custom obliged relatives to gift livestock as a start-up to newly married young couples to breed their own herds. When animals get old and stop yielding, they are not discarded, but are cared for by the community until they die. The value of livestock is reflected even in the Maldhari language, where they greet one another with "Are your animals healthy, with no illness?", followed by "How much milk is your animal giving?" The White Revolution, based on principles of profit, eliminated traditional caring practices such as bij, which had provided a safety net within the community for people in need, and for members who had no means to produce or pay for milk themselves. The loss of this safety net increased poverty at the Maldhari community level.

Operation Flood, also known as the White Revolution, refers to the highly successful dairy cooperation movement in Anand, Gujarat, begun in 1970, which created a National Milk Grid connecting milk producers and consumers throughout the county, "reducing seasonal and regional price variations while ensuring that the producer gets fair market prices in a transparent manner on a regular basis". Begun as a rural development initiative to create jobs and income for rural communities, it was considered a major economic success for India's rural milk producers, and for facilitating easy access to dairy products for the consumer, with more than seventy thousand dairy cooperatives in the country by the late 1980s.[39]

38 In Gujarat, the two main breeds are Gir and Kankrej. The Kankrej cattle are identified by magnificent curved horns. In India, the Gir is found only in Saurashtra. When the Portuguese held Goa, Daman and Diu as protectorates on India's west coast, during the colonial era, Saurashtra fell under Portuguese protection geographically and the Portuguese exported the Gir cows to Brazil. The Brazilians expanded this industry and today export Gir semen and embryos all over the world and have developed Gir milk productivity to a maximum of fifty litres per day. In India, the Gir cow still produces only half that amount and has remained undeveloped as an industry.

39 ('Operation Flood' taken from the National Dairy Development Board website www.nddb.coop/about/genesis/flood).

One of the leaders of the pastoralist NGO[40] was my host in Gujarat, of Maldhari ancestry, and whose family was from Becharaji town, close to Meru. His family lost all their cattle in the 1985 drought. Consequently, they were forced to move to Ahmedabad, the capital of Gujarat, where the family bought two buffaloes from the mother's brother. His mother took care of the buffaloes, which comprised the family income at that point as his father was not earning. His father went into community leadership and began a struggle against landlords who were encroaching on common property used by Maldharis for livestock grazing. Dependence on climatic conditions is one part of the story. The other is dependence on the current political situation, in which the Maldharis of Mera District have decided to participate in order to shape their own struggle for land rights through political activism.

The Bharatiya Janata Party (BJP), a right-leaning party under the then Chief Minister of Gujarat had been in power for fifteen years in Gujarat when I visited in 2013.[41] Gujarat had a two-party system with Congress and BJP. In Gujarat, a senior BJP leader, rebelled against the party leadership and resigned from the BJP in August 2012, launching a new political party called the Gujarat Parivartan Party (GPP).[42] The rebel leader's community were traditionally pastoralists, who in turn were part of the marginalised communities, which also included Dalits, Adivasis (tribals), Kohlis, and others, many of whom joined the newly formed GPP.[43] In Gujarat, a part of the civil society had been trying to get rid of the BJP ever since the notorious 2002 Hindu-Muslim riots in which more than a thousand people, predominantly Muslim, were killed by Hindu mobs.[44] After the riots, the civil society in Gujarat campaigned for the Congress, as a strategy to avoid splitting the vote. In spite of this, the BJP won with a big margin in 2007. Subsequently, a movement was spawned in order to create alternative leadership independent of either the Congress or the BJP, headed by a Member of Legislative Assembly (MLA).[45] The NGO was part of an organisation of marginalised communities in this area of Kutch in Gujarat, which included pastoralists, who protested against land violations by the government in collaboration

40 I had met this Maldhari community member in Jordan, at the Dana +10 workshop I was facilitating for mobile Indigenous peoples in 2012.

41 In 2014 Narendra Modi won the national elections to become Prime Minister of India.

42 Traditionally, the Patels formed the leadership of the Maldhari community. It was an inherited title. The Patels have since become a sedentary community. My host was also of the Maldhari community, and part of the NGO working with the Maldharis whom I was visiting, aspired to politically represent the marginalised communities in this district of Gujarat.

43 Other marginalised communities in India are officially named by the Indian government as Other Backward Classes (OBC).

44 Narendra Modi has been accused of encouraging sectarian violence and as being complicit in the Gujarat riots. See Majumder, 'Narendra Modi "Allowed" Gujarat 2002 Anti-Muslim Riots'; Mishra, 'The Gujarat Massacre'.

45 An MLA is a representative from a specific district elected to a State Legislature in India.

with this new alternative movement which was independent of both the Congress and the BJP.

Land Violations

Land expropriation by private individuals and the sale of gauchar lands by the government to private individuals and industries formed part of local land violations. The particular community that I studied did not use legal mechanisms, but instead used political action such as protests, advocacy, and lobbying in order to assert their land rights.

One such example was the action by Mahuva farmers, to protest a BJP government land violation in 2010. Previously, in the Taluk of Mahuva in the Saurashtra region of Gujarat, cultivation was widespread on lands that had been desalinated and recharged through government efforts to build reservoirs. Besides providing irrigation for agriculture, these reservoirs engendered rich ecosystems populated by more than forty species of birds. The most significant change for the community was their increased affluence. The threat to the main water source for farmers was prohibited by law.

The BJP state government sanctioned 3,460 hectares of fertile farmlands with reservoirs for the construction of a cement factory, threatening the livelihoods and the ecosystem of this area. It would have destroyed local livelihoods, pastoral grazing lands, and a prevailing rich ecosystem.[46] The sanctioning of the land to the Nirma cement factory was unbeknownst to the farmers, who only discovered it when the date of the environment public hearing was announced.

In 2010, with women leading the protest, the farmers began to mobilise to reclaim their lands. This included a now-celebrated 350 km protest march, which lasted fifteen days and ended at the state assembly to voice their concerns. Their struggle was supported by civil society organisations and prominent activists. The pastoralist NGO joined the mobilisation efforts to reclaim their lands and, with the help of the local Member of Legislative Assembly, took the battle for their lands to the Supreme Court, eventually winning their case. Eventually the farmers won their case in

46 The Indian government policy of 2012 on gauchar lands: 'No pastoral land to be given to industrial or commercial purpose. Government will also ensure these are not encroached against the interest of local community; If gauchar land is in middle of an urban area, the government will denotify and sell the land and develop pastures at an alternate site; New gauchar (pastoral) land policy to comply with the last year's Supreme Court order asking state government to not sell government owned pastoral land for industrial or commercial use; If gauchar land is in middle of an urban area, the government will denotify and sell the land and develop pastures at an alternate site; In some cases, the government has given land for some public purposes, for instance, schools, which require adjoining gauchar land. In such cases, we will sell the land to them and use the money in developing new pastoral land'. Taken from Desh Gujarat, 'Gauchar Land'.

2011, when the Supreme Court of India ruled against the Nirma cement factory's right to environmental clearance.[47]

The White Revolution of milk production in Anand in India, though very successful for mainstream communities, broke the traditional pastoralist marketing system as all their produce went to the dairy cooperatives. The newly enforced dependency on the dairy cooperatives also pushed them into a more semi-nomadic lifestyle. Earlier they were migratory pastoralists and used their livestock for the production of milk.[48] The traditional division of labour between the Maldhari pastoralists and the settled farmers maintained a system in which the Maldharis had animals and the Choudaris, another non-mobile tribe, had land. The Choudaris, however, were more powerful and had taken over the selling of milk products to Anand and had pushed the Maldharis out of this market. Traditionally, the Maldharis had provided veterinary care for the animals. The Choudaris also took over this community task, and the Maldharis lost this source of income as well.

Pastoralists, like other farmers, are reliant on the weather. The year I was visiting, the rains were too little and too late. In previous years, the pastoralists had been able to rely upon a predictable three-year cyclical weather pattern, with one year of good rains followed by a year of adequate rains and a third year of drought. Between 1985 and 1987, however, they had three consecutive years of drought, during which large numbers of livestock died, and they had to keep migrating in search of water. Between 2001 and 2011 they had no drought in any year. In 2012, while this data was being gathered, there was no rain. The drought was severe, with no rain from Jamnagar to Kutch, both of which were points along the seasonal migratory route. Life was uncertain, and land violations added to the problems caused by natural weather conditions.

The Role of Panchayats in Land Violations

Gujarat law states that pastoral lands, known locally as gauchar land, cannot be changed, and that the privatisation of gauchar land is illegal, as I have outlined earlier.[49] All *Panchayats*[50] have a register of all the livestock in the district.[51] The reason for this is to ensure the ratio of grazing land to livestock. By legislation, there must be 40 acres of grazing land for every one hundred animals. The Panchayats in this area of Kutch have not honoured this law.

47 Desai, *Subaltern Movements in India*, 76; Jha, 'Mahuva Farmers' March Ends'; Kanekal, 'Nirma's Cement Plant'.

48 The change for the Maldhari communities which was created by the White Revolution was explained to me by a member from the community.

49 Desh Gujarat, 'Gauchar Land'.

50 'Panchayat' is the term used to describe a village council made up of five governing members who have been elected as an organ of village self-government.

51 The livestock register does not include goats.

They changed the rule unilaterally, compelling the Maldharis to file a police charge – a First Information Report (FIR) – to oppose this new regulation.[52] The powerful landlords threatened to file a counter FIR, which would have disallowed the Maldharis to continue their communal tradition of grazing on the landlords' fields after harvest. The Maldharis stood their ground, and eventually the landlords promised to let them graze as usual. This promise, however, was not honoured. In addition, the landlords also arbitrarily decided that the Maldharis were not allowed to graze on temple land. Temple land traditionally belongs to the whole community, and Maldharis had always grazed their livestock on temple lands in the past.

Initially, the Maldharis asked the Panchayat to urge the landlords to stop these new arbitrary restrictions, but the Panchayat did not comply. When the Maldharis started a protest in reaction, the police tried to mediate, promising to "stop the action, and we will sort other grazing lands".[53] No grazing land was provided, however, after the Maldharis stopped their protest. Post-conflict, the Maldharis' source of income was rescinded, with landlords no longer requesting their labour. Now, having lost their gauchar grazing land, the Maldharis can only graze their cattle on the edges of farms, which is also causing problems, and the landlords have lodged a new police complaint against this. The farmers have also lodged false police cases, charging the Maldharis with encroaching, which has pushed the police to arrest the Maldharis. These issues are increasingly marginalising the Maldhari community and severely restricting their access to justice.

Gender Dynamics in the Maldhari Community

The loss of gauchar land for grazing had increased Maldhari women's workload. The new task of having to gather fodder added to a workload that started between 4 a.m. and 5 a.m. in order to complete domestic chores such as cooking and laundry. The ponds, which had dried up with the conversion of pond areas into private cultivated fields, no longer provided the Maldhari livestock with drinking water. The farmers began charging the Maldharis a fee to use tube wells for watering their animals. Since the farmers seized the grazing lands, the animals have to be grazed further away, adding to the women's time spent on this task. This had caused new tensions within the community, especially after the farmers appointed security guards who chased away and intimidated the women. The women had to resort to gathering fodder for the animals rather than

52 A First Information Report (FIR) is the first step for a civilian in reporting a crime or offence according to Indian police rules. It is filed with the police by a victim of a crime. It is important because it sets in motion the process of criminal justice and investigation.

53 Quote from an interview of from the Maldhari community in Gujarat.

allowing them to roam free. They began carrying between 50 and 60 kilos of fodder and walked about 4 km more each day, which added to their workload and proved detrimental to their health. When the cows started giving less milk, due to the change of nutritional status, the women were blamed. Seasonal migration of cattle, which occurred at the start of the monsoon seasons, was undertaken by the men, forcing a gender division of labour, with the women at home taking care of domestic work, the children, and the elderly. The general division of labour had men herding livestock every day and the women going to the market. There were small markets every 7 km from each village, and big markets 18 km from each village. Traditionally, the women pastoralists in Gujarat traded in the markets and therefore controlled the money. However, the Amul milk cooperatives from Anand in Gujarat changed the dynamic negatively for Maldharis, since they could no longer control the marketing of their milk produce. This has a direct gender connotation for women, who lost control of marketing, finances, and economic independence.

The assets that a woman owns and brings to the marital home had diminished since the White Revolution. The traditional custom for married women was that the woman would go back and forth from her own family to the marital home on visits. This is called 'Ana'. The final return to the marital home, which is called 'Jiana', occurs six months after the birth of the first baby. During the Jiana, the woman brings back livestock given formally to her by her relatives, which are her own assets. The White Revolution destroyed this livestock exchange in several ways, and also negatively affected how livestock is valued. Now, instead of livestock, people desire television sets and other electronic goods. The White Revolution has also changed the value of milk animals, because now each milk animal has a price. Prior to this, animals were not priced individually. Instead, value was placed on the herd as a whole. Animals were therefore given freely to newly married women by their relatives. This rarely happens now, which has diminished the financial worth of the assets a newly married woman can contribute to her household.

The villages I visited included Finchdi and Sitarpur, where an NGO supported the activities of the Maldhari pastoralists. Residing near the Maldhari villages in huts built in the traditional pastoralist dwellings, where the NGO worked, I met with groups of pastoralists, both women and men, although the women did not play an active role in the discussions. The head of one of the Maldhari families, whose home I visited, accompanied us on the village visits. The group discussions entailed descriptions of how the community had advocated for retaining their grazing lands – lands that are steadily being encroached upon. The language was a local Gujarati dialect, and an NGO staff member acted as an interpreter. The village was crowded and busy, with lots of activity and numerous heads of cattle with remarkable long horns. We sat in a circle with a group comprising members of the tribe, mostly men and children. There were no signs of affluence. Gender differences were starkly apparent in the children. The boys were well groomed, with neatly combed, oiled black hair. All the girls looked unkempt in contrast, their untidy hair dry and brown, a sign of malnourishment. Traditionally in these communities, men and boys eat first, girls eat second, and women eat last. The boys had solid silver bracelets, a traditional piece of jewellery worn by men of the Maldhari caste, while the girls wore only cheap plastic bangles. These superficial details could be perceived as revealing gender being valued differently, and more negatively for females.

The Economics of Maldhari Livestock Rearing

The economics of Maldhari livestock rearing was described in detail.[54] The cost of fodder was Rs. 15.00 per kilogram. Each animal needed either 8 kilograms of dry fodder or 30 kilograms of green fodder, which was approximately Rs. 120.00 per animal. In the autumn of 2012, during my visit, the cost of feed because of drought was Rs. 12.00 per kilogram. Cattle feed

Figure 2.1 Gathering for a focus group at Sitarpur Village, Gujarat, with the Maldhari pastoralists

Photo by the author

54 This information was given to me by the community during data collection interviews.

was normally lower than the cost of fodder, but now, with the drought, it was the opposite. Instead of costing Rs. 120.00 per day to feed an animal, under drought conditions it now cost between Rs. 150.00 and Rs. 170.00 per day, creating a financial loss for the Maldharis. Traditionally, the farmers followed a custom in which they were not allowed to cultivate after the harvest without offering free grazing rights to pastoralists for one or two days after the harvest. This was a customary right. One or two days were called 'one round' of grazing. If the farmer did not give permission for the pastoralists to graze freely, traditionally the pastoralists could allow their animals to destroy the farmer's crops.

Before the White Revolution, the Maldharis of Kutch were mostly making ghee from their milk, which was sold. By custom, buttermilk that they produced was not allowed to be sold but was kept as food for the calves and for free distribution to neighbours, a solicitous aspect of communal living. Raw milk was also not allowed to be sold in the past, the custom being that only a value-added product from milk, such as ghee, could be sold. Even in contemporary times, camel milk had generally been free, though this practice was changing. Traditionally, during a wedding, the celebrating family invited camel owners who came and distributed free camel milk. The main income of camel owners was from transportation. Pastoralists believed that Momai, the Gujarati goddess who rides a camel and whom pastoralists worship, does not allow the sale of camel milk. A camel, which feeds on trees, is traditionally entitled to feed freely on whatever trees it encounters. In 1935, the price of one sheep and the price of the wool of one sheep was the same. No one, therefore, ever killed an animal. Eighty years ago, before independence, when the silver coin with Queen Victoria's head, called 'rani chaap rupiya', was in use, the price of one silver coin (one *bigha*) and one cow was the same.

The White Revolution had encroached on land because the Anand dairy needed land to grow fodder. This encouraged a bigger market for cattle, and many farmers who had formerly only grown crops started investing in livestock, which had always been the exclusive occupation of Maldharis, creating competition and reducing the Maldharis' income. In addition, pastoralists traditionally received free fodder in the form of wheat and other grasses from farmers when the latter had an excess. Farmers had no tractors then, and they used the bullocks and organic manure from pastoralists. The pastoralists would graze their herds to get rid of weeds that grew after the monsoon. While the herds grazed on the weeds, they would drop their dung, which farmers then used as fertiliser. The increased competition created by Anand had destroyed this mutual interdependence between farmers and pastoralists. Because of all these changes, pastoralists were slowly facing increasing impoverishment. Pastoralists, for example, use local breeds of livestock; the White Revolution introduced the Holstein, Fresian, and Jersey cows. These foreign cows are not free range, which pushed out the pastoralists. There are eighteen district-level dairy unions, only two of which include pastoralists.

Traditionally, land was not valued very highly among the nomadic Maldhari community. Finchdi village comprised thirty-nine families, of which only three owned enough land to survive sustainably. Three or four families owned between one and four *bighas*.[55] The rest of the community was landless. We visited the home of two residents of Finchdi village, who had been so involved in land issues that they were invited to represent Maldhari land issues at a global gathering in Sweden. In the Finchdi areas, there were three hundred Maldharis, and the village, with the help of the NGO, had carried out research on changes in land and crops. The quality of a certain crop called *jejwa*, which was used for fodder, had greatly diminished for several reasons: less land to grow seasonal crops, failed monsoons and increased drought, and too much pressure on a small area of land. Previously, this family had owned 150 cows, and they had had access to 6 or 7 square km of gauchar land, which was traditionally collective grazing land. Now, they owned only ten to fifteen cows, and all the collective grazing land was under cultivation with castor beans. The cows gave them an income of Rs. 6,000.00, which was now halved due to the rising costs of fodder. Traditionally, the Maldharis had a good life; they made lots of ghee from the milk from their cows and were able to sell it. A bull used to be sold for one hundred rani chaap (silver coins), much more than they brought in now.

During the focus group meeting at Finchdi village, the group explained that the gauchar land, which used to be collective grassland, had now been broken up and privatised. The privatisation of gauchar land is illegal. Starting twenty-five years ago, Babul trees had been planted in grassland, and these thorny trees now cover 27 acres next to the jungle, terminating the grazing for their cattle. Another change was the illegal conversion of pond areas into private, cultivated fields. Some of the collective grasslands had been fenced off under a government grant scheme for the planting of vegetables and other crops. Due to the encroachment by these powerful individuals, both private and government, there was no longer any collective property in Finchdi. Wanting to avoid conflict, the Maldharis had not challenged these changes. There were also future plans for a Maruti auto plant to be built in this area. The local Panchayat changed part of the gauchar land into a fenced plantation called Panchwati. In Gujarat, the law states that gauchar land is protected,[56] but the plans for change were processed illegally by the Panchayat. The increasing impoverishment of the Maldhari community as a consequence of loss of land and constrained livelihoods was very apparent.

55 A bigha is a local unit of land measurement in square metres in India. It varies considerably, but in Rajasthan it is roughly 2,500 square metres.

56 Agarwal, Flintan, Pandya, Assefa and Eba, *Land Tenure Security and Governance Dynamics in Gujarat, India*, 25.

Sitarpur village had 350 acres of gauchar land. The first community there were the Thakurs. There were now also Patels and Maldharis who occupied Gaikwad District, Mehsana, Surendranagar, Ahmedabad, and Pattan. Sitarpur was the centre for these five districts. In 2009, a powerful landowner called Puraji Darbar, with the help of his own community, took over the gauchar land for a period of about ten years. The Maldharis protested this takeover with the NGO's help. The Maldhari leaders, called Patels,[57] called for a meeting with the Darbaris (to which this powerful man belonged), but this meeting was unsuccessful. The Darbaris refused to give up their land. The night of the refusal, the Maldharis held two meetings. All of them, including men, women, and children, decided that they wanted their gauchar land back at all costs, even if it included violence. They resolved to stay united. In July 2009, in cooperation with Maldharis from three other villages, Finchdi, Hasalpur, and Naviani, they organised a sit-in action on the gauchar land with seventy people – men and women – and five hundred animals. The leaders called the people together with the communication, "Whoever has pastoralist blood must arrive at 8 a.m.", making it a matter of community pride and responsibility to attend. The Darbaris quickly sought the aid of the local police, who came to threaten the Maldharis. The organising NGO, however, attended the Maldhari sit-in with a video camera, which forced the police to withdraw for fear of being held accountable for unfounded harassment of the Maldharis. This movement snowballed into activism in six or seven villages, adding Mera, Manavada, and Tuvad to the original list of four villages. The Darbaris filed an FIR at the police station and reported the names of all the Maldharis at the sit-in. The NGO supported the Maldharis by dealing with the red tape and explaining the injustice of the situation, and within two days they managed to obtain grazing access to the gauchar land. The fact that the Maldhari community had representatives in the local Panchayat also further strengthened their land claims, as it gave them the necessary political clout for successful land activism.

Ninety Maldhari households have been in the district of Mehsana for about four hundred years. Between October and May, fifty households migrate seasonally to Kutch, 100 km away. The full family migrates, but before 1985 only the men and animals did so, while the women stayed back to look after the young and the old. After 1985, they had three years of drought, so the whole family started migrating in search of food and grazing land. In 2012, during my visit, they were facing drought again. Another problem was that gauchar land was government land, but the government had recently been giving this land away for privatised ownership. About four Maldhari families have bought land; the rest only have income from their livestock. The Maldharis recently started selling milk through cooperatives

57 Each Maldhari community has one or two leaders called 'Patel', which is an inherited title.

to the Mother Dairy, which was centralised in the whole state. They were not supported by any other NGOs.

There were many 'false' FIRs filed every year against the Maldharis. It costs them thousands of rupees to fight these unfounded cases. The police demand bribes, which adds to the cost, to which the many Maldhari people and NGO staff I spoke to attested. Many Maldharis were too busy with their livestock to enter into legal action. In addition, the lack of education results in an unawareness of the potential protection offered by land legislation. After the sit-in with three other villages, Sitarpur village, with the NGO's support, united with the other villages to form a local support organisation. Previously, the Maldharis were not united, had no strategy, and lacked trust among themselves. The NGO seemed to have brought them together to form a united front to challenge the continuing land violations.[58]

The lack of protection of a minority in order to enable them to pursue their traditional livelihoods and lifestyles might be perceived as 'state violence'. The shared traditions of the Maldhari pastoralists, such as bij, the free distribution of milk, and the custom of community contribution of cattle as a start-up investment for newly married couples, guaranteed that no community member was in need. Reliant on customary traditions to protect each other from calamity or accidents, and caring for each other, with a modest lifestyle that involved only rearing enough animals to match their capacity for animal husbandry, ensured a strong in-built non-hierarchical community welfare system. This traditional communal welfare system was being destroyed by the land violations carried out by the government and other non-nomadic groups.

Traditionally, gender dynamics were relatively equitable, with women controlling income from the sale of produce at the market. Women also brought their own assets to the marital relationship, assets that remained their own. Both these traditions offered women economic independence. However, these communal safety nets were being eroded by the economic squeeze caused by the erosion of the pastoralist livelihood and by the various forms of modernisation in India, such as the corporate milk production of the White Revolution. Private industries, such as the cement factory mentioned earlier, would also destroy the delicate eco-balance of former fertile farmlands.

The Mera District Maldharis rebelled against the socially divisive politics that the state of Gujarat experienced, which culminated in 2002 with the Hindu-Muslim riots, in which a considerable number of Muslims, a minority religious community in the state, were massacred while the government stood by and took no protective action. Forming a new political party, the marginalised communities in Gujarat, including Maldhari pastoralists, religious

58 NGO staff recounted a strategy they used to encourage unity among the Maldharis, which was to encourage the use of the traditional Maldhari language by singing local songs such as 'There's Something Wrong with Your Water'.

minorities, Dalits, Adivasis, and Kohlis, came together in protest against the prevailing discordant politics of the state. The Maldharis, by participating in this new political party, have taken a strong stand against mainstream politics that has colluded with the economic elite to displace them from their lands and further marginalise them.

The Maldharis had not used the legal system to help them in their land claims, preferring to take the political route. One of the reasons for this might have been that in their seasonal migration with their cattle, they did not use forest lands, and the Forest Rights Act applies to forest lands. Another reason was that the choice of strategy to claim land rights was often dependent on the priorities of the NGO working with communities. In this case, the NGO was interested in using political action as a strategy. This theme of NGO influence runs through each case study.

Case Study: 'Look for a Yellow Turban'

The Dhangar Pastoralists of Ahmednagar, Parner Block, Maharashtra

Four hours after departing from the large city of Pune, we left the road, and the jeep bumped along the dry grassy terrain for a while. The vague directions we had were simply to "look for a yellow turban".

After stopping a few times while the veterinarian doctor tried to connect to the pastoralist community on her mobile phone, two vividly yellow-turbaned men on a motorbike approached us in a cloud of dark dust. Mahindra, one of the yellow-turbaned men on the bike, joined us in the red jeep and piloted us to a pastoralist camp in the distance. Abandoning the jeep at some point, we continued on foot towards a group of bright blue tarpaulin-covered tents. Leaping over a stream where a few horses browsed, we approached the Dhangar community of women, men, and children.

The Dhangar pastoralists herded sheep and goats, with their migratory corridors ranging from the Konkan coast in Western India, through the forests and into the Western Ghats, the hills of the Deccan Plateau. This particular group was slowly being edged out of their ancestral migration routes by the government and private industry. I was visiting them in the Deccan Plateau of Maharashtra. In the autumn of 2012, the hilly Deccan Plateau of Ahmednagar, Parner Block, looked thickly green and wooded, belying the actuality of the rain-deprived dryness of that year's failed monsoons. The monsoons are vital for watering the herds. The veterinarian doctor, from an NGO called Anthra,[59] was driving out to check the goats of the Dhangar pastoralist

59 Anthra was an idea developed by a group of women veterinary scientists, who work specifically with rural livestock farmers and pastoralists focusing on women. The NGO was started in 1995 with an all-women governing board. Anthra carries out research on veterinary

community. She described the situation of the failed monsoons, which had completely disrupted the annual migration plans of this Dhangar community.

Community Profile

The Dhangar mobile Indigenous community was the main sheep-raising community in Maharashtra. They were pastoral even five hundred years ago, and might then have had cattle in addition to the sheep and goats they had at present. They no longer had cattle, but the 'hero stones'[60] depict cattle being stolen from the pastoralists in Maharashtra. Their migratory routes from Maharashtra took them towards the Konkan along the coast, up to Goa and on to Gujarat. Their eastward migration varied, depending on the quality of the grazing. The sheep clear stubble in farmers' fields after the harvest and leave their dung behind as fertiliser. Dhangars rear black Deccanese sheep as well as new breeds, such as Madgyal sheep from other parts of Maharashtra. The origin of the breeds is scientifically unclear. The British brought breeds such as Suffolk and Merino, among others, and established a research centre in Pune, in Maharashtra.[61] The traditional *gairann*, the local name for grazing fields for cattle, was part of every village which had open greens for this purpose. The government re-allocated this gauchar land to private individuals and industries, destroying the pastoralists' access to traditional grazing lands.[62] The Dhangar community in 2012 did not use legal mechanisms to claim their rights; however, they were being informed and supported by Anthra, a local veterinary NGO, to educate themselves on legal avenues for redress using the Forest Rights Act.

Sitting on mats strewn under the trees, where tiny kids and lambs tethered to the trees were closely watched by guard dogs,[63] we met the community in a group. While the veterinary doctor gathered test tubes of evidence to be taken back to her laboratory, Mr. Pranav was raising awareness in relation to land claims and advocating for access to their traditional grazing lands. Mr. Pranav, an Anthra staff member dedicated solely to advocacy work, explained to the group the importance of land deeds and the consequences of not having them. He talked about the Forest Rights Act, of which they knew very little. The Dhangars had been paying house tax (*ghar patti*) for as long

science, builds local capacity and advocates on behalf of communities on issues related to livestock, livelihoods and biodiversity.

60 Hero stones are historic, inscribed stone tablets, which record heroes in battles and are found all over India.

61 Taken from an interview with Nitya Ghotke.

62 Taken from an interview with Nitya Ghotke.

63 When we entered the camp, escorted by a couple of men from the community, we were met by very noisy, aggressive barking sheepdogs. These dogs protected the sheep from wolves, and the pastoralists told us that they rear these crossbred mongrel dogs from birth.

as they could remember. The community had to prove that they had been residents here for a long time in order to reclaim their grazing rights. They were not interested in ownership rights because they did not want to settle or build homes. They needed to continue to have access to this land, and they wanted their children to continue to have grazing rights and seasonal lodging. Since this is the dry area, they only stayed here for four months during the monsoons and then returned to the Konkan. They wanted rights to all the grazing routes they used, and Anthra planned to map their traditional grazing routes and help them place their land claims.

The Dhangar community, despite their spartan, nomadic existence, was a wealthy community. One of the community members explained that the group had seven hundred head of sheep. The community also owned a few horses, used only as pack horses for their annual migration. This community member had three children and had known three generations of life on this land. His youngest daughter was about four years old and travelled with the group. His other two children were 10 and 12 years old and attended school in the Konkan, living with extended family and grandparents. Since the 300 km trek was undertaken on foot, the only people on the Deccan Plateau were young able-bodied families with their children; the older members of the community no longer migrated, but stayed in the Konkan, on the western coast of India in the state of Maharashtra. Schooling and old age separated families during the migratory period. The community suggested to us that they thought their mobile lifestyle might change in the near future, as some of the educated children may not want to remain pastoralists. While in the long term this appears an inevitability, some of the children in this community who were not schooled would probably continue this nomadic lifestyle in the near future.

After the Hindu festival of Dussehra[64] in October, the group travelled 300 km back to Dahanu on the west coast of the Konkan and stayed until June, when the monsoons hit. During the four monsoon months, they returned to the dry lands of the Deccan Plateau, settling in the rain shadow of the foothills of the Ghats, as the wet in Dahanu during the monsoons can bring disease to the herds. The community's homes comprised only tents. The tents were covered by bright blue and yellow tarpaulins held up by bamboo poles. Surrounding three sides of the tent was a small mud wall with an open front. The square tents[65] were lined on one side with large, highly polished brass pots containing water and possibly food. Wicker baskets containing clothes were neatly positioned against the wall. At the front of the tent near the opening was a mud-built stove fed by firewood. The day of our visit was the bull festival, and on arrival in the village we were invited to sit down

64 The Hindu festival of Dassera celebrates the victory of good over evil.
65 The square tents are roughly 340 to 510 cm on each side.

Figure 2.2 Blue tarp tents, Dhanger Camp, Deccan Plateau, Maharashtra
Photo by the author

in one of the huts and were served a sweet dish cooked with broken wheat, peanuts, coconut, ghee made from goat's milk, and *jaggery*.[66] After this dish, we were served rice with lentils and vegetables. The cooking pot was enormous and served the whole community of roughly twelve households.

Despite the relative affluence that their seven hundred head of sheep afforded them, the non-material, ancient Dhangar nomadic lifestyle remained a choice, and tent habitation was a definite preference over a fixed and more permanent abode. They showed us several interesting objects such as home-made woven rope catapults which they used to keep away the wolves, who prey on their herds of sheep, and large pendants of pressed silver imprinted with different Hindu deities, each accumulated over the years from city jewellers. The jewellery was further evidence of their relative affluence, which was superficially contradicted by their nomadic and very basic lifestyle. Water had to be fetched daily from nearby streams, and the outdoors was used for sanitary purposes, emphasising that their nomadic lifestyle remained a very definite choice, rather than something externally imposed. Even in Konkan, where older community members lived year-round in extended families with school-going children, they chose to live in tents rather than traditional concrete or brick structures, which they could have afforded if they felt it was necessary to own a house. Though economically not wanting, they could be perceived as being

66 Jaggery is pure, unrefined brown sugar, with a distinct caramel flavour.

socially deprived, since the members who migrate had no easy access to either healthcare or education.

The community speaks a dialect of Marathi. The conversation I had with them centred around the present failed monsoon of 2012, which they said felt like a repeat of the very severe drought of 1972. Their migration from Dahanu in the Konkan had been disrupted by the failed monsoons, and they got stuck somewhere along the 300 km trek, unable to proceed due to lack of water in the Deccan Plateau. Eventually they decided to continue the trek and had been here for a few weeks, having set up their tents. However, the rains remain elusive, and there is not enough water for their pack horses, who need much more water than sheep. Each family has about five horses, and they don't have enough grass to graze on. The goats consume the fine grasses, and so the lack of the normal monsoon vegetation has not affected them as much. Given the lack of water, they may have to turn around and start retracing their 300 km journey by the end of the week. Their daily grazing is limited to 15 to 20 km in total; they do not stray out of this grazing boundary, and other groups do not encroach on their limits. This is part of their customary laws.

Land Dispossession

Two hundred years ago, before the time of their great grandparents, the military took away their land and gave the Dhangar community very little compensatory money. The military now used this land as a firing range, and the Dhangars no longer had freedom of movement. They had recently built a low wall in order to retain what little water they had left after the failed monsoons. The military was now questioning them about the wall.

This community had bought land in Karjat and Ahmednagar in Maharashtra. Two politicians, one of whom was the Deputy Chief Minister, and an ex-Forest Minister, however, owned sugar factories in the area and were encroaching onto the grazing land of the Dhangar community, trying to claim it illegally. The government declared this grazing land an Indian Conservation Area, which they were calling the Black Buck Sanctuary. While declaring it a conservation area, however, government officials excluded their own sugar factory land from the sanctuary. The mobile Indigenous peoples' land had been demarcated as part of the conservation area, and the government had sent them a notice indicating they would be compensated with Rs. 15 lakhs per acre[67] for irrigated land, and less for non-irrigated land. On 30 August, the NGO Anthra had planned a meeting for the Dhangar community to educate them on their land rights. This meeting was dependent on whether the community would return to the Konkan if the rains continued to evade them.

67 One lakh is 100,000.

Land dispossession, first by the military and then by local politicians and government officials, mirrored the same events as the case of the Maldharis, with different actors. The NGO working with the Dhangar community, Anthra, from Pune, was committed to using the legal system in the form of the Forest Rights Act, and was raising awareness and mentoring the Dhangar community on their legal rights. The role of civil society was vital in the struggle for land rights in India. They were taking over this role from the government, who were invisible in these case studies as protectors of the peoples' rights. The challenge for the Indian government was to comprehend their role of protecting the rights of India's communities, and to recognise whether they had the capacity to administer the procedural rights of the Forest Rights Act.

Conclusion

The historical chronology of laws in India has had long reverberations that are still affecting Indigenous peoples in contemporary India. The Criminal Tribes Act 1871 targeted nomadic communities specifically, followed by the Scheduled Districts Act XVI, 1874, the Government of India Act 1919, and the Government of India Act 1935, all designed to force migration and to change ownership of forest lands from mobile Indigenous peoples, and settled Indigenous communities' customary rights to lands, to sovereign governance. Nomadic tribes have faced the harshest consequences of these changes, alienated from their lands and still, in contemporary India, alienated from the benefits of economic development.[68]

For mobile Indigenous peoples, the onus of pursuing a legal strategy to claim land rights and to avoid forced migration has fallen on the people themselves. Administrative justice and protective governance mechanisms are not reliable. This is due to government complicity with land expropriation, which, as the earlier examples show, are the central threats to the land rights and subsistence of Indigenous groups in India. The examples in this chapter of such complicity are many and varied: the politician who built a sugar factory on ancestral grazing lands of the Dhangar community in the Deccan Plateau; the military who expropriated Dhangar lands for their firing range; the Maldharis who lost their gauchar lands to other, more powerful communities, connected to the Anand milk production, part of the national White Revolution movement in India. All these cases reflect the neoliberal aspect of India's capitalist system, in which the needs of the economic elite supersede those of communities who have less economic power and who are left marginalised and unprotected by the state.

It is significant that not all the communities are necessarily using land legislation such as the Forest Rights Act to assert their land rights. Some groups

68 Heredia, 'Denotified and Nomadic Tribes', 7.

such as the Maldharis favour political action and do not utilise legislation. Others such as the Dhangar have been introduced to the Forest Rights legislation in order to access justice. The common thread running through all these advocacy efforts has been support from civil society such as NGOs. The NGO in Gujarat was initiated by members of the Maldhari community themselves, while in Maharashtra, Anthra was external to the nomadic communities. The choice between taking political action or legal action seemed to depend on two factors: the awareness of the NGOs of how to take advantage of legislation; and their capacity to do so. It is evident that the legal capacity of mobile Indigenous communities to use legislation was dependent on civil society support.

Bibliography

Baxi, U. 'Postcolonial Legality'. In H. Schwarz and S. Ray (eds), *A Companion to Postcolonial Studies*. Blackwell, 2005, 178–94.

Desai, M. *Subaltern Movements in India: Gendered Geographies of Struggle against Neoliberal Development*. Routledge, 2015.

Desh Gujarat. 'Gauchar Land Not to Be Allotted to Industries'. *Desh Gujarat*, Ahmedabad, 22 April 2012. www.deshgujarat.com/2012/04/22/no-gauchar-land-allotment-for-industry-commercial-activity-gujarat-govt-coming-up-with-a-new-policy-on-pasture-land/.

Gadgil, M. 'Conserving Biodiversity as If People Matter: A Case Study from India'. *Ambio – Economics of Biodiversity Loss* 21(3) (1992), 266–70.

Gadgil, M., and R. Guha. *This Fissured Land: An Ecological History of India*. Oxford University Press, 1992.

Heredia, R.C. 'Denotified and Nomadic Tribes: The Challenge of Free and Equal Citizenship'. *Occasional Paper Series*. University of Poona, 2007.

Jha, P.K. 'Mahuva Farmers' March in Gujarat Ends, But Movement Continues'. *DNA*, 18 March 2011. www.dnaindia.com/india/report-mahuva-farmers-march-in-gujarat-ends-but-movement-continues-1521455.

Kanekal, N. 'Nirma's Cement Plant in Gujarat Faces Relocation'. *Livemint*, 10 May 2011. www.livemint.com/Politics/qUnTd1sGcG2tVVfcC2mpQI/Nirma8217s-cement-plant-in-Gujarat-faces-relocation.html.

Majumder, S. 'Narendra Modi "Allowed" Gujarat 2002 Anti-Muslim Riots'. *BBC News*, 22 April 2011. www.bbc.co.uk/news/world-south-asia-13170914.

Mishra, P. 'The Gujarat Massacre: New India's Blood Rite'. *The Guardian*, 14 March 2012. www.theguardian.com/commentisfree/2012/mar/14/new-india-gujarat-massacre.

Sarin, M., and O. Springate-Baginski. 'India Forest Rights Act: The Anatomy of a Necessary But Not Sufficient Institutional Reform'. *IPPG Discussion Papers* 45 (2010).

Stanley, O.D. 'Wetland Ecosystems and Coastal Habitat Diversity in Gujarat, India'. *Journal of Coastal Development* 7(2) (2004), 49–64.

Notes

Agarwal, M., F. Flintan, N. Pandya, A. Assefa, and B. Eba. *Land Tenure Security and Governance Dynamics in Gujarat, India: Pastoral Women's Perspectives*. LRI

Rangelands Research Report 5, 2021. https://cgspace.cgiar.org/items/94b59e64-c6bb-452d-b388-32d09162cf31

Committee, D.S. *Dana Declaration on Mobile Peoples and Conservation*. O. U. Refugee Studies Centre, WCPA, WWF and DICE, Wadi Dana, Jordan, 2002. https://www.danadeclaration.org/_files/ugd/d6f494_24b4464f3d7b4e4aaf0de72c5d53a728.pdf

Development tUNCoS. *Indigenous Peoples Caucus Major Group Closing Statement*. Nited Nations Commission on Sustainable Development, 2005.

Development WSoS. *Indigenous Peoples' Caucus #39 Statement by Victoria Tauli Corpuz*. United Nations Department of Economic and Social Affairs, 2002.

Nations, U. *The Rio Declaration*. United Nations, 1992.

Nations, U. *United Nations Declaration on the Rights of Indigenous Peoples*. United Nations, 2007.

Pastoralism CCoELoEA. 'Pastoralists Turn Variability into Food'. *Misereor*, 2021. www.celep.info/wp-content/uploads/2021/06/Pastoralists-turn-variability-into-food-FULL-1.pdf, accessed 18 August 2021.

Reduction ISDRISfD. *Hyogo Framework for Action 2005–2015: Building the Resilience of Nations and Communities to* Disasters, Kobe, Hyogo, UNISDR, 2005, 1–23. www.unisdr.org/wcdr

UNISDR. *Indigenous Knowledge for Disaster Risk Reduction: Good Practices and Lessons Learned from Experiences in the Asia-Pacifi c Region*, Bangkok, UNISDR, 2008, 84.

Chapter 3

Gender Resilience and Deconstructing Inequality

Introduction

The two case studies in the previous chapter specifically relate to mobile Indigenous peoples and how they used legislation to claim their land rights, or alternatively, how they preferred a non-legal path and chose to take political action instead. In this chapter, I move to the nomadic Raika camel herders and the settled Adivasi forest community of Bhasla[1] from the hills of southern Rajasthan's Aravalli Range, both of whom have engaged in active struggles for their lands using the Forest Rights Act 2006, and both of whom were led by women. The broad historical introduction to the Adivasi community of India and to the Raika later introduces examples of the gendered change that new legislation has rendered in some village communities. These particular scenarios from my field work substantiate different aspects of the struggle for rights to self-determination,[2] gender equality, and access to justice, and serve to deconstruct gender inequality and the evolution of a community's empowerment.

One of the most significant aspects of the lives of forest communities affected by dispossession of lands and forced migration was the damage to security and forest-based livelihoods facilitated by new laws under the colonial government. These laws were designed either to extract forest resources for profit by the governing bodies, or to protect wildlife within a conservation framework. The neoliberal culture that divided the security and rights of forest communities from the priorities of industry profit or the safety of wildlife failed to recognise that forest communities had been an integral part of forests for centuries. Forest ecology was fiercely protected by tribal peoples in order to sustain Indigenous livelihoods and cultures. Indigenous women

1 Names have been anonymised.
2 The concept of self-determination is used here as it is used in the Forest Rights Act in the sense of recapturing of agency and of local control over lands and natural resources rather than the broader terminology used in the case of the right to self-government which occurs in a political split of a geographical area from a nation or state.

DOI: 10.4324/9781003589488-4

played a vital role in this protection. In India, tribal women's dependence on natural resources in the forest both for domestic purposes and livelihood needs is significant.

The self-determination of tribal communities in India was quickly eroded by the normative framework enacted from the late 1800s onwards, to defend the privatisation of nature norms of forest governance. The Forest Rights Act 2006 changed the legal culture that had governed forest legislation implemented by the Indian government after independence, and by the colonial government before independence. Since it aims to restore lost lands and customary rights, and to reverse the historical injustice of land expropriation from tribal communities in India, it has increased rights to self-determination, which in turn has positively influenced the livelihoods of forest communities.

National and international policies fed off each other to develop regional and national legal instruments recognising women's rights. Awareness of women's rights has evolved since the development of the concept of human rights, with treaties such as the International Convention on the Elimination of All Forms of Discrimination against Women (CEDAW).[3] Discrimination against Indigenous women takes multiple forms, focusing on their indigeneity and cross-cutting their gender.[4] CEDAW does not mention Indigenous women's rights specifically, and nor does the United Nations Declaration on the Rights of Indigenous Peoples (UNDRIP) specifically refer to women's rights.[5] Women still hold the unenviable position of comprising the majority of the poor globally, feminising the actuality of poverty.[6] Staudt explains the concept of feminisation of poverty as "women's increasing and disproportionate presence among those in poverty".[7] Poverty alleviation strategies have never been gender neutral. Land, especially, has been the domain of men, and economic development policies have been blind to the gender division of agricultural labour and to the contribution of women to land-based production. Funding and policies have been aimed at men as 'farmers', and women have neither been recognised as farmers nor as heads of households. Reflecting this bias, legal progress in the past had not taken into consideration gender asset sharing,[8] or inheritance or control of land. The Forest Rights Act's requirement of at least one-third of the Gram Sabha's participants being women has contributed to changing the paradigm of gendered decision making at the local level.

Forests, where Indigenous peoples live, are resource-rich areas. Development-induced displacement has therefore been concentrated in forest lands in India, with 40 to 50 per cent of communities displaced by development being

3 Holtmaat and Tobler, 'Cedaw and the European Union's Policy', 399.
4 Tugendhat and Dictaan-Bang-oa, *Realizing Indigenous Women's Rights*, 157.
5 Tugendhat and Dictaan-Bang-oa, *Realizing Indigenous Women's Rights*, 157.
6 Staudt, 'The Feminization of Poverty', 216.
7 Staudt, 'The Feminization of Poverty', 217.
8 Staudt, 'The Feminization of Poverty', 219.

tribal, despite comprising less than 8 per cent of the nation's population. More than 40 per cent of land illegally acquired for development and mining belongs to tribal communities in India.[9] In contemporary India, tribal women have been prominent protestors, advocating against dispossession of their lands caused by extractive industry.

Adivasis in India

India's Adivasi Indigenous tribal communities are officially categorised as 'Scheduled Tribes', or 'STs', who comprise about 8.6 per cent of India's total population.[10] Adivasi tribes, scattered all over India, are culturally and ethnically diverse.[11] They are minority populations in all states except in the Northeast,[12] living mostly in the hills and in forests and nurturing a profound identity with their lands.[13] Many Adivasi communities still depend on the forests for their livelihoods, fuel and raw materials for handicrafts, and honey for economic transactions, and timber for house-building materials.[14] They adhere to ancient customs that serve to maintain ecological balance.[15] A statement by mobile Indigenous peoples framed for the Rio+20 Conference of 2012 claims: "The capacity of Mobile Peoples to innovate and to conserve biodiversity is a resource that can help guide the world in its transition towards a more sustainable future".[16] This ecological harmony is gradually being destabilised by land-based 'modernisation' and commerce.[17] The Adivasis themselves, who have been pushed into smaller and smaller areas of habitation by insidious and recurring government evictions, are being forced to overgraze their decreased lands, and are losing their finely tuned, ecologically sensitive practices.[18]

During and after the colonial period in India, tribal communities have had an exploitative history, with their lands

> eroded by the penetration of market forces, and integrated with the British and princely administrations [for tax purposes]. . . . [They] were

9 Sigamany, 'Destroying a Way of Life', 160.
10 2011 Census Primary Census Abstract; 8.6 per cent Adivasis number approximately 113,520,000. https://censusindia.gov.in/2011census/population_enumeration.html. Accessed 2014.
11 Jackson,'Women/Nature or Gender/History? A Critique of Ecofeminist "Development"'.392.
12 Government of India, *Ministry of Tribal Affairs Annual Report*, 37.
13 Gilbert, 'Nomadic Territories', 693.
14 Cobo, *UN Subcommission on Prevention of Discrimination and Protection of Minorities*, 137.
15 Bhengra, Bijoy and Luithui, *The Adivasis of India*, 3.
16 Chatty et al., 'Workshop Report', 25.
17 Chatty et al., 'Workshop Report', 25.
18 Chatty et al., 'Workshop Report', 25.

> increasingly engulfed in debt and lost their land to outsiders, forced to migrate and often being reduced to the position of agricultural labourers, sharecroppers and rack-rented tenants.[19]

Colonial rule transformed their lives, and the immigration of farmers from the plains contributed to the start of the destruction of forests and the impoverishment of many Adivasi communities, who lost their means of livelihood, their homes, and their environment when displaced from the forests. Missionaries, convinced of their own European cultural superiority, were "destroying [tribal] art, their dances, their weaving and their whole culture".[20] Verrier Elwin, who came to India during the British colonial era and lived among Adivasi communities, recorded that under British rule Adivasi communities

> suffered oppression and exploitation, for there soon came merchants and liquor-vendors, cajoling, tricking, swindling them in their ignorance and simplicity until bit by bit their broad acres dwindled, and they sank into the poverty in which many of them live today.[21]

Expropriating large tracts of forest lands for the use of the state, the colonial rulers instituted new laws designed to consolidate lands for commercial use and revenue for the British Crown. Adivasi communities were evicted from their ancestral lands, to which they had no titles, restricted from shifting agricultural practices and from usufruct rights.[22]

Adivasi ownership and usufruct rights, under customary laws predating those of all invaders and colonisers, including the present Indian government, render questionable the ethics of any contemporary laws that do not recognise Adivasi customary rights.[23] The British enacted the Land Acquisition Act of 1894,[24] which began the erosion of Adivasi land rights. The continuing destruction of the unique Adivasi lifestyles triggered numerous tribal uprisings, the most significant of which took place in 1820, 1832, 1855–1857, and 1890.[25] These rebellions were systematically crushed by the British rulers, and more new legislation was introduced, such as the Forest Act of 1927,[26] which, by classifying forest lands as protected and conservation lands, proclaimed that all forest lands belonged to the state. This was calculated to treat any Adivasis who continued to live and work in the forests as 'encroachers' on their

19 Chandra, Mukherjee and Mukherjee, *India since Independence*, 135.
20 Chandra, Mukherjee and Mukherjee, *India since Independence*, 136.
21 Chandra, Mukherjee and Mukherjee, *India since Independence*, 136.
22 Chandra, Mukherjee and Mukherjee, *India since Independence*, 136.
23 See Chapter 3 for a more detailed outline of forest legislation in India.
24 Bhengra, Bijoy and Luithui, *The Adivasis of India*, 3.
25 Government of India, *Report of Working Group*, 9.
26 Bhengra, Bijoy and Luithui, *The Adivasis of India*, 10.

own lands. It effectively displaced Adivasis from land required by the British for their timber industries, creating impoverishment, exclusion, and the beginning of the forced migration that continues today. Independence from British rule did not change this trajectory of economic development, and new legislation and policies, such as the Forests Conservation Act of 1980, the Procedure of Reservation of Forests, the Coal Bearing Area (Acquisition and Development) Act of 1957, and the National Minerals Policy of 1993, have reinforced development-induced displacement and led to deprivation.[27]

> A major proportion of India's coal, forest, hydro-electric and mineral resources are located in traditional Adivasi lands, yet most Adivasis have never gained a share of the wealth generated through exploiting these assets. Eighty-five per cent of Adivasis reportedly live below the official poverty line.[28]

This national land expropriation, a policy that has developed since 1874[29] and which every government has adopted before and after independence, takes place all over the country, especially in mineral-rich forests where tribal communities live. The identity and livelihoods of women in forest tribal communities have been closely rooted in natural forest resources. In the context of gender inequality in predominantly patriarchal societies, the threat to forest-based livelihoods and loss of lands is experienced more acutely by women, whose productive and reproductive roles are so closely interlinked with forest lands, forcing them into a vulnerable position.

Women can be perceived both as victims and, when they challenge these vulnerabilities, as actors. This chapter, which describes the land rights issues of tribal women in southern Rajasthan, unpacks the dichotomy of the dual roles of women as victims and of women in control of their lives. The existence of a strong gender imbalance, in which women are at the bottom of the power hierarchy, pushes women into the role of victim, in which they have unequal land rights and poor access to claiming land ownership. The FRA, which offers, in principle, increased rights to ancestral lands, has reordered the paradigm of land rights of Adivasi communities. This change has also transformed the gender dynamics within the community, as recounted in my field visits to the Bhasla and Kumbhalgarh villages, illustrating a growing gender empowerment. Although their struggles might not necessarily have culminated in a uniformly empowering outcome in other areas of the Aravalli Range, the Raika and Adivasi women were proactive agents in their own struggle for land titles.

27 Bhengra, Bijoy and Luithui, *The Adivasis of India*, 10.
28 Bhengra, Bijoy and Luithui, *The Adivasis of India*, 3.
29 Bhengra, Bijoy and Luithui, *The Adivasis of India*, 3; Dash and Kothari, 'Grabbing'; Gadgil and Guha, *This Fissured Land*; Karanth and Defries, 'Conservation and Management'.

Tribal Women and the Feminisation of Poverty

Ever since the acknowledgement of the feminisation of poverty, it has been established that women share a disproportionate burden of poverty. The reasons for this would be the same as those that limit women's access to justice more than men's. In terms of forest lands, Agarwal argues that poorer women have been "victims of environmental degradation in quite gender-specific ways", demonstrating that they have also played a significant role in environmental conservation practice.[30] Some of the ecofeminist[31] discourse presumes connections between women's biology and ties to nature. I do not expand on that aspect in this book, and am aware of the danger of essentialising women's connection to nature. But I will emphasise the increase in workload specifically for tribal women, whose division of labour includes gathering firewood, fodder, water, and minor forest produce, and cultivation of food. This workload is increased with the degradation of forests and loss of forest rivers through hydroelectric dams,[32] and the impact of the erosion of natural resources on which they are so dependent affects their livelihoods.[33] In India, women have historically been part of the active opposition to the increasing land dispossession of forest peoples, starting with the much-publicised Chipko movement of the 1970s when tribal women hugged trees in order to prevent logging and deforestation.

Land ownership in many tribal communities is often collective, which changes the gender dynamic of land rights. The FRA gives individual land *pattas* in the combined names of spouses. However, before the FRA, any land claimed was in the name of the male member of the household, the exception being the matrilineal Hindu communities of Kerala, and the Khasi communities of Meghalaya in north-eastern India, in which women, rather than men, historically hold the rights of land ownership.[34] The enactment of the FRA may have changed the perception of women's status in the home. Land ownership, which is generally the domain of men, offers a certain social and economic power, which encourages the view that women's work is subordinate to that of men. This perception propels land rights into the gender equality

30 Agarwal, 'The Gender and Environment Debate', 119.

31 Ecofeminism posits that 'there are important connections – historical, experiential, symbolic, theoretical – between the domination of women and the domination of nature' (cited in Curtin, 'Toward an Ecological Ethic of Care', 61). 'The term ecological feminism or eco-feminism refers to a sensibility, an intimation, that feminist concerns run parallel to, are bound up with, or, perhaps, are one with concern for a natural world which has been subjected to much the same abuse and ambivalent behavior as have women.' Cheney, 'Eco-Feminism and Deep Ecology', 11.

32 Jackson, 'Women/Nature or Gender/History', 389; Agarwal, 'The Gender and Environment Debate', 119; Mawdsley, 'After Chipko', 36; Shiva, *Staying Alive*, 55.

33 Xaxa, 'Women and Gender', 360.

34 Xaxa, 'Women and Gender', 354.

debate. In any stratum of society, women's rights to property or land are often dependent on their marital status, especially if the inheritance of land is patriarchal. Tenure security then becomes dependent on marital status, and on the success of marital relations.[35] The husband controls family resources, which in turn lowers the status of the wife and leaves her with less economic power. As highlighted in a report from the former UN Special Rapporteur on Adequate Housing:

> In almost all countries, whether "developed" or "developing", legal security of tenure for women is almost entirely dependent on the men they are associated with. Women headed households and women in general are far less secure than men. Very few women own land.[36]

When forest lands were acquired by the government, whether Indian or colonial, the practice of shifting cultivation was misunderstood and suppressed. This permanently reshaped tribal relationships with their lands, with the sedentary shift impacting their social and financial economy.[37] The keepers of the rich ethnobotanical knowledge of biological diversity conservation and its sustainable utilisation were most certainly women, which had given them authority and respect within their communities. This important source of power had begun to be lost, both to the women and to the community, with land displacement. The traditional tribal communities lived in forest villages in a communal order, which was dismantled when the then colonial government imposed 'revenue villages' to facilitate forest governance. This opened up the secure forest environment to non-tribal communities, which introduced new patterns of exploitation by moneylenders and other traders.[38]

The loss of traditional livelihoods during displacement can lead women into mainstream society to look for jobs. Given the cultural differences between mainstream and tribal communities, the relocation of employment can lead to various forms of exploitation. The sudden switch from being self-reliant and independently engaged in the forests that were their own lands, to loss of their lands, forced migration, and daily wage labour under oppressive working conditions can be detrimental to mental health and well-being, as well as to economic circumstances. The aggression of colonisation, extractive industrialisation, development in the name of modernisation, and deforestation experienced by tribal cultures have led to more than economic impoverishment, and violate the human rights of Indigenous women.[39] During the period between

35 Gilbert, 'Land Rights as Human Rights', 115.
36 Singh, *Legal Rights of the Poor*, no page numbers.
37 Tribal Rights Resources Unit (TRRU), *Tribal Women's Rights on Land*, 2.
38 Tribal Rights Resources Unit (TRRU), *Tribal Women's Rights on Land*, 2.
39 Tribal Rights Resources Unit (TRRU), *Tribal Women's Rights on Land*, 2.

the 1850s and 1930s, displacement from their natural resources, homes, and livelihoods, and unfair tax policies, precipitated tribal uprisings in many parts of India, including Rajasthan, which took both violent and non-violent forms. In south Rajasthan, where I was located for my data collection, rural communities such as those from Bijola in the Mewar region and the Garasias had launched protests. Others, such as the Bhils, negotiated a joint charter drafting their requirements.[40] During this period of unrest, the power of the governing forces was also displayed through various atrocities against tribal communities, including gender-based violence against women.[41]

After independence, central government policies and five-year plans included financial assistance and Tribal Commissioners for tribal development. Between 1992 and 1997, the Eighth Five-Year Plan prioritised participation and local control in an effort to combat the insidious growth of exploitation of tribal communities. Contemporary development strategies have recognised the tribal belt as vulnerable. Nevertheless, the forest lands, which comprise a major part of the tribal belt, though more mineral rich than any other ecosystems in India, also happen to be conducive to the highest concentrations of poverty in the country. The gender implications of this signify the feminisation of poverty, in which extreme poverty and exclusion are most devastating for women.[42] This dynamic maintains a systemic inequity of women's access to natural resources, which in turn erodes the control they have over economic and social aspects of their lives.

Rajasthan scores consistently low in terms of gender inequality, especially in terms of literacy and participation in the workforce.[43] The literacy level of tribal women in the Aravalli hills of southern Rajasthan, for instance, is 36 per cent, compared to 51 per cent for men, and 32 per cent of males have attended school, compared to 13 per cent of females.[44] In the target community that the NGO Astha works with, statistics indicate that most girls are illiterate, with the few literate girls having only basic literacy skills, while boys have better opportunities to attend school.[45] This gender disparity evidences gender discrimination in opportunities for formal education, and reinforces the gender biases prevalent in tribal societies.

40 Tribal Rights Resources Unit (TRRU), *Tribal Women's Rights on Land*, 3.

41 Tribal Rights Resources Unit (TRRU), *Tribal Women's Rights on Land*, 3.

42 Tribal Rights Resources Unit (TRRU), *Tribal Women's Rights on Land*, 4.

43 Rajasthan (along with Bihar, Uttar Pradesh, Madhya Pradesh and Orissa) has consistently low scores on both the UNDP Human Development Index and Gender Development Index. See Ministry of Women and Child Development, Government of India, 'Gendering Human Development Indices: Recasting the Gender Development Index and Gender Empowerment Measure for India. Summary Report', 2009, www.undp.org/content/dam/india/docs/gendering_human_development_indices_summary_report.pdf.

44 The state level of literacy for Rajasthan is 44 per cent, which is lower than the national level of 47 per cent. Taken from TRRU, *Tribal Women's Rights on Land*, 4.

45 TRRU, *Tribal Women's Rights on Land*, 4.

Gender Empowerment

With a strong commitment to gender equality and empowerment, Astha Sansthan, a local NGO in Udaipur, focuses on land rights of tribal communities in the Aravalli hill range of Rajasthan. It also works with human rights, self-determination, and governance. In a study conducted by Astha,[46] it was reported that most of the communities in the study lived in a nuclear patrilineal family system, in which the land title was usually in the name of the oldest male in the household. Only in five out of ninety cases had daughters inherited land from their birth family. Women who inherit land usually do so when they are widowed. Tribal families have a high dependency on land – both personal land for food security, and communal lands for livestock grazing. They also use common forest lands for the collection of minor forest produce, which they trade commercially. Since the majority of them own no more than three *bighas* of land, they fall into the poverty category. Any curtailment of access to open resources necessitates a reliance on daily wage labour, which is known for its exploitative aspects and barely ensures survival levels.[47] Astha reports that the FRA is connected to better access to common lands and open revenue lands on a usufruct basis.[48]

In southern Rajasthan, where I collected my data, land titles were written in the name of a male in the family, either a husband or father.[49] Women rarely inherited land titles. If a woman did hold a title, it would only be in the case of the death of her husband. Only five women out of 476 women interviewed by Astha held titles in their name. "A separated or divorced woman with no land and a family to care for often ends up in an urban slum, where her security of tenure is at best questionable."[50] Since ancestral land is the source of livelihoods, habitat, and a key to maintaining Indigenous culture, it plays a vital role for Indigenous women. In many Indigenous communities, women are the main food producers, knowledge holders, healers, and

46 These data were gathered by Astha from random samples from ten selected village hamlets across five districts in southern Rajasthan. One hundred and sixty-one participants from ten villages across five districts participated in the study. TRRU, *Tribal Women's Rights on Land*, 38.

47 'Income levels of 4% of households is less than 10,000. For majority of households (70%) income is between Rs. 10–Rs. 20,000 p.a. from all sources. Only 26% of households have income over 20,000. This implies a very low per capita income rate if we assume an average family size of 5–6 members. Most of the population of this region covered by our study falls therefore under the official category of the poor in India. Even some of the 24% who have reported a land holding size of more than 5 *bhigas*, report an income from all sources less than 20,000 indicating a low land productivity due to the seasonal character of agriculture being rain fed. There is a heavy reliance on other sources of income across all categories, but more among the poorest for even survival needs.' TRRU, *Tribal Women's Rights on Land*, 38.

48 TRRU, *Tribal Women's Rights on Land*, 29.

49 TRRU, *Tribal Women's Rights on Land*, 29.

50 Gilbert, 'Land Rights as Human Rights', 115.

keepers of the culture. When lands are lost, women lose their self-reliance in food production. They lose their knowledge in natural resource management, biodiversity, and medicinal plants, which is not only a loss to them but to their communities too, especially in transferring Indigenous knowledge to the next generation.[51] The Bhil, Garasia, Damor, and Kathodia tribes of the Aravalli Range have been identified by academics as:

> the custodians of local indigenous knowledge. The surrounding plants form an integral part of their culture and the information about plants gets passed on from generation to generation only through oral folklore although many times kept secret. . . . This traditional knowledge developed over years of observation, trial and error, inference and inheritance has largely remained with the indigenous people. The knowledge of tribes on the value of plants has helped them to have a sense of responsibility in judiciously utilizing the plant resources and also to conserve and pass on the wisdom on plant resource utilization to the posterity.[52]

According to an Astha report, it was a "deep rooted belief" held by both men and women in the Aravalli hill communities that women owning land was an anomaly.[53] Patrilineal lineage was a fact accepted by the community. Women and young girls who might expect land rights were seen as a threat to the accepted social dynamics, and could potentially disturb the unequal social order.

> Men from Ramgarh reported that other men would protest on occasion when land was given to daughters as it set a wrong precedence and women would start demanding more rights if any woman was allowed to inherit or was given property by her father.[54]

For a woman, moving away to her marital home was perceived as an obstacle to her owning ancestral land. Astha found that

> the entitlement of land to women implies the possibility of women challenging the entire power structure and its impositions on women's lives, and hence men collectively and individually resist the claims of women through assertions of lineage and denial of knowledge and resources to claim these rights.[55]

51 Tugendhat and Dictaan-Bang-oa, *Realizing Indigenous Women's Rights*, 158.
52 Katewa et al., 'Traditional Uses of Plant Diodiversity from Aravalli Hills of Rajasthan', 2.
53 Astha, *Women's Land Rights Report*, 40.
54 Ramin, *For Forest Land and a Way of Life*, 43.
55 Ramin, *For Forest Land and a Way of Life*, 42.

The one exception was a village called Bhalai, deep in the forest, where women were aware of the FRA and were planning to take advantage of the option to file for joint land titles for spouses.[56] Either way, men often made unilateral decisions without including women in the process of claiming land rights, and women still lacked awareness and knowledge of the law, which created strong obstructions to accessing justice and claiming land rights.[57]

Case Study: Changing Gender Perspectives Among the Raika Pastoralists

Rajsamand District and Pali District, Rajasthan

In the Rajsamand District and Pali District of Rajasthan, the fight to protect the usufruct rights of the Raika camel herders was led by a Raika woman leader, a capable community leader whose community was using the Forest Rights Act with the support of a local veterinary NGO. Unusual in Rajasthan's patriarchal history was the fact that this leader was a woman, a visible symbol of the successful recognition of gender equality and leadership within a community, and the community's potential to advocate for their land rights.

The leader no longer wore her *dupatta*[58] purdah fashion, as many Hindu Rajasthani women did, covering their faces with their veils and watching the world through a film of thin coloured cloth. She now looked people directly in the eye while leading her community in advocating for land rights and challenging government discrimination against her Raika community of camel pastoralists in Sadri, in Rajsamand District, Rajasthan. She was also a member of the board of LPPS,[59] a local NGO supporting the Raika camel-herding pastoralists. She had built a small 'kachcha'[60] house twenty years ago in her small village on Ranakpur Road, in spite of much local opposition. The opposition focused on her being a newcomer to the village and therefore an 'outsider'. LPPS supported her and, recognising her strength and potential, later trained her to be the community leader she had developed into. Capable and well travelled, this leader had advocated for mobile Indigenous land

56 Ramin, *For Forest Land and a Way of Life*, 42.

57 Ramin, *For Forest Land and a Way of Life*, 47.

58 A dupatta is a veil worn by women around their shoulders, or thrown over their heads, and in some parts of western India such as Rajasthan and Gujarat, states where women respond to a more patriarchal convention than their sisters in many other Indian states, to veil their faces.

59 LPPS: Lokhit Pashu Palak Sansthan is Hindi for 'welfare organization for livestock keepers'. It is an NGO supporting Raika camel pastoralists since 1996. It works towards people-centred livestock development and the sustainable management of biodiversity-rich agro-ecosystems. Taken from www.lpps.org/, accessed 2014.

60 A 'kachcha' house is a 'rough', unrefined house usually built of a mixture of mud, wood and thatch. The opposite of this is the 'pukka' house, a sturdier house built of concrete and brick.

Figure 3.1 The Latada Forest is known locally as Sandiya Dhari Took, an old Raika name which simply means 'where the camels sit'

Photo by Anisha Wilmink

rights both in India and abroad, including in Canada, Germany, Kenya, the Netherlands, Spain, and Switzerland.

Community Profile of Rajsamand and Sadri

The Rajsamand District of Rajasthan, where the Raika camel herders resided, was arid and drought-prone, near the Thar Desert. Camels as livestock comprised a sustainable livelihood for pastoralists, as they played a socio-economically significant role in Rajasthani lives. Local folklore traces the origins of the Indian camel back to Afghanistan.[61] The grazing corridors for Raika camels included the Kumbhalgarh forests in western India. Most of the forest had been converted into the Kumbhalgarh Wildlife Sanctuary situated in the Aravalli Range of hills.[62]

61 Interview with, Raika Camel Herders of Sadri, Rajasthan (2012).

62 New legislation for conservation, such as the Forest Conservation Act of 1980, was passed. 'The Wild Life Protection Act of 1972 had already severely restricted the rights of Adivasis in the wildlife sanctuaries and removed their rights in national parks. The 1991 amendment to the Act took this a stage further. The 147 wildlife sanctuaries and 75 national parks (of which 18 are tiger reserves) covering 4.26 per cent of the land mass are planned to increase. These moves, with the financial backing of the World Bank and other international agencies, have forced Adivasis to further restrict or altogether abandon their survival activities in the forests.' Bhengra, Bijoy and Luithui, *The Adivasis of India*, 10.

The historic Fort of Kumbhalgarh was visible from our camp.[63] The campus where we stayed, which belonged to the LPPS, bordered the forest which was home to diverse wildlife and birds, including leopards, wolves, and antelope, along with many other endangered species. LPPS was a support organisation for the Raika camel herders of Rajasthan, and advocated for the conservation of livestock biodiversity and land rights. They also provided veterinary services and encouraged income generation from camel breeding, sheep, and goats. LPPS emphasised ecologically sound methods of dryland use and livestock rearing and also sought to raise awareness of Raika practices and to preserve the heritage of the Raika community. They promoted Indigenous knowledge and pastoralism as a sustainable form of livelihood. They engaged in participatory research into camel rearing practices and desert ecology focused on 'bringing the camel back'.

The head of LPPS, explained that the camel was not Indigenous to India and was brought by Mahmud of Ghazni from Afghanistan when he invaded India repeatedly from 1000 AD.[64] The Raika community was said to have come with Ghazni, and they are considered Indigenous pastoralists, though not necessarily Indigenous to India. Before 1941/42, the Raika migrated only within Rajasthan. Raika is a specific name for the pastoralist communities of camel herders in Rajasthan. In the last five years, 60 per cent of Raika have settled and are semi-nomadic. Before 1941/42, there was little agricultural activity in Rajasthan, with the only crop locally grown during monsoon season being millet.[65] The Rajputs, a warrior clan, also had livestock. The Rajput maharajas used camels for warfare, and also for trade and transportation, rendering it a very valuable commodity, owned by the wealthy.[66] Prior to 1940, the Maharaja of Bikaner constructed a canal in Ganga Nagar, using camels as draught animals, before which most areas except Pali District and Udaipur were desert. The Raika had always been camel breeders in Rajasthan,[67] and the camel population in the 1940s was very high. There were about ten thousand camels

63 Our host claimed that the impressive walls of the fort, which extend for thirty-six kilometres, were the second longest in the world after the Great Wall of China.

64 Srivastava, *History of India*, 13.

65 The wealthier people ate wheat, which is imported into the state, but poorer people and pastoralists ate millet. Wheat crops were introduced only after the 1950s.

66 Kohler Rollefson and Rathore, 'Participatory Approaches', 36.

67 Raika were vegetarian and did not use their camels for meat. They believed that their role in God's eyes was to look after the camel. They regarded themselves as 'guardians of the camel'. The community had outlawed the sale of female camels, and female camels were used as part of a dowry in a marriage. Over the centuries, the Raika had accumulated a large body of Indigenous knowledge about camel breeding and management, veterinarian science related to camels. 'For this reason, they were referred to as "native camel doctors" by colonial veterinarians.' Kohler Rollefson and Rathore, 'Participatory Approaches', 36.

Figure 3.2 Brass jug used to serve camel milk, Latada Forest, Rajasthan
Photo by Anisha Wilmink

in any one village,[68] for example, while now there were only about eight hundred in a village. This decline began partly with the decrease of grazing land due to conservation and the lack of interest of the younger generation in herding, which forced them into sedentary pastoralism. They now had a varied source of income, which included cotton and dill cultivation, and the sale of buffalo milk and butter. Although they were once purely camel specialists, they now herded buffalo, goats, and sheep as well. Some Raika, who herd only camels, continued to practise nomadic pastoralism. Today the Raika communities generally have low levels of education and adhere to conservative gender roles.

Community Profile of Latada

A camel breeder from a Latada village, owned between thirty and thirty-five camels. His family was semi-nomadic and traditionally used the same route. More recently, however, the family migrated only 100 kilometres during the hot summer season in search of grazing pastures, going anywhere where the farmers invited them to graze. During the harvest, pastoralists were invited to graze their animals on the refuse from the harvested crop, which helped the

68 'Camel populations are decreasing in most Asian countries. The majority of camels in India are found in Rajasthan.' Kohler Rollefson and Rathore, 'Participatory Approaches', 35.

farmer to 'clean up' the post-harvest remnants. A camel now sold for between 40,000 and 45,000 rupees, while only ten years earlier it cost Rs. 5,000.00. Camels were therefore more lucrative today, and, besides camel manure, their milk and wool were also sold. The breeder's family sold camel manure to farmers for fertilisation. Over steaming brass bowls of camel milk, served by Raika men wearing their splendid traditional turbans of bright red, we met with a village focus group on the edge of the Latada Forest. The resident Raika group recounted a story of a successful protest using the Forest Rights legislation.

In another part of the Latada Forest, on the next day of my data collection, we visited a family home in a village with LPPS. The village was thickly wooded, and I recognised neem trees, the leaves of which are used in India for Ayurvedic medicinal purposes, and the twigs for cleaning teeth. The house we visited bordering the Latada Forest was a large, rough mud house painted white with red tiles placed on a roof made of sticks and twigs. The old wooden string cots stacked against the wall outside the house were evidence that the family slept under the stars in the cooler night temperatures of the hot summer. Seated outside on attractive brown, black, and white patterned blankets woven from camel wool, with three brothers, and their mother from the Raika pastoral community, we discussed the pastoral way of life and its accompanying dependence on land. A 6-year-old daughter of one of the brothers nestled close to her grandmother, who sorted through a platter of fresh green chillies and peeled garlic during the discussion. Two 10-year-old boys joined the group and ran around freely, unlike the little girl who played quietly with an empty purple plastic bottle of the sort that vitamin tablets

Figure 3.3 Pastoralists in Latada Forest

Photo by Anisha Wilmink

come in. I wondered if the freedom the boys had to run around while the little girl sat quietly with her grandmother was indicative of differing gender roles. After the focus group meeting, however, as we were leaving the village, we encountered the little girl leading the goats and sheep to pasture, with her grandfather bringing up the rear of the herd. The young boys were nowhere in sight. Perhaps they were in school? Was the little girl in school too? These remained unanswered questions about the cultural conditioning of gender roles.

The Latada Forest bordered both Mewar and Marwar districts of Rajasthan, and the Raika had access to both sides of the border. Before Indian independence in 1947, these two districts were separate states, and the Raika had no permission from the colonial Forest Departments to cross the borders. Traditionally the Raika lived outside the village, always staying near the forests. Their houses were built as temporary structures. During the monsoon rains, they built a small *Dhani* or colony, and used forest lands for pasturing. They also had access to pasture their herds in the seasonal grasslands. In the winter, the herds, using their instinctive knowledge, migrated away from the forests, and the Raika followed. The Latada dam, built for irrigation purposes, was where the herds were watered. The Latada Raika's day started at 7 a.m. when the cows were milked at home. The cows and buffalo streamed into the *chook*[69] by themselves and numbered about two hundred. They waited there patiently for the Raika herdsman to arrive, and then followed him after he signalled to them with a special calling sound. Every village paid the Raika herdsmen to graze their cattle for them. This was part of the Raika's livelihood.

Land Issues

Land issues for this community focus primarily on the struggle against the Forest Department for access to the forest for seasonal grazing, which the pastoralists had always used freely for the grazing needs of their livestock. This changed with the transformation of forests into a protected area called Kumbhalgarh Wildlife Sanctuary. Forty-three villages were affected by the loss of grazing rights and Kumbhalgarh Wildlife Sanctuary's negative effect on their livelihoods. The Raika found themselves in constant conflict with the Forest Department, which objects to the Raika grazing their camels in the Kumbhalgarh forests. This was contrary to a Rajasthan High Court ruling in 2002 recognising the customary rights of communities inhabiting the Kumbhalgarh peripheries. LPPS lodged a court case against the Forest Department for disallowing camels in the forests. The FRA specifies that Gram Sabhas[70] have the authority to make decisions on land use in their territory. By these rules, the Forest Department is subject to Gram Sabha decisions on the use of forest lands. The Forest Department, in having to accept the new authority

69 A 'chook' is a part of the village where the herds assemble before being taken out to pasture.
70 Gram Sabhas are village councils comprising all adult women and men in a village. They are permanent bodies and cannot be dissolved.

of the Gram Sabhas vested by the FRA, has lost its power over the forests, which it has ruled since the colonial government converted them into sovereign property in 1871.[71] This loss of administrative power has led to administrative injustice and non-compliance on the part of the Forest Department. The Forest Department, as well as the *Patwari*,[72] do not attend meetings to which the Gram Sabhas invite them.

During my meeting with the Raika community, they explained that in August 2011, about ten thousand Raika women, men, and children from Sadri used their livestock to close three or four roads in order to protest the inaccessibility to the Kumbhalgarh forests and to demand their customary rights to the forests. Another irregularity was the illegal and exorbitant 'fees' that the Forest Department charged the pastoralists to use the forest for grazing. In the past, the Forest Department would charge Rs. 1.00 per sheep for grazing, and Rs. 5.00 per camel. Today, these fees are Rs. 25.00 per sheep and Rs. 500.00 per camel or buffalo annually. The politicians wanted Rs. 20,000.00 from each village to pay for grazing rights.[73] The Raika community was challenging the Member of the Legislative Assembly's decision to charge fees, which was a contradiction of their customary grazing rights. The protest was successful, and the Raika community received permission to access the forest again for grazing. They also reclaimed the rights to graze their herds in the forest for only Rs. 5.00 for the small animals and Rs. 10.00 for the larger animals, as was the custom previously. The Raika now demand receipts for any payments they make, which introduces an element of accountability into the practice.[74]

The leader of the community explained to me that in her role as a community leader she negotiated land issues with government officials. When forty-three villages found themselves harmed by the conversion of their territory into a wildlife sanctuary, the civil society network rallied and organised a public hearing in 2012 with public officials and journalists, which included issues of Right to Information (RTI), the National Rural Employment Guarantee Act,[75] and the Kumbhalgarh National Park. The leader, representing

71 'The most detrimental legislation, passed by the British in 1871, was the Criminal Tribes Act and the Indian Forest Act 1927 . . . which excluded traditional forest dependents and dwellers from forest lands reserved for economic timber harvesting for the Crown's treasury, and legalised the expropriation of forest lands from tribal and other forest peoples.' Sigamany, 'Destroying a Way of Life', 62.

72 A Patwari is a government official from the Forest Department who is responsible for mapping the forest for the purposes of determining land leases.

73 These facts were related by the community leader and staff of LPPS who acted as interpreters.

74 These facts were related by the community leader and staff of LPPS who acted as interpreters.

75 NREGA is the National Rural Employment Guarantee Act, 2005, later named the Mahatma Gandhi National Rural Employment Guarantee Act (MGNREGA). This Act provides for the enhancement of livelihood security of households in rural areas of the country by providing at least one hundred days of guaranteed wage employment in every financial year to every household whose adult members volunteer to do unskilled manual work and for matters connected therewith or incidental thereto.

the national park issue, stressed the need for usufruct rights and access for grazing for the 120 forest villages that existed on the periphery of Kumbhalgarh, and spoke to the Chief Minister of the state of Rajasthan.[76] He directed her to the Assistant Chief Secretary of the Ministry of Environment and Forests, Mr V.S. Singh, who promised to send a high-level committee to Sadri to investigate the local opposition to the national park. Three hundred Raika pastoralists and other tribal stakeholders affected by the national park gathered for a meeting with the Divisional Forest Officer (DFO). The policies applicable to national parks in India were categorised differently according to wildlife protection legislation. Some parks were 'inviolate' and bar human beings from 'trespassing'. The problem this caused derived from the fact that forest communities, whose forest-dependent livelihoods were recently threatened by 'inviolate' policies, historically inhabited these 'inviolate' zones. The community in Sadri had taken a decision to petition for collective forest rights.[77] The Raika community in this area was actively using the Forest Rights Act to claim their rights, in addition to taking political action.

The battles for forest access in Latada, Pali District in Rajasthan, which LPPS supported, predated the Forest Rights Act.

The forests around the Kumbalgarh Fort in the Aravalli hills in Rajasthan were notified as the Kumbhalgarh Wildlife Sanctuary (KWLS) in 1971.[78] Historically, the forests were used as hunting reserves by local kings and rulers, and after 1885, under colonial rule, the Aravalli hills were exploited for commercial forest timber.[79] After Independence, and even after official forest protection as a sanctuary, forest peoples still exercised forest rights for grazing and other forest livelihood and sustenance. In 2000, the Supreme Court of India issued an order which eventually resulted in a list of 'prohibited' activities of residents in what were now wildlife sanctuaries and national parks. The Raika pastoralists lost grazing rights, which affected their livelihood.[80] Many camels died of starvation as a result, and the camel population declined by 70 per cent, while the sheep and goat populations declined by 35 per cent.[81] Another reason for the decline of the herd populations was that the younger generations were not necessarily committed to the nomadic lifestyle of their parents. A significant problem faced by the Raika related to the lack of administrative justice, primarily through corruption. For example, the local government requires a 'commission', which can be anywhere

76 This interview took place in August 2012.

77 The FRA includes collective forest rights, which is significant since many tribal communities behave collectively and have traditions of sharing commons.

78 Tatpati, *Kumbhalgarh: A Flawed Conservation Story in the Making*, 12.

79 Tatpati, *Kumbhalgarh: A Flawed Conservation Story in the Making*, 12.

80 Tatpati, *Kumbhalgarh: A Flawed Conservation Story in the Making*, 19.

81 Statistics quoted by the community and the NGO being interviewed.

between 10 and 40 per cent of any government grant the pastoralists apply for related to camel projects, whether veterinary care or income generation.

The Latada District Raika followed similar legal strategies to the Sadri District Raika communities. They took their claims to the Forest Department, to the Chief Minister of Rajasthan, or to the state High Court. The members of the focus group were confident that they could gather hundreds of community members within twenty-four hours for a land claim protest. Before the arrival of the mobile phone, they used runners bearing the news from one village to the next. The Gram Panchayat of every village in the district filed a claim for their customary rights while plans were being made to convert the forest to national parks.[82] The village formed the Aadhikar Samiti (Forest Rights Committee), a requirement of the Forest Rights Act, as it formally asks the people to make the claim. A report was sent by the Samiti to the Sub District Commissioner. The claims included producing proof of dwelling before 2005. This proof requires either seventy-five years of dwelling or three generations of dwellers in the forests. Another requirement was a visual map called 'Najriyar Naksar', which the Forest Department has to provide. LPPS arranged for an affidavit through the Rao or scribe,[83] which was then sent to three government offices.[84] The state makes the decision. The Rao records show that the Raika community arrived in the Marwar District of Rajasthan around three hundred years ago, from about 100 kilometres away. The Rao/Charan still used the Maharaja of Jodhpur to describe the geographical area, and had still not adopted the Government of India's state of Rajasthan. The Forest Rights Act requirement of having to prove forest residence for seventy-five years is not procedurally user-friendly, especially when many forest communities are illiterate.

The semantics of the Forest Rights Act also caused problems for mobile Indigenous communities because initially the Act only described 'Scheduled Tribes' (Adivasis) and excluded pastoralists. Pastoralists and civil society organisations all over India took up this issue, and the wording of the Act was changed to include 'other traditional forest dwellers', which includes pastoralists.[85] LPPS, on behalf of the nomadic communities, met with the Ministry for Tribal Affairs in Rajasthan in order to petition for the removal of punitive fines.

On 10 July 2012, a letter with twelve signatures from the Pali Jila Congress Committee was written to the Chief Minister of Madhya Pradesh, Gujarat,

82 The Gram Sabha's book of minutes is called 'prasthav', in which all the land claim proceedings are recorded.

83 The Rao are scribes from the Charan community who traditionally record population statistics in an old language called Dingal.

84 The three government offices were the Sub District Office, the District Office, and the State Committee.

85 Government of India, The Scheduled Tribes and Other Traditional Forest Dwellers (Recognition of Forest Rights) Bill (adopted 15 December 2006, No. 158-C of 2005).

Punjab, and the Mewar District of Rajasthan. This letter requested that the restrictions and fines imposed upon pastoralists should be reconsidered with more compassion and understanding when they return to the forests during the grazing season. It also called for gauchar lands (grasslands) to be 'notified' (officially classified) for grazing. Two Raika representatives spoke of the Forest Department's role in strong terms: "The Forest Department really tortures the mobile Indigenous peoples when they return for grazing during monsoon season. The cattle belong to Raika, Bhil, Gujjar, Grazia, and Rawal. Of these groups, the Raika have the greater share of cattle".[86] The Raika were discovering, however, that the conflict with the Forest Department had unexpected dimensions. When the Raika tried to help the Forest Department (FD) to capture poachers, the FD did not appreciate it. The Raika were recognising that the reason for this was because the poachers themselves were from the FD,[87] which was a serious allegation.

The Raika community's campaign to reclaim their deteriorating land rights used both political and legal strategies. Their battles to protect their usufruct rights began before the Forest Rights Act was enacted. Without the law to support them at that time, they staged protests to force the government to recognise their rights. With the Forest Rights legislation, they have an additional mechanism, proving that the recognition of substantive rights is indispensable for any action or legal redress. Civil society here, in the form of the NGO LPPS, has played a vital role not only in forcing the land rights issue onto the national agenda and raising the capacity of the pastoral community to fight for their own land rights, but also in creating visibility and giving shape to gender participation, voice, and leadership within the Raika pastoral community.

Analysis: Empowerment and Vulnerabilities

The power and political acumen generated by their determination, as introduced in the Introduction Chapter of this book, resulting in a successful conclusion, was not lost on the women of Bhasla village. They explained at the meeting that they felt empowered and strong. Some of them felt they needed to eschew the gungat, which they now perceived as keeping them in the background and had, they felt, kept them sheltered from community decision making. The Community claims that they had been strengthened by the participation of these politically mobilised women who affirmed that they were ready to fight for their lands. They stated that although they had previously never been out of their village, they were now ready to travel to Udaipur – perceived as the 'big city' – to fight for their

86 Interview with, Raika Camel Herders, Rajasthan (2012).
87 Interview with, Raika Camel Herders, Rajasthan (2012).

land rights and attempt to access justice. The men at the meeting confirmed that they were now aware of the women's new-found strength, which has changed their attitude towards the women in their community and has produced a realisation of the formerly hidden potential of women. According to the norm, men have a monopoly on political and economic power, whether on the domestic front, in national politics, or in the international arena, and they therefore have more opportunities for participating in their own legal emancipation. They have more confidence in approaching the legal system. The legal system itself is staffed with more men than women, which immediately limits access for women and may hold an unintentional gender bias within legal decision making. Although the Bhasla village experience provided a glimpse of hope that norms can change, access to justice for women remains more difficult than it does for men.

The Kumbhalgarh and Bhasla village narratives of changing gender attitudes might be rare occurrences, but they did not obscure the fact that the gender dynamics of land rights for Indigenous peoples in India presented an uneven picture. It is difficult to make generalised statements about tribal women in India, since tribal peoples lived in many states and differed widely from each other.[88] Women in different tribes enjoyed different levels of equality. Some tribes were traditionally matriarchal, and some were matrilineal. Some, such as the southern Rajasthani women, had been Sanskritised, and some were converted to Christianity, and had assumed certain patriarchal traditions of other religions that were formally alien.[89] Customary rights to land inheritance differed within tribes in different parts of India. In some areas, such as the north-eastern states and Kerala, customary matrilineal inheritance laws prevailed. The forests had provided a certain amount of geographical distance from mainstream societies, which had in some instances maintained a degree of isolation from patriarchal elements of Hinduism and Islam, and therefore less widespread gender discrimination. The general endemic gender power imbalance, however, cannot be denied, and was seen to be "shaped not only by gender discrimination within Indigenous and non-Indigenous arenas, but by a context of ongoing colonization and militarism; racism and social exclusion; and poverty-inducing economic and 'development' policies".[90] On a macro scale, the gender imbalance also related to a global feminisation of poverty, in which "women comprise the majority of the poor".[91] The global

88 Xaxa's article on tribal women in different groups all over India makes clear the potential inaccuracy of generalised conclusions given the major differences in behaviours and status of women within these groups. Xaxa, 'Women and Gender', 350.

89 Xaxa, 'Women and Gender', 350.

90 Raya, 'Indigenous Women Stand against Violence', 100.

91 'First coined two decades ago, the phrase "the feminization of poverty" focused on women's increasing and disproportionate presence among those in poverty. Two phenomena contributed to this trend: first, the overrepresentation of women among minimum-waged and

reality of women being excluded from the mainstream was compounded for tribal women who faced the double discrimination of being excluded as part of tribal communities and also, in parts of India such as Rajasthan, as being separated as women within the patriarchal tribal culture.

Customary tribal land traditions respected land as communal. Within the communal context, the concept of private property and ownership created a conflictual reality. The communal system had never required documentation of private land rights.[92] Customary tribal traditions were based on the community's shared relationship with natural resources, within which the role of women was vital to the sustainability of the use of natural resources as a body of knowledge used for health and nutrition. Women's contribution to this system formed part of their livelihoods. When ownership and power dynamics changed with both colonial and Indian governments assuming control of forest lands, property ownership concepts crept in that were alien to customary land traditions and which disconnected women from their historical relationship with natural resources based on shared lands. The FRA, promising empowerment and equity through a progressive articulation of substantive rights, also introduces a dichotomy of expectations raised by the ability to claim private land titles which contradicts the historical collective use of lands. Within this conceptual inconsistency, the legal provisions of Community Forest Rights (CFR) assume a gravity and significance that has not been developed as fully as it could and should have been.

NGOs who worked with forest land rights in southern Rajasthan were staffed mainly by people belonging to mainstream communities. Reflecting their own private property traditions of ownership, they were maybe slow to realise the importance of claiming CFR in their work of raising awareness and supporting claims to forest rights. They focused considerably more on private claims to hereditary forest lands. The government authorities who granted CFR might have been prejudiced by the threat to the status quo of their loss of power of jurisdiction over forest lands. Claiming CFR therefore faced more constraints than it deserved. This affected the domain of women's livelihoods, identity, and collective work with natural resources. It would also affect women's reproductive tasks of caring for the community, which are dependent on interpersonal, communal interactions, and communal properties, and which are intrinsic to the maintenance of tribal culture and identity, and to control over local resources and land. Claims for land titles were part of a process that was heavily biased against women, and the contemporary gender paradigm was deeply embedded in a patriarchal structure in southern Rajasthan, mirroring the global gender stereotype of land ownership. This gender aspect, combined with the dichotomy of private land

unpaid workers; second, the rising percentage of women who headed households with dependent children.' Staudt, 'The Feminization of Poverty', 217.

92 Interview with, NGO staff, Astha Sansthan, Rajasthan.

title claims within a historical context of communal and shared land traditions, renders potential land rights for women even more elusive.

The Astha survey reported that the Forest Rights Act had facilitated the ownership of land for women.[93] Conventionally, land titles had been written in the name of a male family member, and women had rarely inherited land titles, unless a husband died. Out of the 476 women interviewed, only five held titles in their own names. The FRA, however, provided for the registration of land titles in the joint names of both spouses. Since women cared for livestock, they claimed the goats and poultry as their property, and they also claimed the income from the sale of their livestock. This income was used for family consumption. When a family owned larger herds, the income was usually not controlled by the women, and the larger herds were not considered a woman's assets. If the sale of a larger number of animals took place in the market, the men controlled the income from those assets. The sale of milk and minor forest produce generated income for women. However, if the sale took place in the markets and was of a higher value, the men would control the transaction, and the women would not be able to claim income from that transaction as part of their own assets. The Astha study calculated that the Work Participation Rate (WPR)[94] was higher among women than men in more than half of the villages covered in the study, inferring that "the land holding size does not impact WPR among women and that women's work contribution as household or wage labour, in foraging and cultivation is significant in all households".[95] Women in the Adivasi communities in southern Rajasthan, therefore, although their productive and reproductive contribution in general within the gender division of labour was higher than that of men, still had limited financial access and exercised limited control to assets such as land. By controlling assets, men also controlled women, which dangerously limited the economic and social freedom of women within these tribal communities. In the next chapter, I expand on the gender experiences of the Adivasi community of the Aravalli hills, in the context of gender analysis and empowerment, and its effect on land rights.

The Forest Rights Act advocates equal land rights for women and men, and requires a stated percentage of women's participation in community decision-making bodies such as the Gram Panchayat. The procedural rights that grant women systemic power still have to be negotiated within the inherent patriarchal power structures of the Aravalli hill tribal communities, to which women had not been traditionally invited. The Bhasla village example provided an instance in which women had uncovered their strength in order to challenge the dominant cultural patriarchy. It was not a smooth

93 Astha, *Women's Land Rights Report*. 51.

94 The definition of Work Participation Rate (WPR), as used in the Census of India, is the percentage of total workers to the total population. 'Indian Census in Perspective: Census Terms – Census of India', accessed 2014, censusindia.gov.in/Data_Products/Library/Post_Enumeration_link/eci6_page3.html.

95 Astha, *Women's Land Rights Report*, 31.

transformation, and necessitated violence at some level. To use the Bhasla women's own analogy, "camels do not grow horns." This, as a mechanism for change in gender status, cannot necessarily be relied upon as a methodology for structural equality within Adivasi communities. However, the existence of the FRA is a welcome tool in order to access justice and begin changing the existing gender paradigm of inequality.

Conclusion

In dealing with the issue of women's empowerment, I use the example of Bhasla village, which epitomises the struggles of women to achieve control over their lives. The patriarchal culture of the southern Rajasthani Adivasis ensures the ownership of land remains primarily a male domain. Women's traditional control over natural forest resources has to contend with this patriarchal culture of land ownership in addition to the offer of individual land titles permissible under the FRA, which goes against the grain of collective land resource use and women's vital control of these resources. It is well evidenced that women's ownership of property and land, which increases their economic strength, also impacts favourably on better nutrition and health for the family, on child mortality, and education.[96]

International aid and local NGOs have often directed both funding and programme inputs at men, reflecting a patriarchal bias that reinforces the inability of women to own property and to engage in community decision making. Women's labour load is often as heavy or heavier in local agricultural production, but they have historically not been regarded as 'farmers'. Rather, as in Western culture, they were regarded by development NGOs as 'farmers' wives'. Funding, agricultural extension, and new technology have historically been aimed at men. This bias has been introduced by civil society development organisations, which has greatly impeded women's access to assets and economic control.[97]

Displacement from land, of the sort that southern Rajasthani forest communities are trying to counter by using the Forest Rights Act, has proven more detrimental to women with their loss of access to natural resources. This impacts not only their livelihoods but also their domestic food production and control. India's land rights legislation reflects a commitment to social justice, but is dependent on the state and the judicial machinery for equitable enforcement. In the case of tribal communities, the state, in its failure to meet legal standards of protecting citizens and ensuring access to justice, is circumventing existing legal frameworks. Given that the patriarchal status quo dictates an inequality that leads to a systemic feminised poverty, the state

96 Xaxa, 'Women and Gender', 345.
97 Xaxa, 'Women and Gender', 345.

has an added obligation to respond to the needs of women, who could be perceived as a vulnerable sub-section of any community. Yet rights-based legislation that should promote social justice and inclusion is still implemented arbitrarily and is dependent on gender-blind practice.

The case studies in this chapter and in the previous one reveal that within the mobile Indigenous groups studied, gender equality is present within both the Maldharis and the Raika communities, the former having in-built traditions which are gender-friendly, while the Raika have had gender equality inorganically introduced by supportive NGOs who are part of the land rights struggle. These are positive examples of the importance of non-discriminatory patterns of gender, which strengthen the collective voice and ability of these peoples to unite and advocate for their rights.

Returning to the Raika and Bhasla women's experience, in which the women held the power, there is hope that organic, endogenous empowerment is not as impossible as a camel growing horns.

Bibliography

Agarwal, B. 'The Gender and Environment Debate: Lessons from India'. *Feminist Studies* 18(9) (1992), 119–58.

Astha. *Astha Women's Land Rights Report.* Unpublished, 2012, 1–84.

Bhengra, R., C.R. Bijoy, and S. Luithui. *The Adivasis of India.* Minority Rights Group International (MRG) Report, 1999.

Chandra, B., M. Mukherjee, and A. Mukherjee. *India since Independence.* Penguin Books, 2008.

Chatty, D., et al. 'Workshop Report, Dana+10 Declaration, 11–13 April 2012, Wadi Dana, Jordan'. *Nomadic Peoples* 16(2) (2012), 95–136.

Cheney, J. 'Eco-Feminism and Deep Ecology'. *Environmental Ethics* 9(2) (1987), 115–45.

Cobo, J.M. *UN Subcommission on Prevention of Discrimination and Protection of Minorities, Study of the Problem of Discrimination against Indigenous Populations.* United Nations, 2014.

Curtin, D. 'Toward an Ecological Ethic of Care'. *Hypatia: A Journal of Feminist Philosophy* 6(1) (2008), 60–74.

Dash, T., and A. Kothari. 'Grabbing: Dangers of the Green India Mission'. In K. Kohli and M. Menon (eds), *Banking on Forests: Assets for a Climate Cure?* Kalpavriksh and Henrich Boll Stiftung, 2012.

Gadgil, M., and R. Guha. *This Fissured Land: An Ecological History of India.* Oxford University Press, 1992.

Gilbert, J. 'Land Rights as Human Rights: The Case for a Specific Right to Land'. *Sur: International Journal on Human Rights* 10(18) (2013), 114–35.

Gilbert, J. 'Nomadic Territories: A Human Rights Approach to Nomadic People's Land Rights'. *Human Rights Law Review* 7(4) (2007), 681–716.

Government of India. *Ministry of Tribal Affairs Annual Report.* MoTA, 2010–2011.

Government of India. *Report of Working Group on Empowerment of Scheduled Tribes for the 11th Five Year Plan.* Government of India, 2007.

Holtmaat, R., and C. Tobler. 'Cedaw and the European Union's Policy in the Field of Combating Gender Discrimination'. *Maastricht Journal of European & Comparative Law* 12(4) (2005), 399–425.

Jackson, C. 'Women/Nature or Gender/History? A Critique of Ecofeminist "Development"'. *The Journal of Peasant Studies* 20(3) (1993), 389–418.
Karanth, K.K., and R. Defries. 'Conservation and Management in Human-Dominated Landscapes: Case Studies from India'. *Biological Conservation* 143(12) (2010), 2865–964.
Katewa, S.S., B.L. Chaudhary, A. Jain, and P. Galav. 'Traditional Uses of Plant Biodiversity from Aravalli Hills of Rajasthan'. *Indian Journal of Traditional Knowledge* 2(1) (2002), 27–39.
Kohler Rollefson, I., and S.H. Rathore. 'Participatory Approaches to Using the Camel in Combating Desertification'. In D. Faye and P. Esenov (eds), *Desertification Combat and Food Safety: The Added Value of Camel Producers*. IOS Press, 2005.
Mawdsley, E. 'After Chipko: From Environment to Region in Uttaranchal'. *The Journal of Peasant Studies* 25(4) (1998), 36–54.
Ramin, J. *For Forest Land and a Way of Life: The Story of the Adivasis' Struggle in Southern Rajasthan*. Astha Sansthan Publications, 2007.
Raya, M.I. 'Indigenous Women Stand against Violence'. *Australian Indigenous Law Review* 11(2) (2007), 100–01.
Shiva, V. *Staying Alive: Women, Ecology and Development*. Zed Books, 1988.
Sigamany, I. 'Destroying a Way of Life: Indigenous Peoples, the Forest Rights Act of India and Land Displacement of Indigenous Peoples'. In I. Satiroglu and N. Choi (eds), *Development-Induced Displacement and Resettlement: New Perspectives on Persisting Problems*. Routledge, 2015, 159–69.
Sigamany, I. 'Land Rights and Neoliberalism: An Irreconcilable Conflict for Indigenous Peoples in India?' *International Journal of Law in Context* 13(3) (2017), 369–387.
Singh, N. *Legal Rights of the Poor: Foundations of Inclusive and Sustainable Prosperity*. Author House, 2014.
Srivastava, A. *History of India: 1000 A.D.–1007 A.D.* Shiva Lal Agarwala, 1971.
Staudt, K. 'The Feminization of Poverty: Global Perspectives'. *The Brown Journal of World Affairs* 5(1) (1998), 215–24.
Tatpati, M. *Kumbhalgarh: A Flawed Conservation Story in the Making*, 2022. https://kalpavriksh.org/kumbhalgarh-a-flawed-conservation-story-in-the-making/?srsltid=AfmBOoqsGmGe2xeSHNeOQ-DOwSDgPvDNDeitcgJOj25umAadt89FeQAh
Tribal Rights Resources Unit (TRRU). *Tribal Women's Rights on Land and Other Natural Resources: Southern Rajasthan*. Astha Sansthan, 2012.
Tugendhat, H., and E. Dictaan-Bang-oa. *Realizing Indigenous Women's Rights: A Handbook on the CEDAW*. Tebtebba Foundation, Forest Peoples Programme, Asia Indigneous Women's Network (AIWN), 2013.
Xaxa, V. 'Women and Gender in the Study of Tribes in India'. *Indian Journal of Gender Studies* 11(3) (2004), 345–67.

Chapter 4

Livelihoods and Forest Rights

The Struggle for Self-Determination

Introduction

Tendu *patta* refers to the leaf that tobacco is rolled in to make 'beedis' or hand-rolled cigarettes. The two examples of the Tendu *patta* struggle for control of land-based livelihoods and of the Amba villagers and their struggles against imminent displacement from their lands serve to review the broader context of the global trend of land dispossession and forced migration of Indigenous peoples, and how legislation is used in order to access justice. Both the Amba Adivasi forest community's land rights campaign and the Tendu *patta* livelihoods operation are based in the hills of Rajasthan's Aravalli Range and have been engaged in forest rights and access to justice.

The normative framework of new state laws in Rajasthan and others preceding them govern forest rights in India. They contribute to the expropriation of forest land by the government and explain the transition of the Adivasi community from exploited labourers to business owners through a process of awareness raising and political mobilisation. The eventual progress towards self-determination through the formation of cooperatives resulted in economic independence and a price war, with which the Adivasis succeed in hiking up wages substantially. The legal impact of the Tendu *patta* changes supported the campaign for the enactment of the Forest Rights Act, with the hope of revolutionising Indigenous land rights.

The remote and isolated Amba forest village experienced land violations but endogenously developed strategies with the support of local civil society organisations to challenge imminent displacement from their forest homes. The implementation of the Forest Right Acts, a progressive development, is starkly juxtaposed with the antiquated forms of governance and administrative justice relating to Amba's land rights claims. The conclusion highlights the uneven administrative justice of the law, and the dichotomous role of civil society actors with differing agendas.

DOI: 10.4324/9781003589488-5

Figure 4.1 Aravalli hills, Rajasthan
Photo by the author

Aravalli Hill Range of Southern Rajasthan

In the Aravalli hills of southern Rajasthan, an Astha (NGO) survey[1] concluded that the level of income for the households surveyed was low, precipitated by low productivity caused by poor land quality and predominantly rain-fed agriculture.[2] The majority of families had a small landholding, less

1 Tribal Rights Resources Unit (TRRU), *Tribal Women's Rights on Land*; Government of India, *Ministry of Tribal Affairs Annual Report*; Ramin, *For Forest Land and a Way of Life*. The Astha survey was conducted across ten villages in five districts of tribal communities, in the Aravalli hills of southern Rajasthan. Age group of male and female participants in the study = 30–50 years; average number of children = 3.7; average household size = 5.65; average landholding = 3–5 *bighas*. TRRU, *Tribal Women's Rights on Land*; Astha. *Astha Women's Land Rights Report.*

2 Four per cent of households earned less than Rs. 10,000 per annum, 70 per cent of households earned more than Rs. 10,000 but less than Rs. 20,000, and only 26 per cent of households had an income of more than Rs. 20,000 per annum from all sources. The 24 per cent of households who had more than 5 *bighas* of land reported an average income from all sources of less than Rs. 20,000. TRRU, *Tribal Women's Rights on Land.*

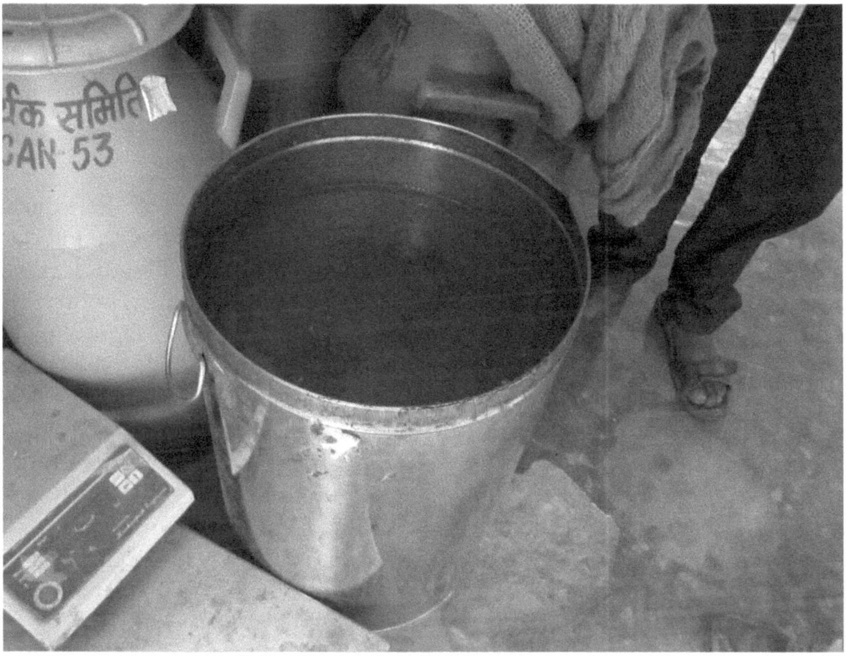

Figure 4.2 Minor forest produce of raw honey
Photo by author

than three *bighas*,[3] and were dependent on supplementing their income with external labour and migration outside the community. They had poor food security for some parts of the year. Even three to five *bighas* of land did not provide enough agriculture, forcing a dependency on external labour and the collection of minor forest produce. The forests provide "a variety of nutritious foods as edible tubers, roots, rhizome, leaves, shoots, flowers, fruits, nuts, [and] seeds".[4] Wild edible plants are an important source of daily nutrition for tribal peoples of southern Rajasthan, making vital their access to minor forest produce from common property resource areas. Land rights therefore not only sustain land-based, traditional, tribal livelihoods but also food sources.[5]

Minor forest produce and labour returns remained a struggle. The next section traces a labour campaign in the Tendu *patta* forest-based trade in

3 One bigha is the equivalent of 1,618.7 square metres. See www.sizes.com/units/bigha.htm, accessed 2014.
4 Katewa et al., 'Traditional Uses of Plant Diodiversity from Aravalli Hills of Rajasthan', 2.
5 Katewa et al., 'Traditional Uses of Plant Diodiversity from Aravalli Hills of Rajasthan', 2.

the Aravalli hills and the community's evolution from exploited labourers, threatened by forced migration, to empowered owners collectively in charge of their own trade.[6]

Tendu *Patta* Livelihood in the Aravalli Hill Range

For about three weeks in May, in the forested Aravalli hill range, the women and children of the Adivasi communities rise at 4 a.m. and walk deep into the forests to climb Tendu trees in order to gather Tendu *patta* (Tendu leaves). These are the most highly charged minor forest produce in India, politically, legally, and economically. Tendu *patta* are used for rolling *bidis*, Indian hand-rolled cigarettes.[7] The women pull their long *gaghras*[8] between their legs and tie them up behind to facilitate climbing trees with the children in order to reach the good leaves. As they are picked, the leaves are stored in cloths tied around the women's and children's waists. By mid-morning, after about six hours of plucking, they return home with the collected leaves, which they drop on the floor inside the house. While the men and children begin the bundling of the leaves, the women start their morning chores of fetching water and cooking. After everyone eats, the women join the bundling teams. With fifty leaves per bundle, and about five thousand leaves per morning, it is an extremely labour-intensive month. The bundled leaves are carried by the men to the collection depot, called *fud*, and the *fud munshi*[9] counts the bundles and pays the gatherers at a piece rate per hundred bundles. The women rarely accompany the men to the fud; contact with the munshi is usually handled by men in Rajasthan, meaning they also control the profits earned. This has a negative connotation in terms of gender equality. In the early 1990s, in one season a family could make Rs. 3,000 at a rate of Rs. 7.50 per bundle. That was considered a lot, despite the exploitation and low daily wage.

Tendu trees grow in the forests of central India; most of this land is in Adivasi territory. The stakeholders in the lucrative Tendu competition are the Tendu *patta* gatherers, who are impecunious Adivasis; the buyers of Tendu *patta*, referred to as traders, buyers, or contractors; the state; and corporate bidi industries. Corruption existed at the level of the buyers or contractors,

6 (see note 2).

7 There are twelve different forms of minor forest produce (MFP) identified by the Ministry of Tribal Affairs (MoTA): (i) Tendu, (ii) bamboo, (iii) mahuwa seed, (iv) sal leaf, (v) sal seed, (vi) lac, (vii) chironjee, (viii) wild honey, (ix) myrobalan, (x) tamarind, (xi) gums (gum karaya) and (xii) karanj. Taken from Press Information Bureau, *Identification of 15 Minor Forest Produce*. Tendu *patta* (Diospyros melanoxylon) leaves are used for making bidis, Indian hand-rolled cigarettes. 'The Tendu Leaf', DownToEarth, 28 June 2015, www.downtoearth.org.in/coverage/the-tendu-leaf-12528.

8 Gaghras are long, brightly coloured, ankle-length skirts.

9 Munshi is a Hindi word used to describe an actuary, accountant, clerk or secretary.

who bid for the right to buy the collected Tendu *patta* but who underpaid the primary gatherers and under-reported the collections. Since the forest lands and Tendu trees belonged to the state, the state encountered revenue losses caused by the under-reporting amounting to millions of rupees. This compelled the enactment of new laws in the late 1950s drafted to protect the state from revenue losses.[10]

The Normative Framework Governing Forest Rights in India

Laws in India include both federal and state laws. Laws that are enacted by individual states are separate from national legislation such as the Forest Rights Act. Laws enacted by individual states therefore are not necessarily replicated in every state. In this section, I describe a few laws that specifically govern Rajasthani forests. These laws were particular to the state of Rajasthan and were not national laws. The original laws governing the forests were formally designed for the state to expropriate forest lands during colonial rule, forcing the migration of Indigenous communities. These laws were continued, and new laws were created by the Indian government after independence. This illustrates irrational governance. This subversive governance maintained the forced migration of Adivasis, treating them as 'encroachers'. This led to the prohibition of Adivasis collecting Tendu *patta*, one of the few lucrative trades they could engage in.

Under the Indian government after independence, forest lands were divided into Reserved Forests, Village Forests, and Protected Forests, in an attempt to further consolidate them under government management and forcing more migration. The Rajasthan Forest Settlement Rules 1958 outlined policy for the demarcation of forest boundaries, to be carried out by the Forest Department. The enactment of these rules immediately restricted tribal communities' access to the forests, and obstructed their traditional livelihoods, putting the onus on the Adivasis to claim back the ancestral rights they had lost to the policies of Reserved Forests. These ancestral rights, under the Rajasthan Forest Settlement Rules 1958, needed to be sanctioned by the local government (Part IV, Section 16).

The rules acknowledge the existence of villages in the forests and incorporate claims to be made by persons from Blocks and villages. These claims include 'rights' and 'concessions', as highlighted here:

> The first step to be taken by the Forest Settlement Officer is the publication of a proclamation under section 6 of the Act as given in form 'L' specifying the situation and limits of the proposed Reserve as published in

10 Chadana et al., *Status of Adivasis/Indigenous Peoples*, 8.

> the Official Gazette, explaining the consequences which will ensue on the reservation of the forest and requiring all persons claiming any right in or over such forest, to specify within the prescribed period, either in writing or verbally, the nature of such rights and the amount and particulars of the compensation (if any) claimed in respect thereof. (Page 346, Part IV, 'Investigation of Claims', Section 11 (b)).

The 'claims' mentioned here were land claims referred to in Section 14 (a). An interesting aspect of the Rajasthan Forest Settlement Rules 1958 is that in Part IV, Section 6, the claims can be presented either on behalf of a family or on behalf of a tribe or community, therefore recognising the communal rights of a forest tribal group. It also recognised usufruct rights, and access to minor forest produce. However, the access was no longer free, but had to be sanctioned by the government, impairing tribal communities' rights to self-determination.

The ensuing laws that consolidated state monopoly over forest lands and prevented Adivasi control over their ancestral lands included the Rajasthan Reserved Forest Act 1960, which restricted both habitation and farming on the lands within Reserved Forest areas, and declared the gathering and collection of minor forest produce a punishable offence. This not only forced migration but reduced the Adivasi communities to the status of encroachers on their own lands, thereby criminalising them. The restriction of access to pursue their traditional livelihoods also led to impoverishment. Many Adivasis either became wage labourers on their own lands, bonded to the government, or had to leave the forest to look for menial jobs that paid low daily wages. In 1972, the Central Government passed the Wildlife Protection Act. The Forest Department takes responsibility to protect the wildlife in any game sanctuary. This task, however, took priority over the needs of forest communities. The Act stated that forest peoples and other people dependent on the forests are not allowed to sell forest resources and minor forest produce. This destroyed livelihoods, especially those of the most marginalised tribal families who are highly dependent on the sale of minor forest produce and on limited farming on their own lands.[11] The Act protected wildlife, an important development, but it came at the cost of the resident forest communities. The 1980 Rajasthan Protected Forest Act did not criminalise the forest communities in the same way as the very restrictive Rajasthan Reserved Forest Act of 1960 enacted twenty years earlier. However, people still needed an official pass to take dry wood or forest produce for consumption from the forest, and it was only legal to collect one head load of minor forest produce per person per day.[12] With the enactment of the Forest Rights Act, the one head load restriction was changed, and the community could use bicycles or

11 Chadana et al., *Status of Adivasis/Indigenous Peoples*, 79.
12 Chadana et al., *Status of Adivasis/Indigenous Peoples*, 79.

bullock carts, but not two-wheel or four-wheel vehicles since they would add to forest degradation. This vehicle law changed in 2013, and the restrictions were lifted. The Congress Government also drafted new welfare policies that provided funds for community development. Panchayat[13] members received a stipend from the government and had access to development funds, but the funds had not been spent well on the community for improvement of livelihoods.[14] The Forest Rights Act 2006 was part of these new Congress Government welfare policies.

In Rajasthan, in order to counter the revenue losses, and to regulate the trade in the interests of the government, the state enacted the Rajasthan Tendu Leaf Trade Regulation Act 1974.[15] The main aim of creating a state monopoly in the Tendu leaf trade was to consolidate the profits under the government. The state monopoly of the Tendu leaf trade was outlined within the following provisions: Section 5, which restricted purchase to the state government or an agent chosen by them, disempowering the community and exposing them to potential exploitation; Sections 7 and 9, which fixed the price of Tendu leaves in consultation with a government committee and bound the buyers to purchase the leaves at this price; Section 10, which required growers to register themselves with the state government; Section 11, which required manufacturers of bidis and exporters of Tendu leaves to register; and Section 22:

> Rajasthan Forest Act, 1953 and other laws not to apply to Tendu leaves for purposes covered under this Act. – (1) Nothing contained in the Rajasthan Forest Act, 1953 (Rajasthan Act XIII of 1953) shall apply to tendu leaves in respect of matters for which provisions are contained in this Act.

This legal regulation not only ensured that the Adivasis remained impecunious, daily waged labourers, but it was also disempowering for them to have the state controlling their livelihoods on what used to be their own ancestral lands. The profits were not shared with the Adivasis by the state.

13 The Panchayat is the local governing body at the village level. The village is called 'Gram'. The Panchayat is usually referred to as the Gram Panchayat, to be differentiated from the Gram Sabha, which is the village committee formed by every adult member of a village. If a village has fewer than 1,500 members, it is grouped with other villages in order to form the Gram Sabha. The Gram Sabha elects the 'panchas' for the Gram Panchayat, holds them accountable and conducts village meetings. The Gram Panchayat is in charge of organising the development of the villages, which includes all welfare, social justice and economic activities for the community. https://pria.org/panchayathub/panchayat_text_view.php.

14 The development schemes include the Indira Gandhi/Chief Minister housing grant and the National Rural Employment Guarantee Act (NREGA), which guarantees each rural household one hundred days a year of wage employment. This incorporates building roads, dams, bunds, protecting forest walls and other construction jobs.

15 Rajasthan Tendu Leaves (Regulation of Trade) Act, 1974. Latest Laws.com, accessed 2016, www.rajforest.nic.in/writereaddata/Revised_Rules_1974_English.pdf.

Rajasthan state forest laws and land rights campaigns, and federal forest laws.

- 1958: Rajasthan Forest Settlement Rules demarcated forest boundaries controlled by the Forest Department. They restricted tribal communities' access to the forests and obstructed their traditional livelihoods, putting the onus on the Adivasis to claim back the ancestral rights they had lost to the Reserved Forests policies. These ancestral rights, under the Rajasthan Forest Settlement Rules 1958, needed to be sanctioned by the local government.
- 1960: Rajasthan Reserved Forest Act restricted both habitation and farming on the lands within Reserved Forest areas; gathering and collection of minor forest produce became a punishable offence. Adivasi communities were criminalised and perceived as encroachers on their own lands.
- 1972: Wildlife Protection Act (Central Government). Forest communities' needs became subordinate to the protection of the wildlife in any game sanctuary, regulated by the Forest Department. The sale of forest resources and minor forest produce by forest peoples was restricted.
- 1974 Rajasthan Tendu Leaf Trade Regulation Act. Regulation of trade to create a state monopoly in the Tendu leaf trade, and to consolidate the profits under the government.
- 1980: Rajasthan Protected Forest Act lessened existing restrictions that criminalised forest communities, but retained control through imposition of official passes to collect dry wood or forest produce for consumption from the forest, with only one head load of minor forest produce allowed per person per day.[16]
- 1993: TDF (Tribal Development Forum) was established in the Kotda Block of Udaipur for tribal self-rule rights-based approach on progress. They collected poor and marginalised tribal peoples from four Blocks and established leaders to encourage a strong community alliance of tribal peoples for land rights.
- 1995: Jungle Jameen Jan Andolan, a people's organisation for tribal land rights, was formed by affected tribal communities of southern Rajasthan. A major effort and struggle for forest rights ensued.
- 2002: CSD (Campaign for Survival and Dignity). States became involved jointly in the struggle on a national level to outline a framework for a new forest act. People's organisations helped by beginning to pressure the government to pass a forest act to protect villagers from displacement.
- 2006: Scheduled Tribes and Other Traditional Forest Dwellers (Recognition of Forest Rights) Act, 2006 (also known as the Forest Rights Act) was finally passed by the federal government.

16 Chadana et al., *Status of Adivasis/Indigenous Peoples*, 79.

Transitioning From Labourers to Owners

The years 1986, 1987, and 1988 were drought years in the Aravalli hills of southern Rajasthan. The rains came in 1989, breaking the cycle of drought, and by 1990 people could look beyond hunger, drought, water, and food. Livelihoods became a focus, and in the early 1990s the communities in Kotda Block of Udaipur District started taking stock and analysing how much they were being paid for labour-intensive gathering work. The Forest Department, Panchayats, and *Zilla Parishads* (district Panchayats or councils) showed no interest in people's rights, their livelihoods, or the formation of cooperatives for minor forest produce, and the community did not know much about it, nor did they know their rights.

With the support of Astha, an NGO focusing on land rights, the tribal communities chose the Tendu *patta* micro-industry as a Block-wide shared priority.[17] The goal was to get a better rate for their labour, and this was the start of a long-term advocacy movement that changed the dynamic of Tendu *patta* as minor forest produce and income generator for Adivasis. Astha lent strong support to the advocacy movement and, using village-level staff, organised the tribal communities into a strong union. Astha's objective was to create people's organisations that would eventually stand independently. They began with small, issue-based meetings, in which people began analysing the Tendu *patta* rate. The first meetings discussed the issue of the levels of exploitation of poor communities living in resource-rich areas. The questions posed were: what strategies did the communities need to undertake in order to avoid exploitation by more powerful stakeholders, and how could they make sure they could use the resources to their advantage? With Astha's help, communities in Kotda Block petitioned the Forest Department (FD) to initially raise the minimum rate to Rs. 10.00. Because the FD makes the most royalties from Tendu *patta*, historically it suited them to not list Tendu as part of the minor forest produce that forest peoples were allowed to access. At that point in 1990, there were about forty thousand Tendu *patta* collectors in Kotda Block. The contractors, usually rich outsiders, sometimes even from outside the state of Rajasthan, were heavily dependent on this large number of labourers. The contractors, in 1990, paid royalties to the Forest Department of between 1.5 lakh rupees and 13–14 lakh rupees.[18] These royalties gave them the right to collect the forest produce from a specific unit, a

17 Initially, Astha had ideological reservations about supporting the Tendu *patta* trade because smoking was so bad for health. However, it was the only industry that was shared throughout the whole Block that could be used as part of the advocacy for improvement in livelihoods. Astha therefore went along with this choice of trade. The ultimate goal was to spread any advancements made with this strategy to other minor forest products so that the communities could take control of their own resources.

18 One lakh = 100,000.

geographical piece of land from which they could collect, buy, and transport the Tendu leaves.

The community strategy was a strike action, stopping the collection of Tendu leaves until the rate per bundle was raised from Rs. 7.50 to at least Rs. 15.00. Initially, three Gram Panchayats organised themselves. Tribal Panchayats often include up to fifteen villages. Later, they organised into five clusters, with all the leaders of the Gram Sabhas forming an organisation called Sangarsh Samiti with about fifty people from all over the Block. This core group spread the word using *pad yatras* (foot pilgrimages), through songs and more meetings. The communities began a strike action that lasted sixteen days. Initially, the contractors tried to break the strike by hiring a jeep with microphones which they drove through the villages announcing that the strike was over. The *fud munshi* made some bundles of leaves to try to convince people that the strike was over. But the strike continued. The contractors still had to pay royalties to the Forest Department, whether they had Tendu *patta* or not. They arrived at Astha's doorstep offering a 'donation' to Astha if they would stop the protest by making an offer. Astha declined, explaining that this was not their campaign but the people's, and that they did not have any power. Since paying royalties worth lakhs of rupees without leaves was an expensive option, on day seventeen the contractors agreed to pay a minimum of Rs. 15.00 per bundle for leaves collected. This rate was flexible, as it was only a minimum. For example, if the contractor wanted the tribal people to collect the last leaves of the season, they were prepared to pay more. The strike action had thus been a success.

Self-Determination Through Collaboration and Cooperatives

The following year, in 1991, the Sangarsh Samiti community organisation that had been formed before the strike action in 1990 with the help of Astha began to analyse the Tendu *patta* trade: their profits, the buyers, and the rates of sale.[19] It was a capacity-building exercise to understand the trade, and the tribal communities soon felt they had a handle on the Tendu leaf business. It also led to the realisation that they were being paid a pittance considering the profits. The tribal community decided that they wanted to control the business themselves without using middlemen, especially as the traders were so exploitative. They found a sympathetic Indian Administrative Service (IAS) officer, the managing director of the Manohar Kant Raja Sangh (Rajasthan Tribal Federation), who encouraged the formation of cooperatives and offered to finance the venture.[20] He suggested that they, the community, become a contractor. This entailed attending the auction and bidding for a

19 Information supplied by Astha staff who were supporting the change action.

20 The budget covered renting a *godown* (warehouse) to store the leaves, buying gunny sacks to put the leaves in, and a 10 to 15 per cent sum of money to cover the Forest Department royalty fees.

unit – a specific area of the forest in which the successful bidder is allowed to gather Tendu leaves. Following the Rajasthan Tribal Federation advice, the Kotda community formed a cooperative called Adivasi Tendu Patta Sangrahan Sahakari Samiti, Kotda (Tribal Tendu Leaf Collectors Cooperative). For self-determination, this was a significant achievement and the first of its kind for the Adivasis of Kotda Block.[21]

The cooperative attended the auction and managed to win three units using the grant from the Tribal Federation. The Forest Department accepted their bid. Besides gathering Tendu leaves, the successful bidder has the right to count the leaves, pay the gatherers, bring the leaves to the *godown* (warehouse), and sell them to the bidi manufacturers or bidi leaf traders. The manufacturing of bidis is an all-India trade, with different brands. The majority of the rolling is done in south India, although Tendu leaves are grown in the central belt.[22] Locally, the preparation of Tendu leaves is complicated, and preparing them for transport from the forests in the central belt to the bidi-rolling factories in south India takes a few days.

For the cooperative, taking control of the Tendu business became a labour-intensive venture. The *fud munshi* and his team slept and lived in the fields in order to guard the Tendu *patta*, as the bundles were laid out in an empty field to dry after being counted. If the field used for the drying of the leaves had difficult access to the road, it created a problem for those who brought their Tendu *patta* for drying, and it also made it difficult to transport it to the *godown*. The priority was access to the field for those bringing the leaves. Camels would transport the leaf-filled gunny sacks from the fields to the road, where they were loaded onto trucks waiting to depart for the *godowns*. The *godowns* kept the bags dry in case of pre-monsoon showers. Re-drying was possible if there were one or two showers, but if early rains wet the leaves, they would become discoloured, immediately lowering the purchase price.[23] The next step in the process involved the buyers. They examined a sample of five *boras* – big gunny sacks, which were considered the 'standard bags'. Small gunny sacks were called *bori*. A price was agreed with the buyer by the cooperative's secretary or president after the leaves had been inspected.[24] Once the price had been settled, an agreement was drawn up in writing and binding documents were signed. In the first year, the Adivasi

21 In 1995, all the Tendu *patta* cooperatives merged to form one organisation called Samarthak Samiti. Since Tendu *patta* is seasonal and only lasts for one month, the cooperatives focused on other minor forest produce for the rest of the year, such as honey, honey wax, black plums, amla products, bel fruit, custard apples and so on.

22 The central belt of India includes northern Andhra Pradesh, Orissa, Chhattisgarh, Rajasthan, northern Maharashtra, northern Gujarat and Madhya Pradesh.

23 The Tendu *patta* season starts on 1 May. The monsoon starts in the middle to end of June, but pre-monsoon showers could wet the bags.

24 The Kotda Block was initially supported by Mr. Rathod, who managed the Samarthak Samiti or self-help group SHG, in negotiations with buyers.

Tendu Patta Sangrahan Sahakari Samiti cooperative in Kotda made a net profit of 6.5 lakhs,[25] a significant success for self-determination and much more than a mere profit margin for the Adivasi Tendu *patta* trade.

The commercial success that the cooperative enjoyed lent a confidence and power that was used to stabilise the minimum wage. The Kotda cooperative had wanted to pay their Tendu *patta* gatherers Rs. 30.00 per bundle. In spite of the seemingly high rate, they calculated that they would still make a profit. The government had increased the minimum collective rate to Rs. 20.00 per bundle, and other contractors were still also paying that rate. On 2 May 1991, the Kotda cooperative called a meeting under a tree at Sulau Choraha, where three roads come together. The contractors resisted any raise and tried to keep the rate at Rs. 20.00. The community, who were members of the cooperative, persisted, and the meeting dragged on for five hours, resulting in a compromise of Rs. 26.00 per bundle. The main objective for the Tendu *patta* cooperative in raising the rates was so the gatherers or leaf collectors could share in the profits, and also to force the other contractors to raise their rates. This was achieved successfully. Actions such as the Tendu campaign gave birth to tribal rights activist groups, one of which was called the Jungle Jameen Jan Andolan. In 1995, the Jungle Jameen Jan Andolan took its campaign to the larger cities, in order to pressure the government to draft and pass legislation recognising tribal land rights. Rallies were held in the streets of cities such as Jaipur and New Delhi in order to grow the movement beyond the state and onto a national level, with the message of resource extraction causing the displacement of forest communities. This contributed to the 2006 enactment of the Forest Rights Act.

In the next case study, the threat of imminent displacement of the isolated forest community of Amba village, and the legal strategies formulated by them with the help of civil society, emphasises the land insecurity that remains part of forest peoples' lives.

Community Profile: Amba Village, the Phulwari Ki Nal Wildlife Sanctuary, Kotda Block, Udaipur

Phulwari Ki Nal is one of eleven Forest Blocks[26] in the District of Udaipur, about 120 km from the city of Udaipur.[27] Phulwari Ki Nal was

25 6.5 lakhs is Rs. 600,500.

26 The local word for 'forest' is 'van'. Forest Blocks are called 'van khand'.

27 The district is the principal subdivision within the state. There are 476 districts in India; districts are subdivided into tehsils, areas that contain from two hundred to six hundred villages. The tehsildar, who serves in much the same capacity as the collector, is the chief member of the tehsil revenue department and is the pre-eminent official at this level. Government of Rajasthan, Department of Forest, 2010. https://forest.rajasthan.gov.in/content/raj/forest/en/home.html# Accessed 2013.

'notified'[28] in 1983 as a wildlife sanctuary, and is described as a "hilly and undulating part of Southern Aravalli Hills".[29] It forms a part of the largest continuous forest tract in the arid Aravalli Range of hills in Rajasthan and is rich in fauna.[30] The sanctuary, stretching to 511.41 square km, comprises eleven *van khands* or Forest Blocks, one of which is Phulwari. A total of 365.92 square km is Reserved Forest, and 145.49 square km is Protected Forest.[31] The sanctuary houses about 134 forest villages that have existed for many generations and form an integral part of the area's biodiversity. Amba was the smallest village in this district, with thirty-five households. The Bhil tribe who lived here were identified by the names of three sub-sections of the Bhil tribe: the Khair, Dama, and Kapariya. Set deep in the forest, the village was isolated, with poor access and infrastructure and no running water or electricity, even in 2013. The nearest school was in the next village, ensuring low literacy levels.

I visited Amba village in the Phulwari Ki Nal Wildlife Sanctuary with Astha staff members. One aspect that struck me during my visit was just how inaccessible the village remained. There was no road to the village, which meant that only four-wheel-drive vehicles could access it. Our only options were to walk or use a motorbike. Soon after we crossed the borders of the sanctuary, marked by a large yellow signboard announcing the entrance to the Phulwari Wildlife Sanctuary, the road disappeared, and we continued into the forest on a dirt track. Leaving the dirt track, to my surprise, the driver aimed his motorcycle at the river, and we rode bumpily along the dry winter riverbed. During the monsoons, the river would be full. For now, however, it made for the most direct route into Amba village.[32]

Set among the trees, the houses in Amba were predominantly built from thatch, twigs, branches, and other forest material. One house, half built, was

28 'Notified' is terminology maintained from the Indian Forest Act 1927, enacted during the British colonial period when forest lands belonging historically to tribal communities were notified in order to extract forest resources for industry. Heredia, 'Denotified and Nomadic Tribes: The Challenge of Free and Equal Citizenship', 6.

29 Government of Rajasthan, Department of Forest, 2010, accessed 2013, https://forest.rajasthan.gov.in/content/raj/forest/en/home.html#.

30 The fauna recorded are leopard, hyena, chinkara (Indian gazelle), wild boar, four-horned antelope, flying squirrel, pangolin and 120 species of birds. The four-horned antelope, pangolin, flying squirrel and deer species are of 'conservation interest'. Government of Rajasthan, Department of Forest, 2010, http://rajforest.nic.in/?q=phulwari-ki-nal.

31 Government of Rajasthan, Department of Forest, 2010, http://rajforest.nic.in/?q=phulwari-ki-nal.

32 Mountain riverbeds, however, are not sandy, and for me, the pillion rider, it became painfully bone-jarring as Sarfraj skilfully navigated the bluish, large, smooth riverbed stones, which were sometimes covered by large puddles of water. As an outsider from urban India, I was astonished by the fact that in the year 2013, in India, known at that point as one of the fastest growing economies in the world, there were still isolated villages and hamlets with no modern infrastructure such as roads and running water or electricity.

being constructed with stones and cement, the owner being a beneficiary of a government housing benefit scheme.[33] Any natural clearings in the jungle had been converted to fields. Most of the community could be said to be living below the poverty line, dependent on minor forest produce for their livelihood, supplemented by seasonal migratory work. No claims for land rights had been filed with the Gram Sabha, either by individuals in the village or the community as a whole. Awareness of the Forest Rights Act was low, and the state government, who, by provisions of the Act, were obliged to acquaint the communities with their rights had not only neglected to do so but in this instance were exploiting the lack of community awareness in order to refuse these rights.

Land Violations, Forcing Migration, and Strategies

The sense of urgency in the Phulwari Ki Nal Wildlife Sanctuary was obvious. Four of the smallest villages had been served a notice from the District Collector via the *Sarpanch*,[34] summoning them to a meeting at which the *Sarpanch* was to inform the community that a survey team was being formed by the Forest Department in order to conduct a survey of the villages. The community was to complete a survey questionnaire recording the value of their assets on 9 January 2014. This was allegedly the first stage of the government's process of displacing communities from the wildlife sanctuary. The survey form could then be used to prove that the community could be rehoused or rehabilitated elsewhere. This information could potentially be used in order to change the status of the sanctuary to a 'critical' wildlife sanctuary which would then become 'inviolate'. A critical wildlife sanctuary, which was inviolate, would prohibit forest peoples from inhabiting the area, forcing them to migrate from their ancestral lands.

At first *glance*, the format of the survey form appeared benign, including the name of the village, the size of the population, the measurements of the land area, individual landholdings, and whether the houses were *'kachcha'* or *'pukka'*.[35] If one looked carefully, however, at the end of the survey form, space was provided for a signature or thumb print, which indicated voluntary agreement to vacate the lands. The requirement of a signature to voluntarily

33 This scheme was a government social welfare programme started by Rajiv Gandhi in 1985, which offers subsidies and cash assistance for the construction of houses to people living below the poverty line (BPL).

34 The villages served the notice were Bhimatalai, Vaviran and Shisvair under Medi Panchayat and Amba in Mahad Panchayat. The district collector is the highest official in a district, and is a member of the Indian Administrative Service. A *Sarpanch* is an elected head of the Gram Panchayat, which is the governing body at the village level in India.

35 'Kachcha' means 'rough' or 'flimsy' and refers to homes made of mud and thatch, while 'pukka' homes are 'solid', 'firm', 'strong' and refer to homes made of concrete, stones or brick.

abandon their own lands seemed to exploit the fact that the community was predominantly illiterate and would sign the form without realising that they were being complicit in dispossessing themselves from their own properties. The Astha field worker, noticing this, immediately contacted the NGO lawyer,[36] who issued a notice to the Forest Department pointing out that the plans to displace the community were illegal according to the FRA under the present circumstances, in which forest rights had not yet been vested in this community.

The nature of the plans to convert the status of the Phulwari Wildlife Sanctuary to a critical wildlife sanctuary was very strange. The Astha staff member from the local community managed a marketing organisation called Samarthak Samiti, which sold minor forest produce for the community, including honey, woollen blankets, wax, resin, wood oil, and medicinal plants, among other non-timber products. Coincidentally, he shared the same name as someone else who was part of a District Level team devising the plan for the conversion to critical wildlife status, which would displace certain communities. The team comprised the Collector, the District Forest Officer, the Conservation Forest Officer, and other members. The Astha staff member, on 29 December 2013, received a letter of invitation to the meetings a week before the survey was issued to the community intended for someone from the District Level team. His attendance at the meeting was serendipitous as he could alert Astha when he realised what was being planned.

The threat felt by the community was palpable. Upon arrival, an old man came up to me in greeting, and the first thing he said was, "Where there are Adivasis, there are forests. We are the caretakers of the forests. I am now over seventy years old, and have never lived anywhere else. If they displace us, where do we go?" This question captured the essence of the Gram Sabha meeting I attended in Amba that day, 11 January 2014. The NGO had planned the agenda around a discussion of the best strategy to use in order to avoid being displaced by the Forest Department, who were trying to change the status of the wildlife sanctuary to a 'critical wildlife habitat', thus making the area inviolate. Astha staff explained at the meeting that the Amba community was under no obligation to sign any papers. The community should interrogate any outsiders as to their purpose in entering the village. The community should initiate a discussion with the Collector and ask questions about the plans being launched for the Phulwari Ki Nal Wildlife Sanctuary, the lack of transparency of the process, and whether the process complied with the Forest Rights Act. The community were cautioned about giving anyone, even from the Forest Department, permission to conduct a survey. The advice given included: "Do not act obsequiously to any government official, and always question their

36 The lawyer attached to Astha and working with the tribal communities, donated his services to the organisation free of charge.

encroachment on the village". The meetings began with traditional communal singing, spelling out a commitment to self-determination: "We planted the mango trees; this land is ours; we won't lose our land; In Jaipur, in Delhi, the government is in charge . . . on our land, we are in charge, we are the government". With an increasingly activist pace, the Gram Sabha meeting was followed up the next day with another strategy meeting at the Astha Training Centre at Kotda village in Kotda Block in order to consolidate the strategies against displacement, and the next week a meeting for all the villages from Kotda Block was facilitated by Ramesh Nandvana, the legal counsel for Astha, in order to build the community's legal capacity. The strategies were based on the FRA and the procedural rights that the community could access. These are analysed in the next section on administrative justice in the context of how to respond to the government action calculated to change the status of the Phulwari Wildlife Sanctuary to a critical wildlife sanctuary, in turn displacing the Amba community from their ancestral forest home. 'Inviolate' was a term used in the FRA: a critical wildlife habitat requires areas "to be kept as *inviolate* for the purposes of wildlife conservation".[37]

Analysis: Administrative Justice and the FRA

The Tendu *patta* story, of a rights-based campaign to transform forest livelihoods from an exploitative trade to one in which the Adivasis controlled their own livelihoods, took place a decade and a half before the Forest Rights Act was in place. The southern Rajasthan Adivasis' struggle for self-determination and access to justice had played an important part in the campaign leading up to the Forest Rights Act. The Act affirms many of the rights that were hard fought for in the case study earlier. For example, the FRA defined the term 'minor forest produce' to include all non-timber forest produce of plant origin, including bamboo, brushwood, stumps, cane, tussar, cocoons, honey, wax, lac, Tendu or kendu leaves, medicinal plants and herbs, roots, tubers, and the like.[38] The fact that Tendu is included in the list is significant as it was consciously removed from the list in the past on account of its lucrative

37 Chapter One, Section 2 (b): '"critical wildlife habitat" means such areas of National Parks and Sanctuaries where it has been specifically and clearly established, case by case, on the basis of scientific and objective criteria, that such areas are required to be kept as *inviolate* for the purposes of wildlife conservation as may be determined and notified by the Central Government in the Ministry of Environment and Forests after open process of consultation by an Expert Committee, which includes experts from the locality appointed by that Government wherein a representative of the Ministry of Tribal Affairs shall also be included, in determining such areas according to the procedural requirements arising from sub-sections (1) and (2) of section 4'.

38 FRA Chapter One, Section 2 (i).

attributes. It now 'belongs' to the people again, allowing them access to collect it and to use it as they had done traditionally, within or outside the village borders.[39]

The FRA opened up land access, and more than 30 per cent of households reported access to common lands and open revenue lands.[40] The families who managed successful land rights claims under the FRA tended to have larger landholdings and more access to land in revenue villages. Household incomes were supplemented by ownership of livestock. Poultry and goats were reared for consumption and could provide an important asset to supplement the income of small landholders. Small households might have kept one or a few cows, and larger landholders tended to keep buffaloes. Every household, regardless of wealth, aspired to own a pair of bullocks.[41] Marginal households were dependent on the collection of minor forest produce both for income and consumption needs, while medium landholders resorted more to trade in products from land, forest, and cattle to supplement their income.

As defined earlier in this study, administrative injustice refers to government failure to protect citizens, and behaviour that is unjust, unreasonable, or dishonourable, or does not allow citizens access to justice.[42] The threat to the Phulwari Ki Nal communities came not only from the Forest Department's efforts to dispossess the community of their ancestral lands. Another threat to land security lay in the unreliable access to justice embodied in the terminology of the FRA, as noted later. The wording of the Act specifically leaves the decision of establishing any areas as critical wildlife habitat to the government:

> as may be determined and notified by the Central Government in the Ministry of Environment and Forests after open process of consultation by an Expert Committee, which includes experts from the locality appointed by that Government wherein a representative of the Ministry of Tribal Affairs shall also be included, in determining such areas according to the procedural requirements arising from sub-sections (1) and (2) of section 4.[43]

The government at the forest level is represented by the Forest Department, who have not been known to conscientiously obtain the Free and Prior Informed Consent (FPIC) required both by the national FRA and by international laws such as UNDRIP, nor have they been proven to be sympathetic

39 FRA Chapter Two, Section 3 (c).
40 TRRU, *Tribal Women's Rights on Land.*
41 TRRU, *Tribal Women's Rights on Land.*
42 United Kingdom Administrative Justice Institute, 'What Is Administrative Justice?', AA discussion paper (Nuffield Foundation Series 2015).
43 FRA Chapter One, Section 2 (b).

to or supportive of forest rights, creating a conflict of interest biased against tribal communities.[44]

There were several violations of the FRA legislation by the government via the Forest Department. For instance, in Amba, the concerned Gram Sabhas had not given prior permission for the planning or implementation of any changes. Chapter III. 4 (2) (e) states: "The free informed consent of the Gram Sabhas in the area concerned to the proposed resettlement and to the package provided has been obtained in writing". If the Gram Sabha agrees or gives permission for any changes, then all plans for change or rehabilitation need to be open and transparent, with compensation packages in written agreements. The FRA defines strict prerequisites for protecting forest rights before being able to either create inviolate areas for wildlife conservation, or to resettle or have any other forest rights affected. In Amba, the six criteria recorded in the FRA that had to be met before any change of status, as outlined in the following paragraphs, had not been fulfilled.

Chapter IV. 6 (7): "The process of recognition and vesting of rights as specified in section 6 is complete in all areas under consideration". All individual and community forest rights have to be completed and recognised. This refers to the rights of individuals and communities to make a claim to their land. The Gram Sabha is authorised to verify and consolidate these rights, and to map the area before passing the claim to the Sub-Divisional Level Committee (SDLC) for consideration. The SDLC is created by the state government, as is the District Level Committee (DLC) to whom the claim goes after the SDLC has considered it. The decision of the DLC is "final and binding". The Amba community had not started the process of claiming community or individual rights.

Chapter III. 4 (2) (b):

> It has been established by the concerned agencies of the State Government, in exercise of their powers under the Wild Life (Protection) Act, 1972, that the activities of impact of the presence of holders of rights upon wild animals is sufficient to cause irreversible damage and threaten the existence of said species and their habitat.

As a first step, the state government has to prepare a report that proves there is conflict between the forest peoples and wildlife, and they have to mention any threats that people may be causing to endangered species. Secondly, the

44 United Nations Declaration on the Rights of Indigenous Peoples (adopted 13 December 2007, UNGA Res. 61/295 A (UNDRIP Add 1)): 'Indigenous peoples shall not be forcibly removed from their lands or territories. No relocation shall take place without the *free, prior and informed consent* of the indigenous peoples concerned and after agreement on just and fair compensation and, where possible, with the option of return' (Article 10).

government has to share this report with the concerned Gram Sabhas and the public. No such report had been prepared by the government for Amba village. As the old gentleman said when I arrived in Amba, "We are the caretakers of the forests".

Chapter III. 4 (2) (c): "The State Government has concluded that other reasonable options, such as co-existence, are not available". The argument provided by the Amba community in relation to the earlier two clauses is that they have lived in harmony with the wildlife for centuries. In addition, the state government's decision on whether the tribal communities were endangering the existence of wildlife was unilateral and could be perceived as arbitrary. The threats faced by the community also included the uncertainty of whether the decision made by the state government was biased, and how transparent this decision-making process would be to the community.

The remaining three criteria that were not fulfilled are as follows:

Chapter III. 4 (2) (d): A resettlement or alternatives package has been prepared and communicated that provides a secure livelihood for the affected individuals and communities and fulfills the requirements of such affected individuals and communities given in the relevant laws and the policy of the Central Government.

Chapter III. 4 (2) (e): The free informed consent of the Gram Sabhas in the area concerned to the proposed resettlement and to the package provided has been obtained in writing.

Chapter III. 4 (2) (f): No resettlement shall take place until facilities and land allocation at the resettlement location are complete as per the promised package: Provided that the critical wildlife habitats from which rights holders are thus relocated for purposes of wildlife conservation shall not be subsequently diverted by the State Government or the Central Government or any other entity for other uses.

None of these procedures had been honoured by the government. The Committee that was set up had sent a letter to the *Sarpanch* to inform the community of the survey and plans for impending displacement, instead of obtaining Gram Sabha permission. The government's attempts to displace people from their lands raise another more complex question: what characteristics of the legal and political system enable those charged with carrying out the law to suspend administrative justice[45] and circumvent existing legal frameworks?

45 Administrative injustice is defined as 'when the government, or those working on its behalf, act in ways that appear wrong, unfair or unjust, [and do not ensure] that public bodies and those who exercise public functions make the right decisions . . . [and that] mechanisms for providing redress when things go wrong are not accessible for citizens, consumers, individuals or groups'. United Kingdom Administrative Justice Institute, 'What Is Administrative Justice?', AA discussion paper (Nuffield Foundation Series 2015).

At a meeting I attended in Kotda village, where the community had gathered to meet with Astha regarding the FRA, alleged government violations of forest rights emerged during the discussion. These alleged government violations comprised a long list, as described in the paragraphs later, and confirm a lack of administrative justice, referred to earlier, and the government's failure to protect the forest peoples.

"The Forest Department (FD) is continuing to build walls and fences in forest lands." Before the Forest Rights Act, the FD, which is part of the Ministry of Environment and Forests (MoEF), had complete control of the forests. Walls and fences were often used to keep forest communities out of the forest, as forest lands constituted rich resources from which the government profited. Since the enactment of the FRA, any government activity has to first be approved by the Gram Sabha. The continued building of walls and fences without Gram Sabha authorisation conveys a clear message that the government respects neither the law nor the forest peoples. It also signals that the government is unable to relinquish authority to the community. Self-determination of forest peoples is not respected or understood.

"The Forest Department persists in felling trees for timber." The reasons for this are similar to those discussed earlier. In addition, the FD's actions in felling trees confirm the perception both within forest communities and among scientists that Indigenous peoples' traditional conservation methods are more committed to ecological preservation than many governments, who collude with the corporate sector when they harness mineral-rich forest lands for extractive industries and conservation, continuing to displace Indigenous peoples from ancestral lands.

"Communities are displaced in order to make way for critical wildlife habitats, without the FD complying with the law and eliciting Gram Sabha permission first." This action on the part of the government does not respect the customary conservation practices of the Adivasis as spelt out in the FRA. Chapter II. 3 (i) refers to the "right to protect, regenerate, or conserve or manage any community forest resource, which they have been traditionally protecting and conserving for sustainable use". Critical wildlife habitats taking priority over the needs of people elicits a paradigmatic shift within the conservation debate, with the more recent perspective on conservation challenging the classic conservation policies that involved the exclusion of people. The FD seems unable to let go of the former conservation policy of excluding people, as was at play in the conversion of the Phulwari Wildlife Sanctuary to a critical wildlife sanctuary. The new conservation paradigm advocates integrating the need to protect flora and fauna with the need to protect peoples' livelihoods and culture, especially when their culture is dependent on 'protected areas'.[46] The new paradigm

46 In India, for example, protected areas comprise many categories such as: Reserved Forests; Protected Forest; Protected Areas, which include National Parks; Sanctuaries; Tiger

brings the inclusion of humans into the equation. Conservation with "a human face" acknowledges the fact that human beings are part of nature and that protecting human needs is as important as preserving beautiful wilderness areas. It includes a debate on whether Indigenous peoples (forest peoples) contribute to the destruction or to the protection of the forests. Protectionists do not take into consideration the economic hardship and irreversible cultural impacts of restrictions on Indigenous communities. The sacrifice of human livelihoods does not equate with efforts to protect the "common good".[47] The issue of people versus biodiversity has moved into the human rights arena, and when human rights are situated opposite the rights of nature, it results in win-lose situations which are self-defeating and not conducive to dialogue.[48]

"The government sells forest lands to extractive industries. And the government expropriates forest lands in the name of 'development'." My discussion here refers to the neoliberal analysis discussed in an earlier chapter, which points out the disjunction of economic development schemes that harm human rights and impoverish certain marginalised sections of society. The argument is that the rights of all individuals and communities should be of equal priority, and economic development schemes should not be pursued for the benefit of some at the expense of others, which would deny access to justice for certain sections of society.

"The Forest Department preys on forest peoples." The experience of the forest communities had been of the FD misusing their authority and extracting money from people collecting bamboo and other building materials from the forests for their houses. This goes against community forest rights as outlined in the FRA, Chapter II. 3:

> For the purposes of this Act, the following rights which are secure individual or community tenure or both, shall be the forest rights of forest dwelling Scheduled Tribes and other traditional forest dwellers on all forest lands, namely: right to hold and live in the forest land under the individual or common occupation for habitation or for self-cultivation for livelihood by a member or members of a forest dwelling Scheduled Tribe or other traditional forest dwellers; right of ownership, access to collect,

Reserves; Critical Wildlife Habitats; Conservation Reserves; Community Reserves; Other Lands (e.g. unclassified lands); Revenue Areas.

47 'Many people living in and near protected areas perceive their interest is tangible and immediate and the "common" interest is unclear and intangible.' Wilshusen et al., 'Reinventing a Square Wheel', 25.

48 'Biodiversity conservation programs do not necessarily have to hinder the attainment of human rights for all people living in or near protected areas. The moral argument in favour of nature protection is perfectly defensible as far as it goes. But if nature protection occurs at the expense of humans without accountability based on a separation between humans and nature, then it becomes less defensible.' Wilshusen et al., 'Reinventing a Square Wheel', 17.

use, and dispose of minor forest produce which has been traditionally collected within or outside village boundaries.

The example discussed during the meeting in Kotda in January 2014 was of one young woman who had collected dry wood, which the FD confiscated, demanding Rs. 500 for it to be returned. The clear message from the FD was that the forest lands belong to the FD and not to the tribal communities. Another example was of a man who was weaving baskets and was apprehended by the FD and interrogated about why he had not requested permission to use minor forest produce to weave his basket. The grasses he had collected for his weaving were confiscated by the FD, who wanted him to pay a bribe to retrieve them. The basket weaver reported this incident to Astha staff, who confronted the FD about non-compliance with FRA law. The grasses were returned to the man with an acknowledgement that a mistake had been made. For the tribal communities, however, this erratic behaviour, dictating principles of eminent domain, remains a constant threat.

The illustrations earlier raise the questions of what precisely is the role of the Forest Department in administering the Forest Rights Act, and where does the concept of justice fit in? Firstly, the administration of legislation, which requires initial awareness raising within the department of what rights the legislation is granting and to whom, seems to be lacking in Rajasthan. Secondly, if the government introduces new legislation, the onus is on the government to commit to the new law and to undertake every strategy that this commitment requires. This is not apparent in such aspects as educating staff, not only on how the new law is to be implemented but also on the rationale and background of the legislation and why it was enacted. The goals and purpose of this law need to be thoroughly comprehended by the staff responsible for implementing it, which the evidence earlier does not support. The enactment of the FRA has changed the role and expectations of the FD. Is this change in their role understood by them, and to whom are they accountable for carrying out their duties according to the expected goals? The irony of government employees perceived by citizens to be oppressing them, as in the examples alleged earlier, is that the salaries of these civil servants are ultimately derived from the income tax collected from the citizens whose rights are not necessarily being protected. The FD engaging in demonstrations of power by extorting bribes from Adivasis reveals it to be pitting itself against the rights of tribal peoples who are using the forest according to customary rights deemed legal by the FRA.

The staff in charge of Forest Rights Act matters at Astha query the possible reasons for the seemingly random rejections of claims and awards, and assert that the implementation process is not going perfectly. They point fingers at the Forest Department, who are not fulfilling their duties in helping the community with verification work, as well as the Revenue Department. Verification refers to the obligation to verify aspects such as land records and maps that chart territorial boundaries. In many areas, people did not claim their rights because they did not get the form from the Sub-Divisional Committee to do so in time. Many claim files are still under process. Some are delayed in the Panchayat, some are in FD offices, and some are with the *Patwari*. Patwaris are responsible for demarcating lands and for drawing the maps. Astha staff feel that Patwaris are not cooperating or helping the community in the process of claiming land rights under the FRA.

Conclusion

The Tendu *patta* campaign to claim land rights for control of livelihoods preceded the enactment of the Forest Rights Act and illustrated a concerted effort to claim rights through political strategies and not necessarily legal ones. The success of the Tendu *patta* struggle forced the discussion of how political advocacy is necessary either to support legal claims or to force the issue of eventual enactment of rights-based legislation for marginalised communities. The case study showing the threat of imminent displacement from forest lands faced by the Amba community represented how the Forest Rights Act had been used to access justice for land rights.

Previously, I argued that national legislation and policies do not necessarily improve access to justice for communities and individuals on the national stage. I assert this is mainly for three reasons: administrative injustice and uneven implementation of the FRA; the marginalisation of tribal groups, and societal barriers such as gender inequality which prevent many from using the FRA; and the lack of rational governance, or governmentality, both at the frontline and at the national level to empower Adivasis to access justice. In this chapter, I extend that argument to posit that the FRA's existence confirms that substantive rights are recognised, which is a considerable improvement over having no rights at all. The implementation of the FRA in India is uneven and dependent on the progressiveness of the state administration. Rajasthan is perceived to be one of the more backward states in the administration of the FRA, with the least community forest rights claims awarded compared to the rest of India.[49] This differentiation has to be borne in mind to avoid national generalisations. The nation state in the alleged violations illustrated earlier creates a threat to the human rights of the tribal communities. This causes a dysfunction, part of which is determined by administrative justice, which in turn is dependent on the mindset of the Forest Department, recalling the colonial attitudes of forest ownership lying with the state, as illustrated in my earlier discussion of governmentality.

49 Interview with Madhu Sarin, November 2013. Madhu Sarin is a leading Indian activist, policy analyst a leading Indian figure in the area of forest rights, rural development and gender justice.

The unevenness of the implementation is demonstrated by indications that there are also positive reports that Adivasis are being given legal rights to their lands. In Rajasthan, thirteen thousand Adivasis had received land deed papers at the time these data were collected, in 2013.[50] Evidence that the Forest Department is working hard to implement the FRA in its geographical area is also apparent in the help that some tribal communities are receiving from the FD in claiming legal rights under the Act. The provisions in the FRA outlined in detail earlier have facilitated the submission of land claims for tribal communities. Some forest officials, from top officials to forest guards, are publicising the rights of the FRA in their area of work, and some of them show interest in the rules and procedures that are of help to the Adivasis. There are very few issues of harassment or corruption in dealing with the tribal peoples who submit their claims. The point being made here is that in spite of the land violations experienced by some tribal peoples instigated by the Forest Department, there are other positive aspects that present a contradictory picture.

The extent of awareness raising and training of Forest Department staff dictates the level of success of new legislation. What aspects of governmentality are necessary to avoid setting up new laws to fail? What policies need to be in place in order to remove the apparent animosity demonstrated in the examples experienced by the forest communities in the Aravalli hills? How can these attitudes be replaced with an understanding of their responsibility to implement the law that was enacted by a democratically elected government in 2006? That the FD is part of this elected government requires a show of political morality towards the people they are governing. In addition, both government staff and the communities themselves need to catch up with progressive provisions within the law, such as equality in land ownership for women and men. The law states that women and men are equal. The law states "land to the tiller",[51] particularly for Scheduled Tribes and other traditional forest dwellers. Strategies for legal empowerment need to be "gendered", which means that both women and men have equal opportunities to claim their rights. The law needs to "transform the way that mainstream policies benefit and burden diverse women and men".[52] It needs to consider the multiple forms of discrimination faced by Indigenous peoples who are both tribal and female when in the process of claiming their rights to self-determination and to their communal lands. The new gender equation spelt out by the law requires a change in awareness and acceptance both within the community and among government servants. Patriarchal realities within the Rajasthani tribal culture of land ownership traditions are being challenged by the Forest Rights Act.

50 Interview, January 2014.

51 The expression "Land to the tiller" has long been a rallying cry of radical agrarian movements.

52 Staudt, 'The Feminization of Poverty', 216.

The onus of making communities aware of their rights is on the government. This responsibility, however, is not always conscientiously assumed by civil servants in charge. The forest Adivasi communities themselves are generally illiterate and would be unaware of their legal rights if it were not for civil society organisations assuming responsibility for the community's ability to access justice in regard to the FRA. The support of civil society is welcome in the land rights movement, and may be indispensable. However, civil society support also allows the government to evade their responsibility of protecting citizens' rights. Since illiteracy is an issue, online forms and FRA materials are inaccessible to forest peoples. The Indian government is often results-driven, and focuses on concrete goals such as the number of students in education or the number of trees that have been planted. What they find more difficult to comprehend is the importance of communities being organised so they can access information and training in order to be able to access justice. This has resulted in the protection of the rights of forest communities being undertaken by civil society organisations. For the forest communities of the Aravalli hills, the protection of their rights has not necessarily come from their government, who are vested with the duty and obligation to protect the community's rights and needs.

The Forest Department in India, after the enactment of the FRA, was faced with a change of dynamics in power over forest lands. Prior to the FRA, the government had control and decision-making powers over forest lands. The FRA reversed these powers, giving them back to the forest peoples in line with customary tribal land rights. Rather than committing to the 'spirit of the law', which adheres to human rights, the Forest Department at times seems unable to relinquish the powers that eminent domain gave them. As Robert Reich states, "Without political will and political power – and a movement behind that political will and power – no policy is going to be put into effect".[53] A query that keeps cropping up is what exactly did the government do after enacting the law in regard to building the capacity of the Ministry of Environment and Forests (MoEF) to administer the law, to understand it, and to commit to it? The lack of commitment by the administration has caused harm to the forest communities and to the concept of land rights, and has complicated the use of legal mechanisms for forest rights. In regard to the FRA, the political will was not necessarily consistent or sustained, and tribal communities' access to justice continued to be hindered by industrialisation, administrative injustice, and poor education and legal awareness of Forest Department employees. Compounding these barriers are well-meaning but poorly conceived policies of conservation.

53 Klein, 'Robert Reich on Backing Bernie Sanders'. Robert Reich is an American Professor of Public Policy, an economist, a political commentator and author, and served in the administrations of presidents Gerald Ford, Jimmy Carter and Bill Clinton.

Bibliography

Astha. *Astha Women's Land Rights Report.* Unpublished, 2012, 1–84.

Astha Sansthan. *A Field Based Resource Organization.* Annual Report 2007–2008. Astha Sansthan, 2007–2008.

Chadana, B.S., et al. *Status of Adivasis/Indigenous Peoples Land Series – 8 Rajasthan.* Aakar Books, 2014.

Forest Department Rajasthan. *Rajasthan State Forest Policy 2009.* Jaipur. http://indiaenvironmentportal.org.in/files/forest_policy_draft.pdf, accessed 2013.

Government of India. *Ministry of Tribal Affairs Annual Report 2012–2011*, 2010. www.india.gov.in/annual-reports-ministry-tribal-affairs-0, accessed 2013.

Government of Rajasthan. *Department of Forest*, 2010. https://forest.rajasthan.gov.in/content/raj/forest/en/home.html#, accessed 2013.

Katewa, S.S., B.L. Chaudhary, A. Jain, and P. Galav. 'Traditional Uses of Plant Biodiversity from Aravalli Hills of Rajasthan'. *Indian Journal of Traditional Knowledge* 2(1) (2002), 27–39.

Klein, E. 'Robert Reich on Backing Bernie Sanders, Dating Hillary Clinton, and Making Policy Viral on Facebook'. *Vox*, 5 May 2016. www.vox.com/2016/5/5/11581940/robert-reich-ezra-klein.

Latest Laws.com. *Rajasthan Tendu Leaves (Regulation of Trade) Act*, 1974. www.rajforest.nic.in/writereaddata/Revised_Rules_1974_English.pdf, accessed 2016.

Press Information Bureau. *Identification of 15 Minor Forest Produce for Minimum Support Price.* Government of India Ministry of Tribal Affairs, 2015.

Ramin, J. *For Forest Land and a Way of Life: The Story of the Adivasis' Struggle in Southern Rajasthan.* Astha Sansthan Publications, 2007.

Staudt, K. 'The Feminization of Poverty: Global Perspectives'. *The Brown Journal of World Affairs* 5(1) (1998), 215–24

Tribal Rights Resources Unit (TRRU). *Tribal Women's Rights on Land and other Natural Resources: Southern Rajasthan.* Astha Sansthan, 2012.

Wilshusen, P.R., et al. 'Reinventing a Square Wheel: Critique of a Resurgent "Protection Paradigm"'. *International Biodiversity Conservation: Society & Natural Resources* 15(1) (2011), 17–40.

Conclusion

The Unevenness of Access to Justice

Introduction

In the quest to empirically examine whether the enactment of the Forest Rights Act has changed the accessibility of justice for Indigenous peoples who are claiming rights to ancestral lands, I have developed a holistic conceptual framework for critical analysis. I specifically examine whether legal mechanisms governing land rights in India have made it more difficult for Indigenous peoples to get the resources they need to improve their lives. This book questions whether the Forest Rights Act (2006) of India and its implementation provides a powerful tool for Indigenous peoples to manage their own forests and to advocate for their rights, or whether in reality it increases their vulnerability. When pulling together the various conclusive threads that have emerged from this research, the most significant finding has been that access to justice cannot occur in a vacuum with the introduction of new legislation, however progressive. Rather, it is dependent on crucial nuanced variables, which I have detailed in this book, and which are part of my holistic conceptual framework. The conceptual framework triangulates scholarship and empirical evidence on the major aspects of access to justice, forest governmentality, economic policies, gender equality, legal literacy, and legal history. The framework identifies a nuanced understanding of the political, social, and economic contextual landscape as being vital for a critical analysis of access to justice.

The preceding case study chapters provide a local perspective of the immediate effects of the Forest Rights Act in India, exploring at the micro level the effects of forest rights legislation on the lives of forest peoples in the discrete geographical areas on which this study focuses.

The underpinning causal factors that have emerged from my data acknowledge that access to justice is influenced by the historically and legally biased evolution of land rights, and the political and economic choices of governments. As Rawls theorised, a key tenet of access to justice depends on whether government policies benefit all citizens, or respond only to an elite few at the expense of communities whose cultures do not mirror

DOI: 10.4324/9781003589488-6

the mainstream norms.[1] Similarly, whether embedded social discriminatory attitudes towards gender or nomadism are recognised or not, they also influence access to justice.

My findings indicate that legislation on land rights has divergent and uneven success in improving access to justice for Indigenous peoples. This unevenness is dependent on several political, institutional, and socio-economic factors, which are embedded within multiple levels of the implementation of the FRA and how Indigenous communities realise their land rights through it. These factors can be understood in three over-arching concepts of the law: how progressively the substantive rights within a law are framed and the historical genesis of this framing; whether the procedural rights are well defined and appropriate; and how conscientiously and justly the procedural rights are enacted and realised by citizens. Within these concepts, the following interdependent factors shape the extent of access to justice for Indigenous communities: the impact of historical legislation on contemporary policies; gender bias in governance; the role of civil society in advocating for the rights of marginalised communities; the legal literacy of the community; and administrative justice.

The History of Laws and Legal Literacy

India is a very diverse country, with different forest issues in different states, complicated by federal and state divisions. This results in significant variations between states in implementation of the FRA. Based on the evidence from my data collection, the FRA in general appears to have had uneven success in improving access to justice for Indigenous peoples in the parts of India that I have studied. The evidence from the field work in Chapters 2, 3, and 4 points to the major impediment to access to justice as being administrative injustice. Administrative injustice is evident in local forest governance, unjust national policies, and legal systems that condone this injustice by not providing appropriate redress. It has its roots in the issues emerging from the theoretical framework developed in this research. The analytical framework I advance in this study refers to the history of land laws that I posit were drafted in order for the smooth expropriation of land by colonisers. The ensuing judicial imperialism during the colonial occupation of foreign lands denied people their rights. The dysfunction lies in the concept that justice and ethics underpin the concept and structure of law, yet the legacy of colonial land laws continues to enable contemporary governments to expropriate valuable, resource-rich lands such as forest lands, and to reinforce forced migration in a manner that mirrors internal colonisation.

1 Rawls, *A Theory of Justice*, 9.

I conclude that the historical laws allowing land expropriation have contributed to the evolution of a culture that normalises economic expropriation of forest and other resource-rich lands, and sanctions the forced migration of vulnerable communities. The concept of eminent domain was legally extended to forests from the seventeenth century in India. The Indian national government readily adopted this concept after independence, with a seeming lack of analysis of the potential consequences of retracting rights of vulnerable communities. This lack of analysis has informed the attitudes of government bodies such as the Ministry of Environment and Forests, and departments under this ministry such as the Forest Department. For example, in Gujarat, the government sold to private individuals and industries gauchar lands that the Maldharis used for grazing their herds, and in 2011 the community protested the sanctioning by the BJP government of reservoir construction on fertile farmlands, which would destroy the rich ecosystem on which they grazed their cattle, and thus also their livelihoods. In Maharashtra, two government officials encroached illegally onto the grazing land of the Dhangar and built a sugar factory. Pastoralists were forbidden to use the Kumbhalgarh forests where they had traditionally grazed their camels, sheep, and goats when the government demarcated it as a Wildlife Sanctuary. A high number of the herds died, and the Raika suffered serious losses to their livelihoods. The ensuing attitudes can be perceived as exploitative and disrespectful of the rights of tribal communities. They also strongly influence the administrative justice with which the Forest Rights Act is implemented. The connection between the colonial histories of the Indian forest laws and present forest governance and attitudes remains inextricable and dominant, and presents a barrier to access to justice.

The legal framework that gives people rights is provided by the historical trajectory from which a law emerges, the actors who draft it, and the bodies that enact it. Conversely, I argue that these same processes, actors, and institutions can also collude to deny people their rights. The dominant legal system in India was imposed by a colonial government in the late 1800s and provides the historical trajectory that is rooted in continued land imposition in my case studies. It has eliminated local legal pluralism, which has eroded local legal literacy, self-determination, and access to justice. Today, the traditions of Indigenous communities in apportioning justice necessitate a legal validation of customary laws, and an awareness of national legal frameworks that support their rights. The imposition of a foreign system on a colonised nation injects an element of legal unfamiliarity that is immediately intimidating and excludes sections of the population. This was true of the Adivasis and the mobile Indigenous communities whom I interviewed in areas such as Gujarat, the Dhangars in Maharashtra, and the Raika in Rajasthan. Many of them are illiterate and do not speak the English language, which the legal system requires. These issues have resulted in the FRA being juxtaposed with an embedded judicial imperialism, which can result in the laws not necessarily enabling access to justice. This is compounded by socio-economic inequalities and language barriers within India, which have impaired the legal literacy and capacities of Indigenous communities to use legal institutions on a more equal basis. I conclude that in addition to how a law is framed, the implementation of the law is significant and can create the most difficult barriers to accessing justice. These barriers have rested upon uncommitted governance and poor compliance mechanisms for implementation of legislation, which do not support the spirit of the law or human rights.

Adding to the complexity of legal accountability for human rights is the fact that international regulatory bodies have little power for enforcement, which correlates directly with the weak accountability at the national level for the implementation of human rights. The continuous land expropriation by governments and corporate industries, which displaces Indigenous peoples, highlights the inconsistencies between a growing international human rights body of law and the experience of Indigenous peoples on the ground at the national level. Nation states remain unaccountable to international laws. Even if treaties have been signed by a country, they are not necessarily honoured, and Indigenous communities do not have the capacity to take the fight to the international level. Some declarations and conventions have no teeth and cannot hold countries accountable. Some countries, such as the USA, have not signed up to several human rights treaties. The question therefore remains open as to how the law can support Indigenous communities who are being displaced when there is a gap between international human rights norms and national laws or national enforcement of existing laws. The question of whether international legal norms are inherently biased against excluded groups in any country has evoked a multi-dimensional response. This response highlights the historical benefit to Western nations to which imperialism gave weight. The resultant global economic order has reinforced the north–south economic power imbalance, while overtly attracting the transnational capitalist class of the global south to capitalist values. This has created two opposing dynamics, which have led to increasing extractive industries on mineral-rich ancestral lands of Indigenous peoples, intensifying their forced migration. At the same time, a myriad international treaties and declarations, and national laws morally oriented towards protecting the human rights of marginalised groups are being generated.

FRA Implementation and Administrative Justice

The increase in the decision making and voice of forest peoples that the Gram Sabha village councils offer is a welcome aspect of the FRA. This empowering aspect, however, is diminished in light of the fact that many government and local authorities are poorly educated in the objectives of the Forest Rights Act and how it should be implemented. Governmental bodies and their frontline workers therefore do not always take responsibility in responding to the rights of tribal communities. My case study analysis repeatedly leads back to the issue of poor governance that promotes uneven administrative justice. This poor governance is counterbalanced by a few optimistic examples that evidence how legislation is being implemented in the 'spirit of the law'. In Rajasthan, some Forest Department officials are conscientiously helping tribal communities in claiming their land titles.[2] A few staff members from the Forest Department in Rajasthan have been spreading the word about land rights under the FRA, and some have shown interest in the procedural aspects of the FRA. Importantly, claims that have been submitted are dealt with sincerely for the most part. The implementation therefore remains sporadic, with some positive implementation experiences that offset to a small degree the land violations experienced by some communities.

This book defines governmental attitudes that become hostile to equitable justice by not responding to the needs of forest communities as administrative injustice. The major cause identified by the respondents interviewed on injustice was that the Forest Department and Ministry of Environment and Forests (MoEF) either did not understand the law very well, did not subscribe to the 'spirit of the law', or were unable to relinquish the power of eminent domain. When this is the case, a pattern is set of disempowering the community with the government in control. The FRA was enacted without thorough preparation by the government, who neither disseminated information to the community about their rights nor trained government officials in the provisions of the Act. Consequently, the main goal of the Act, which was to foster empowerment for the community, was lost.[3] This specifically sabotages the provisions of the Act, which offer community control of forest lands and forest resources, and begins to reinforce socially discriminatory practices by the government towards marginalised minorities. Indian forest governance therefore combines to reinforce the disempowerment of forest peoples. This emphasises the fact that the frontline implementation of policies such as the FRA is not a mechanical process but just as political as the policy process that formulates them. Access to justice is therefore highly dependent on how legal rights are recognised or enacted by judiciaries or governments.

The disempowerment created by the politicised implementation of the FRA is further exacerbated by the existing reality of widespread illiteracy and isolation of forest-dependent communities in India, such as the Amba

2 By 2013, during my data collection, thirteen thousand Adivasis had received land deed papers in Rajasthan.

3 Interview data from Madhu Sarin, founder of Campaign for Survival and Dignity, an informal but powerful all India grassroots organisation network of civil society organisations involved with forest rights.

community, and other tribal communities in the Aravalli hills where I worked, which renders many unable to hold forest officials accountable. This, when correlated with poor legal literacy, highlights the impact of socio-economic circumstances on access to justice. Within this context, the role of civil society in supporting forestry communities becomes crucial. It is this factor which I turn to next.

Civil Society Support

Civil society in India, as evidenced in this study, has been active in challenging legal illiteracy and lack of rights, and has played a crucial role in supporting the creation of new rights-based forest legislation. This has had two consequences for the implementation of forest legislation, one being the variable nature of support from developmental NGOs. A relatively unexplored disjunction is caused by the fact that civil society priorities might differ from those of the communities with whom they are working, especially as NGO practitioners often belong to a different socio-economic class than the communities they support. This was discernible in the weighting that was awarded to land claims for individual titles compared to titles for communal property that the FRA recognises. Individual property is a mainstream norm, not a tribal collective one. NGOs are themselves, at times, targets of misleading or outdated policies, and could be perceived as part of the problem. Some NGOs subscribe to supporting the community through welfare programmes that could be perceived as either filling a gap left by the government or creating further dependence among the communities. Other NGOs concentrate on empowerment and creating legal literacy. The type of NGO that a community works with could influence their access to justice and their ability to 'work' the legal system. Some NGOs choose not to work with new legislation, but prefer to advocate for land rights through purely political action and strategies, as in the case of the Maldhari community in Gujarat.

The second consequence of civil society's involvement in land rights has been that civil society is filling a vacuum created by poor governance, which has led to a lack of protection for marginalised communities. Civil society organisations, such as development NGOs, are a critical part of the community's ability to assert their legal rights, as they have staff who actively engage in educating the community on how to access their legal rights, as observed with Astha in Udaipur in Chapter 4. This complication highlights the inability of the government to fulfil its role of protecting its citizens. It also directly contradicts the very existence of legislation recognising the land rights of forest peoples. Legislation is formulated by government bodies, which are entrusted to execute the law in collaboration with local authorities such as the Gram Sabha, but in general they do so ineffectively. In some cases, as referred to in Chapters 3 and 4 of this book, failing to execute the law becomes an active discriminatory effort, which Sircar deems "state violence".[4] Sircar points out that new laws, or more laws, do not necessarily manifest in more rights or more justice, especially in the context of the evidence of laws being circumvented by the state, and state violence against marginalised minorities in the struggle for land and resource extraction. Perfect laws do not necessarily result in justice. They require that those whom the law seeks to protect be made aware of the law, and they require mechanisms for asserting the rights granted by the legislation. The success of the FRA depends on the government agencies implementing the law as written, which, as I have proven in the case study chapters, is arbitrary. More reliable is the support of civil society in India, but civil society organisations are not ubiquitous, and they are dependent on funding that is limited in size and scale. This adds to the sporadic aspect of legal support for empowerment, which creates further uneven access to justice; NGOs are often small islands of success,[5] and many Indigenous communities are not afforded this support. Despite this, however, there is much room for hope as civil society organisations are taking the law further than in an instrumental capacity,[6] and using it comprehensively through national activist platforms, in collaboration with forest peoples.[7]

Gender and Land Inheritance

One of the most marginalised minorities struggling for their land rights are Indigenous women. They face an intersectional double discrimination, both as a part of Indigenous communities and often also within these communities. This is illustrated in the southern Rajasthani case study, where the women of the Bhasla community faced patriarchal domination and were traditionally excluded from land ownership rights within the family. Women's customary responsibility for using land resources collectively, however, might be eroded by the ability to claim individual land titles under the Forest Rights

4 Sircar, 'Spectacles of Emancipation', 527.

5 The NGOs from which I collected data, all of which were extremely successful in their work with land rights, included Astha, Seva Mandir, SPWD (Society for Promotion of Wasteland Development), Marag, LPPS (Lokhit Pashu Palak Sansthan) and Anthra. They all operated in the states of Rajasthan, Gujarat and Maharashtra.

6 Civil society organisations in India are strong and vibrant and have been a powerful force aligning with tribal rights in the country. I met and interviewed organisations such as Campaign for Survival and Dignity and Kalpavriksh, whose work for tribal land rights has been dynamic and influential in pushing through the Forest Rights Act. Another highly participatory forum is the CFR-LA (Community Forest Rights Learning and Advocacy Process), an online environmental portal subscribed to by civil society organisations and community organisations who are also part of the forest rights movement in India.

7 In 2012, as part of the first phase of my data collection, I participated in the National Level Consultation on Forest Rights Act and Protected Areas in New Delhi; and in 2013, I had the opportunity to attend a Public Hearing on Community Forest Rights.

Act. This individual land ownership in the forests reduces customary collective land arrangements and diminishes the control women have enjoyed over natural resources. Control over natural resources in the past has made a significant contribution to women's economic independence, which in turn has had a positive effect on family stability, especially for children's nutrition and health. Given the established gender division of labour, in which it is usually women who collect water and firewood for cooking, the individual claims that have decreased collective forest lands have pushed women further into the forests to look for firewood and water, thereby increasing their workload. Community forest rights under the Forest Rights Act address the gender issues around collective control of natural resources by allowing land titles in the names of both spouses or in the name of single women.

The Forest Rights Act's improvement of access to land ownership has had dichotomous consequences for women, who have been empowered by the freedom gained through the potential for land ownership. The insistence by civil society advocates on the axiomatic aspect of gender discrimination, rendering women more marginalised and vulnerable than men, ensured mechanisms of empowerment within the procedural aspects of the FRA, including the promise of increased and legalised representation in decision-making bodies such as the Gram Sabha and Gram Panchayat, and legal recognition and access to the collection of minor forest produce, which forms a significant part of women's livelihoods. On the other hand, however, women stand to lose control over natural resources and activities, both domestic and economic, that are customarily connected to communal property. The gender dynamics of Indigenous communities, therefore, are another factor that leads to inconsistent access to justice through the FRA for Indigenous peoples. The lack of analysis of these consequences renders the administration of the Act gender-blind, meaning the differential impact on women and men is neglected and unacknowledged.

Moving away from gender issues, the next section addresses the consequences for Indigenous communities of government economic policies that prioritise profit from extractive industries over tenure security.

Capitalism and Extractive Industry

Socio-economic inequalities have dogged tribal land security since forest lands were expropriated by the state in the 1800s. The single most predatory impact on land displacement for Indigenous peoples has been in the name of economic development. Free-market capitalist philosophy, as reflected in the experiences of the threat of imminent displacement by some of the tribal communities I interviewed, is an impediment to government implementation of the FRA.

The communal norms and forest-based livelihoods of Indigenous peoples contrast acutely with the Indian government's choice of capitalism which, as evidenced in this study, puts profits above the rights of Indigenous peoples. The need for resource-rich forest lands serves corporate goals with which the Indian government is complicit. Conservationists similarly have an agenda that conflicts with Indigenous peoples' land claims. In this book, examples of state neglect, which Sircar calls "state violence",[8] are visible in the sugar factory that has encroached upon the grazing corridors of the Dhangar community in Maharashtra, and the struggles of the Maldharis from Gujarat who are faced with the loss of their dairy-based livelihoods following the White Revolution and the corporatisation of dairy produce at Anand. No account was taken by the government of the consequences on these small mobile Indigenous communities living on the periphery of mainstream society with differing norms oriented towards a communal system of sharing resources. These norms, which have evolved over time, contradict the individual profit and state free-market capitalism to which the sugar factory and the corporate dairy industry subscribe. The reinforcement of citizens' welfare as a lower priority than the market compromises constitutional values and the role of courts in upholding justice.[9]

In Amba, the threatening stance taken by the Forest Department in its attempts to dispossess the Adivasi community of their interior forest villages is a form of aggression that is allowed to be maintained by the lack of legal literacy. It is the "lawlessness" that Anderson suggests contributes to poverty, and which is bred through state corruption and the "unchecked abuses of political power"[10] involved in the threat of eviction from one's ancestral lands and source of livelihood.[11] The Indian government's commitment to the private sector's profit intentions contradicts the government's role of protecting the welfare of its most marginalised communities. This comprises neglect and abuse of the socio-economic rights of these communities.[12]

These differing goals compete with the rights of forest peoples to control their own land. Since the government, corporate industry, and conservationists have the power to contribute to a momentum resulting in the displacement of forest communities, the power balance is tilted away from Indigenous peoples, leading to further marginalisation and economic and social impoverishment. The most important aspect of the Forest Rights Act is that, in principle, the promise of substantive rights to claim land changes this power imbalance. The challenge lies in translating the principle of legislated rights.

Since forests are resource rich, they are a prime target for extractive industry, governments, and multinational corporations. These powerful actors are increasingly forming partnerships[13] that covet Indigenous lands,

8 Sircar, 'Spectacles of Emancipation', 527.
9 Sircar, 'Spectacles of Emancipation', 527.
10 Anderson, 'Access to Justice', 3.
11 Anderson, 'Access to Justice', iii.
12 Sircar, 'Spectacles of Emancipation', 548.
13 Suagee, 'Self-Determination for Indigenous Peoples', 673.

contributing to ecological imbalance, violation of Indigenous land rights, and damage to their health.[14] For Indigenous peoples, being able to access justice through legislation such as the FRA in order to challenge displacement from their lands is therefore vital. The government's trading of resource-rich forest lands for extractive industry has been one of the main reasons for the displacement of tribal peoples. The extraction of forest resources challenges the priorities of neoliberal development policies, benefitting some at the cost of others. This undermines the human rights of the communities in this case facing dispossession of their lands. Economic development programmes that do not reflect equality of rights prevent justice for the dispossessed and deny Indigenous communities control of their lives. In the hierarchy of government priorities, within which economic concerns trump those of communities, the economic contribution made to society by these communities is often poorly recognised. The example of the invisible contribution of pastoralists in preserving and managing the ecological balance of grazing lands, which they have done for centuries, emphasises the point. This type of economic contribution happens over an extended time period, is less visible, less recognised, and not ecologically destructive. On the other hand, mining or hydroelectric plants may yield greater short-term benefits but destroy the land and rivers and cause pollution. Much of the financial gain goes to the economic elites and is not widely shared with the communities who inhabit these lands and are dependent on these rivers. As long as this continues to happen, the spirit of laws such as the Forest Rights Act is undermined.

The scholarship engaged in this study, from which an original theoretical framework for analysing access to justice emerged, comprised five major aspects. The first aspect of judicial imperialism has been discussed earlier, that is, how the historical drafting and enactment of land laws has both denied and concurrently provided a framework for land rights. The second aspect is the lack of legal literacy necessary to access justice, which has been maintained by social, economic, and gender disparities.

The third aspect engages with the concept of justice based on a social contract. This development has produced norms of human rights which in turn have helped institutionalise the belief that people have rights that can be legally protected. The dichotomy lies in the fact that the existence of international human rights frameworks does not necessarily protect marginalised communities who do not always have the capacity or legal literacy to access justice, and who have not caught up with existing human rights. This creates a potential hollowness in the human rights norms. The duty bearers of rights are governments and judiciaries. These are staffed

14 Gilbert, 'Corporate Accountability and Indigenous Peoples: Prospects and Limitations of the US Alien Tort Claims Act', 26.

by individuals whose moral compass controls the enforcement of human rights law. The disjunction of the dependency of human rights enforcement on potentially flawed morality, creating vulnerabilities for marginalised communities, is discussed by thinkers such as Rawls, Sen, and Cappelletti.[15] The tenability of just laws and access to justice are directed by egalitarian and inclusive governance.

The ability of Indigenous communities to access justice is reflected in the enforcement of the Forest Rights Act in India, which has many cases of injustice peppered among other cases of due process and justice. Lack of legal literacy is still a formidable barrier, as is the frequent administrative injustice in the form of government officialdom that is not necessarily user-friendly and at times downright abusive. The need for the law to be upheld clashes unhappily with the inappropriately applied policies for economic development that have repeatedly displaced Indigenous peoples from their lands, and continue to do so. The case studies sharply illustrate this point and highlight the systemic legal and political deviations that allow the existing legal frameworks to be circumvented. The case studies also make obvious the inherent incompatibility between the human rights values of the Forest Rights Act and the free-market economic government policies. The duty of the government to enforce justice is violated by the economic policies of the same government, creating a dysfunction in accessing justice, especially for communities made vulnerable by dispossession of their lands. The fourth and fifth aspects comprise postcolonial governmentality and the neoliberal economics conducive to extractive industry and forced migration of Indigenous communities.

Significance of Findings

This book constitutes a significant multi-site research study that critically examines forest rights legislation, Indigenous access to justice, and forest land expropriation. It develops an original theoretical framework to examine the impact of the FRA on access to justice through a dual national and local-level analysis. It is one of the few studies on the Forest Rights Act from the perspective of the continuing bias in the legal history of India since colonialism, which is evident, for example, in the works of Galanter and Cappelletti.[16] Galanter cites examples from the USA, while Cappelletti uses many examples from European countries. This book highlights evidence from India to

15 Rawls, *A Theory of Justice*; Sen, *The Idea of Justice*; Cappelletti and Garth, 'Access to Justice', 203.

16 Galanter, 'Access to Justice in a World of Expanding Social Capability', 115; Cappelletti and Garth, 'Access to Justice', 197.

substantiate the analysis of continuing historical bias in the framing of contemporary laws.

My national-level analysis underscores the fact that the legal response to any demands for justice is driven by the underlying political and economic ideologies of the elected government. The local-level data from the three states of Gujarat, Rajasthan, and Maharashtra, and all the cited case studies in those states, clearly demonstrate these underlying ideologies, expressed at the local level through the institutions of the state. Neoliberal governmentality conflicts with the activist spirit of the Forest Rights Act. The authoritarian governmentality of forest departments often obstructs the progressive rights that the forest peoples are potentially promised through the Forest Rights Act. India's neoliberal governmental policies protect and reflect the priorities of the market, abandoning the true purpose of the justice underpinning laws, the role of courts, and the constitutional framework, which Sircar refers to as the "expansion of the global neoliberal economy [which] is creating a paradigm shift away from the recognition of universal human rights standards".[17] With growing populations necessitating the exploitation of natural and mineral resources, there is a global move to appropriate resource-rich land. The international imperialistic characteristics of resource expropriation are reflected in the historical framing of laws and, at the national level, in the behaviours that many national governments, such as that of India, mimic, in the interface between marginalised populations and national corporate interests. The economic and social conditions created by international institutions on a global scale mirror those necessary on a micro scale within countries such as India, where there is negative evidence of any actual benefits from development trickling down to the Adivasis from Rajasthan or mobile Indigenous peoples such as the Maldharis, the Raika, and the Dhangar, who are losing control over the natural resources on which they depend for their livelihoods, such as community forests. This book adds valuable evidence and detail to show how the confluence of these forces results in an obstruction of the justice promised by the FRA. It highlights how exploitative economic policies are continuing to impoverish forest communities in spite of land rights legislation such as the Forest Rights Act.

Important to the scholarship is the value added by the specific gender analysis in this research. The case studies illustrate the empowering effects of legislation, as seen in the Bhasla case, where the women began to challenge patriarchal traditions that have subverted women's rights to property ownership; the woman community leader in the nomadic Raika community in Rajasthan, championing the land rights cause; and the Maldhari women in Gujarat who traditionally enjoy a more equal role in controlling finances and the sale of their dairy products. The gendered interpretation of the data

17 Sircar, 'Spectacles of Emancipation', 561.

adds a crucial element to any perspective on the land struggles of Indigenous peoples. The three case studies on mobile Indigenous peoples add consequential data to Indigenous scholarship, which in general tends to peripheralise nomadic groups, who are also overlooked by governments because people on the move are harder to govern.

The main thread running through these chapters is the extent to which Indigenous peoples access justice. The main indicator I use in this book is how successful the Forest Rights Act has been in determining access to justice. The definition of access to justice in the Introduction chapter incorporated the 'just' and 'equitable' aspects of legal and judicial outcomes.[18] I point out in this book that the law and justice are not synonymous, although justice creates a foundation for the law. It is assumed that forest rights are conceded with the enforcement of the Forest Rights Act. I have demonstrated, however, that in the case of tribal India, the effectiveness of the government and the roles of the courts and lawyers are not always functional in protecting the rights of citizens, and do not necessarily lead to equitable outcomes. This proves that justice is not always accessible. Rawls associates justice with an ability to trust that the procedures will work within a moral framework and that justice will deliver "fairness".[19] I conclude that for tribal communities in India, who are already socially and economically marginalised, inequality strongly influences their ability to work the judicial system to their advantage, especially when competing with financially comfortable corporate interests. In spite of the progressively articulated Forest Rights Act, being able to claim land rights remains a difficult process for Indigenous peoples.

The Forest Rights Act in India is shaped by constructive and beneficial substantive rights. The substantive rights within the Act are clear and progressive and have been game changing for Indigenous peoples in India. These rights have revolutionised the potential to claim land rights, whether customary or ancestral, which is a great achievement for the tribal and forest communities, and for civil society organisations that advocated fiercely for these rights in collaboration with forest peoples. Whether the procedural rights are similarly sound can be refuted. Separate to the framing of the procedural rights is the execution of the provisions. This is where the biggest impediments emerge. These impediments are framed in this study within the concept of administrative justice and the role of the state. I find that five factors dictate the extent to which administrative justice is delivered and access to justice realised by Indigenous communities: the historical context of forestry laws and the legal literacy of Indigenous peoples; FRA implementation and administrative justice; civil society support; gender and land inheritance; and the effect of neoliberalism and extractive industry.

18 United Nations Development Programme, *Access to Justice*, 5.
19 Rawls, *A Theory of Justice*, 9.

To conclude, in order for these rights to materialise, these five factors must be understood and examined. As evidenced in this study, we still have a long way to go before that can be achieved, especially because many of these factors are the results of entrenched inequalities and the free-market capitalist economic and political forces that sit uneasily with human rights but remain unchallenged. The picture that emerges is therefore often unequal and unbalanced.

Any new legislation, in this case the Forest Rights Act, goes through several steps before it can be engaged to access justice: a protracted advocacy campaign, which for the FRA was launched by both the forest communities and civil society; acceptance by the government of the concept of these particular legal entitlements and the ensuing process of drafting, followed by the enactment; and then the administering of the law. The missing element in the instance of the Forest Rights Act was the preparation by the government of its staff who were entrusted with administering the legislation. Despite this, it is important to acknowledge that the existence of progressive substantive rights is a huge step forward as a channel for the community to secure legal redress for land violations, and has to be protected by honing and strengthening these factors, particularly administrative justice, which is so vital for the success of the forest rights legislation. The framework I have advanced in this research provides a holistic and nuanced understanding of how diverse groups of marginalised Indigenous communities around India are able to utilise progressive legislation such as the Forest Rights Act in their fight to claim land rights. As I have pointed out earlier in this book, access to justice is a means to an end. The end in this debate is Indigenous empowerment, rights to ancestral forest lands, and the control of forest governance.

Bibliography

Anderson, M.R. 'Access to Justice and Legal Process: Making Legal Institutions Responsive to Poor People in LDCs'. *IDS Working Paper* 178 (2003).

Cappelletti, M., and B. Garth. 'Access to Justice: The Newest Wave in the Worldwide Movement to Make Rights Effective'. *Buffalo Law Review* 27(2) (1978), 181–292.

Galanter, M. 'Access to Justice in a World of Expanding Social Capability'. *Fordham Urban Law Journal* 37(1) (2010), 115–28.

Rawls, J. *A Theory of Justice*. Oxford University Press, 1999.

Sen, A. *The Idea of Justice*. Penguin, 2010.

Sircar, O. 'Spectacles of Emancipation: Reading Rights Differently in India's Legal Discourse'. *Osgoode Hall Law Journal* 49(3) (2012), 527–73.

Suagee, D.B. 'Self-Determination for Indigenous Peoples at the Dawn of the Solar Age'. *University of Michigan Journal of Law Reform* 25 (1992), 671–749.

United Nations Development Programme (UNDP). *Access to Justice: Practice Note*. United Nations, 2004. www.undp.org/content/dam/aplaws/publication/en/publications/democratic-governance/dg-publications-for-website/access-to-justice-practice-note/Justice_PN_En.pdf.

Index

Kolibri 360 GmbH
Ferdinand-Jühlke-Straße 7
99095 Erfurt, Deutschland
produktsicherheit@kolibri360.de